THE ROAD ᴛᴏ ᴇAST

A Journey to Singapore

Ben Coombs

'A dream which comes true, leads to other dreams.'

– Gaston Rebuffat, Starlight and Storm

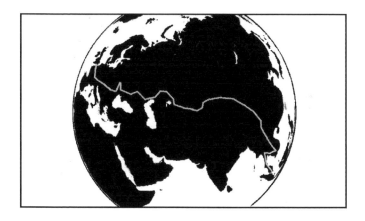

CONTENTS

01	Preface	7
02	Rising to Adventure	13
03	Departure	19
04	The Roof of my World	25
05	Déjà vu	35
06	A New Beginning	41
07	East Again	49
08	First Time East	61
09	The Chameleon Country	69
10	New Worlds	81
11	The Steppe	93
12	Siberia	117
13	Country under Construction	133
14	The Road to Hell	149
15	Through the Wall	163
16	The Rickshaw Run	171
17	Monk Life	203
18	The Last Climb	221
19	Welcome to the Jungle	233
20	The Italian Job	247
21	To Saigon	255
22	Fire and Ice	265
23	The Vietnam Special	277
24	Hunter's Moon	285
25	Going Solo	293
26	A Barge on the Baltic	303
27	To Burma	311
28	Morocco V8	321
29	The Road to Singapore	335
30	Momentum	349
31	Home	357

ONE

PREFACE

28th March 2013
Dartmoor National Park, UK

For miles the road rose and fell, a mottled streak which swept left and right at the whim of the landscape's choppy contours. Thick hedgerows hemmed in the tarmac, beyond which the vivid greens of spring were just beginning to bring the barren moorland to life as winter faded to memory. Inches from my wheels, the grassy verges were punctuated by wild daffodils and bluebells, while foxgloves reached up into the chill air, their scents mingling with that of hot oil and brakes. Above, the sky was a steel blue, dotted with unthreatening puffs of cloud which were periodically obscured as skeletal centuries-old trees scrolled overhead. All around me, a glorious baritone howl ricocheted through the air, echoing among the hedgerows and the granite tors, and changing its pitch and urgency with every sweet gearchange.

I sat low in my classic British sports car, the roof open to the elements and the cold spring air buffeting my hair as we roared along. The road was close to home and I'd driven it many times before. I knew the best line to take through every corner, to maximise visibility and smoothness. I knew that soon, the tarmac would straighten out and I'd drop down a gear and accelerate, revelling in the noise and acceleration as the TVR's trademark roar tumbled from the twin exhausts and bounced between the hedgerows to fill the air around me. I knew that really, the journey was little different to the dozens of other times I'd blasted along here, roof down and the wind in my hair, savouring the experience. But I also knew that despite the similarities to the previous occasions on which I'd driven the road, this time it was different. For in a few hours, I would be leaving on a five month road trip into the unknown and on my return, life would most certainly have changed. That moment, that combination of car, countryside and self so taken for granted over the years, was about to become a memory.

Throughout my life, I had been continuously dreaming up the next adventure, the next grandiose experience which, on completion, would become a memory as I threw myself into yet another undertaking. Some of the dreams took many years to be realised. For instance, as I child, I had dreamed of one day owning a V8-powered, open topped TVR. It had remained a dream for fifteen years before I'd finally purchased the burbling steed named Kermit, in which I was now crossing Dartmoor. Other dreams had been realised almost instantly and had seen me rushing to the far side of the world within a couple of days of an idea forming. And still more – the most outlandish, preposterous or downright scary – remained unaccomplished, waiting for the time and the portents to be right. However I looked at it, dreaming, and then doing, had been a constant in my life for as long as I could remember. An unabating rhythm which had played out ever since I was a child.

Exiting a village, I dropped down a couple of gears and accelerated, sending the big engine's sublime orchestra reverberating between the dry stone walls and etching the moment in my memory. The magnificent noise and vibrations massaged my senses like a sign, a prequel to the main event which was to begin in a few hours' time. For then, a similar soundtrack would be propelling me as I set out to cross half the world. The offbeat thrum of a sports car's V8 engine would be accompanying me through every landscape imaginable, from sandy desert to snow-clad mountain; impenetrable rainforest to urban jungle. As I swung the TVR through a familiar right-left kink, took the bridge across the boulder-strewn brook and accelerated up the hill past the riding stables, I noticed that my impending departure was tinged with a slight sense of melancholy; a vague regret at leaving my comfortable, familiar world. I had returned from every big trip a slightly different person, and so in pursuing my latest dream, I was condemning my present self to become a memory to which I could never return. But life had always been thus. The ambitions which drove me onwards hadn't always revolved around road trips, but they'd always been something larger than the everyday; something which loomed over me and dominated my thoughts until I was drawn out of my comfort zone and dug deep to realise them. Later that day, I would be setting off to drive to the far side of Asia in a Chevrolet Corvette but in reality, that wouldn't be the beginning of the adventure. No, it had begun decades earlier when as a child I had first dreamed of a life beyond the constraints of my age, a dream which formed an ambition that burned bright throughout my youth. That first ever dream is intertwined with my earliest memories and stayed with me throughout my formative years and well into my teens, until I finally achieved it. The dream wasn't travel-based and nor did it involve cars, but it was still an adventure which I aspired to undertake and it had stayed with me until I was able to throw everything I could into its attainment. Through doing so, I had banished the craving, but the result of this was to set in motion the cycle of dreaming, and then doing, which has dominated my life ever since.

No, I thought to myself as I relaxed in the comfort of Kermit's leather and walnut interior, I wasn't about to set off on a brand new adventure that day. When the moment came to board the Corvette and set off for the far side of Asia, I would merely be beginning the next chapter in a continuous adventure which had begun on a fateful day fifteen years before, sat behind a big Lycoming flat-4 engine on an arrow-straight strip of tarmac, 150 miles away.

The experiences of that fateful day had remained engrained in my memory right up to the present time. As the latest chapter of my life's adventure loomed large, I thought back to the inception, all those years ago. The day which had led me to this moment. The day on which it all began.

TWO

RISING TO ADVENTURE

03rd October 1997
Gloucestershire Airport, UK

The runway reached away to the horizon where it merged with a sky that hung like a question mark, beckoning me to open the throttle and begin the adventure. I'd been dreaming of this moment for as long as I could remember. My earliest memories were awash with a craving for the freedom of the skies.

Around me, the tinny fuselage of the Cessna vibrated slightly as the big flat-four engine idled away, swinging the propeller which framed my view ahead. For the first time since I'd started learning to fly, there was no-one sat to my right, only an empty seat. Every time I'd been here before, my instructor had been next to me, watching my every move, keeping me safe. But today was different. Today I had been entrusted to fly solo for the first time, to chase my destiny up into the blue yonder and finally be able to call myself a pilot. Today's adventure was the culmination of a dream which had been part of me for as long as I could remember. At that moment, it seemed like the beginning of something glorious. But little did I know at the time, it was also the beginning of an end.

I ran through the pre-take off checks as I had done many times before during my lessons, reeling off each familiar action like a line in some esoteric chant:

'...elevator trim set for takeoff, throttle friction tight, carb heat set to cold, primer locked...'

Every action had seemed inconsequential before, as I'd carried out the checks full of the overconfidence of youth and with my instructor looking over my shoulder, but now an unfamiliar seriousness shadowed my every check. This time, it was for real.

'...*magnetos on both, fuel on and sufficient, flaps up, DI and compass aligned...*'

A nervous excitement built up within me as the moment of truth drew closer; the moment when I would open the throttle and climb into the blue alone for the first time. I tried to suppress the excitement and focus on the seriousness of the pre-flight checks but doing so was beyond me, such was the gravitas of the moment.

' ...*engine temperature and pressure green, vacuum suction green, no electrical discharge, seat locked, full and free movement of flying controls...*'

After methodically completing the pre-flight checks, I radioed the control tower: 'Golf – Mike Tango ready for departure.'

A reply immediately crackled through my headphones: 'Golf – Mike Tango cleared for take-off runway three-one. Surface wind two-eight-zero, four knots.'

Taxiing onto the runway, I smiled as I grasped the controls, before pushing the throttle smoothly forwards. The engine's previous drone was replaced with a buzzing, rasping roar, sending urgent vibrations pulsing through the airframe. I released the brakes and the whole plane sprang forwards, gaining speed rapidly as its propeller chewed through the crisp autumn air. The rough tarmac buffeted me playfully as I gained speed, keeping the Cessna tracking straight down the runway as I accelerated, just as I'd been taught. Thirty knots, thirty-five, forty. The speed was building quickly now. Once the air speed indicator was reading fifty knots I pulled back on the controls and up rose the little plane's nose, blocking out my view straight ahead. The ride suddenly smoothed out and through the corner of my eye I saw the ground fall away from me. The Cessna's shadow crossed the airfield boundary and then flickered across the familiar patchwork of fields and suburbs, tied together by roads along which rapidly shrinking cars crawled.

Climbing past 700 feet, I turned crosswind, before levelling out and turning again to fly parallel to the runway, already heading back to a point where I could bring the little plane in to land, all the while carrying out a familiar series of in-flight checks to make sure everything was okay with the aircraft's systems. And then, for the first time in the flight, I was able to relax, and so I did what any 18-year old would do when entrusted with an aeroplane. I punched the air in a celebratory fashion and shouted 'get in!' at no-one in particular. I'd been fascinated with aviation for as long as I could remember. My entire life had felt like it was leading up to this moment and now the moment was real. I was a pilot! I'd done it. The dream was a reality. Or at least it would be if I managed to land the plane again.

I throttled back to 1,500 RPM and began the descent, turning finals as the radio crackled 'Golf – Mike Tango, cleared to land, runway three-one. Surface wind is two-eight-zero, four knots.'

I lowered the wing flaps to twenty degrees, slowing the aircraft to its approach speed of sixty-five knots, and then turned and lined up for landing. Fully serious once again, not to mention slightly nervous, I controlled the speed and rate of descent with the throttle and elevator as I guided the little Cessna towards the runway, watching the air speed indicator like a hawk. I closed the throttle as the runway threshold flashed beneath me and the little aeroplane floated just above the ground as I bled off speed for the landing. After a few seconds I had slowed sufficiently for the plane to sink onto the tarmac, the wheels chirping crisply as they touched down. I lowered the nose then pressed hard on the brakes, slowing down to a walking pace before vacating the runway, leaving it clear for the aircraft behind me, which was already turning onto its final approach and would be landing in a few seconds.

I'd done it.

After many years of anticipation, many hours of flying lessons and many months of working night shifts in a local warehouse to pay for them, it was real. As I taxied back to the hangar, I tried to come to terms with what had just happened. I was overjoyed, of course, but it wasn't the perfect moment I'd anticipated. Maybe the dream of flying solo had been built up to such a big thing in my mind that the reality was always destined to fall short. Or maybe flying had already lost its lustre, the romantic freedom of the skies about which I'd dreamed replaced with a reality populated by endless checklists, restricted airspace and barked instructions from air traffic control. Taking to the sky had been my first ever ambition; the first adventure I'd aspired to and done everything in my power to make happen. But through the warm glow of accomplishment, I think that even then I subconsciously knew that it wasn't what I was looking for. My search for a means to express my adventurous spirit seemed destined to continue down other avenues.

After paying for the day's flying and accepting the relieved congratulations of my flying instructor, I walked out of the clubhouse into the crisp evening. Tucked in amongst all the status-symbol Range Rovers and Mercedes which inhabited the flying club's car park, my mum's battered old Fiat Uno looked slightly out of place, but it didn't bother me at all. I pulled up the flimsy plastic door handle, climbed in and immediately felt right at home. The agricultural, rough sounding diesel clattered into life and I headed out onto the road. Thirty miles of sweeping A-roads beckoned and as always, I set about the journey with childlike enthusiasm. The Fiat's lack of power and grip made it the slowest thing on the road, and I relished the challenge of keeping up with the other cars on the sweeping tarmac next to the River Severn, wringing every last drop of performance from the poor little car. The Fiat's sluggishness meant that speed limits weren't the restriction they are in more powerful motors and when behind the wheel I always felt confident and in control, in a way I never did in a plane.

As I hustled the little Fiat home after my first solo flight, I was dimly aware of just how important driving was becoming to me. It may not have been a passion held from the first memories of youth like the world of aviation was, but it was still something I had grown to relish unexpectedly. At the time, I had no idea where this appreciation of the open road would take me, but the more I progressed towards completing my pilot's license, the more my dreams of dancing amongst the towering clouds gave way to other dreams. Dreams of open tarmac, sweeping corners, sports cars and road trips.

THREE

DEPARTURE

28th March 2013
Shaugh Prior, Dartmoor, UK

My drive across Dartmoor in the TVR was almost at an end. Coming into the village, I lifted off the accelerator and coasted, releasing a cacophony of muffled pops and bangs from the exhaust, a sound which I never tired of. Passing the church, I swung the car left down the hill and turned right across the cattle grid at the end of the driveway. It had been a glorious drive, and it reminded me of just how undiminished my enthusiasm for being behind the wheel had remained in the decade-and-a-half since I was flinging that tatty old Fiat Uno around Gloucestershire. The house came into view and I pulled up by the front door, parking next to the bright red Chevrolet Corvette in which I'd be setting off for Asia in a few hours. Shutting down the TVR's engine, silence assaulted my ears as the offbeat thrum of the charismatic V8 died away, replaced by distant birdsong and the sound of the exhaust ticking as it cooled after the morning's spirited drive. I remained in the car and tried to engrave the memory of this latest enjoyable drive into my mind as I listened to the ticking and soaked up the unique aroma of leather, fibreglass and hot oil which the TVR always gave off after being used as intended.

The car was my pride and joy and this was the last time I'd experience it before I left. I didn't want the moment to end.

But end it had to. I climbed out and replaced the removable roof, while glancing over at the Corvette. For two sports cars, the steeds couldn't be any more different. While the TVR's sensuous curves harked back to a more innocent age of motoring, the Corvette's uncompromising

19

bodywork exuded an '80s brashness. The TVR had an old school cabin of leather and walnut, which was defiantly retro next to the 'vette's fighter jet-style cockpit. But the Corvette was comfortable and comparatively effortless to drive, and so it promised to be a fine companion in which to complete this latest adventure, which we'd named the V8Nam Expedition, with the idea being to drive a V8 to Vietnam.

There were still a couple of hours left before I had to leave to collect my co-driver, and I still hadn't begun to pack the car. I set about doing so, pulling together the various piles of things which had built up over the previous few days, each being essential for the trip. There was a clutter of tools on the garage floor and a pile of maps and guidebooks sat on the dining room table. In one room of the house I'd built a small training wall for practising rock climbing and beneath this wall were two further piles; one of camping gear and another smaller pile of climbing equipment. The opportunities for climbing on the trip would be few, but I didn't want to miss out on what chances there were, as climbing had became a very important past-time to me over the years. Indeed, when I gave up flying, the mountains had replaced the sky to become the source of my dreams and aspirations, dominating my life for several years and overshadowing all other opportunities for adventure.

I carried on loading the car, the four-wheeled box which would be serving as my home for the coming five months and 14,000 miles. It didn't have a huge amount of space for the endless paraphernalia but what room there was proved just sufficient and by mid-afternoon it was ready. Before I left, I made a cup of tea and wandered slowly around the house, mentally laying it to rest in my mind. I lingered a little in each room, not wanting to say goodbye, for these spaces represented the life I was leaving. When I closed the front door, it would all become a memory.

I remained longest in the room where I'd built a small climbing wall, touching some of my favourite handholds and cranking out a few pull-ups for old time's sake. As flying had gradually receded to memory, rock climbing had grown to become everything to me; an activity to which I willingly volunteered all my focus and tied up all my dreams and ambitions. Those days had passed, but I still enjoyed the activity in a less obsessive manner and would miss not only my home wall, but also the challenging routes on the granite tors nearby. But this was inevitable. To chase the current dream, previous aspirations had to be put on hold and anyway, the first few days of the trip would be spent in the rock climbing Mecca of Fontainebleau; an enchanting place to which I returned every year. I walked out of the room and made my way to the front door, which I closed behind me, leaving my old life behind.

*   *   *

I lowered myself into the Corvette's cramped cabin which was to be my home for the coming months, and was immediately enveloped within its garishness. Apparently, the way the dashboard – liberally festooned with buttons and digital readouts – wrapped around the driver was modelled on the F-16 fighter plane; however to me the aviation connection was more subtle and personal. The first thing I'd ever noticed about the 'vette's interior was that it smelled exactly the same as the cockpits of the Cessnas in which I'd learned to fly over a decade before. Not only did this latest road trip feel like a continuation of those far-off days of flight, but thanks to some shared glue or material, it even smelled like it too. As omens went, this felt like a good one and just as on those long-gone days when I would climb aboard a Cessna and set off skyward, I found myself infused with a mixture of excitement and trepidation, the sadness at leaving my day-to-day world behind balanced against my anticipation for getting to grips with this latest stage of my life's adventure.

I turned the key and the similarities with a Cessna came to an abrupt end as the Corvette's primeval 5.7 litre V8 engine roared urgently to life, barking like a caged animal and rocking the car on its stiff suspension, before settling down to a lumpy, uneven idle. The rich smell of unburned fuel wafted through the air and electrifying vibrations surged through the cabin. I put the gear selector into 'drive' and wheelspun momentarily on the gravel driveway, before more dignified progress was attained. And so I set off on the first leg of my trip to the far side of the world: a gentle twelve hour cruise down to Dover and across the channel to France, where I'd be spending the first weekend of the trip rock climbing in Fontainebleau Forest. In some ways this first part of the trip was a journey back in time for me, a return to the person who I was before I started taking adventurous road trips, when it was the lure of soaring mountains of rock and ice which consumed me.

FOUR

THE ROOF OF MY WORLD

26th June 2001
Mont Blanc, French/Italian border

I leaned forwards on my ice axe, gasping for breath in the rarefied air as I strained up the narrow ridgeline towards the summit. To my left, a vertiginous snow slope swept down for thousands of feet into France while to my right, Italy beckoned in a similar manner. Looking down, my cold cramponed feet clawed at the compacted snow which made up the ridgeline, maintaining a tenuous link to the mountain. Roped together against a fall, my companions and I had stopped to savour a much-needed drink as we took in our surroundings. We'd been on the move since two in the morning, as we wanted to complete the climb before the sun softened the snow, making progress harder and increasing the risk of avalanches. It was just beginning to get light and the Alps rippled away from us into the dawn, a sea of snowcapped peaks rising from misty valleys still smothered in darkness. Some of them I recognised and aspired to climb one day: the shark's tooth profile of the Dent du Géant, the lofty summit of the incomparable Grandes Jorasses and far in the distance, the unlikely pyramid of the Matterhorn. Yet more of the high points in this sea of peaks had names which escaped me still. Far below, a chaos of glaciers and rocky pinnacles cascaded down to the town of Chamonix, its lights glittering alluringly in the valley below.

I'd dreamed of scaling my first proper alpine mountain ever since I'd given up flying to pursue the considerably cheaper hobbies of climbing and mountaineering. Ten days previously, I'd never set foot in the Alps, but here I was, high on the summit ridge of Western Europe's highest peak.

We pulled our ice axes from the snow and continued upwards. Every step was a struggle for my poorly acclimatised body, but the magnificence of my surroundings kept my mind off the exhaustion. Daylight was building to the east, a horizon of electric blue which glowed brighter with every minute. Not far ahead of us, the ridgeline terminated in a snowy pyramid, the summit of which was now tantalisingly close. Redoubling our efforts, we set about trying to reach it before sunrise, an unlikely race between a few aspiring alpinists and the earth's rotation which ended in a draw.

Ironically given my previous passion for flight, the view from the summit was disappointingly like that from an airplane. Reaching a height of 4,810 metres, Mt Blanc is so much higher than any of the surrounding mountains that you find yourself looking down on the world, with no drama close by to draw and excite the eye. But it didn't matter. The dream had become real and as we started to descend I felt certain that my search was over. In climbing, I'd found the perfect outlet for the adventurous side of my personality.

*   *   *

For several years after that first trip to the Alps, climbing consumed me. I spent my weekends on the end of a rope working my way up the golden granite sea cliffs of Cornwall, while evenings were whiled away on Dartmoor's many tors or training at the indoor climbing wall. Every holiday was a trip to the mountains as I sought to build up my experience and abilities to a level where I could excel on even the hardest climbs.

But it wasn't to be.

While some of my peers went on to tackle ever bolder and more impressive routes in the mountains, I found it incredibly difficult to summon up the self belief needed to feel confident on such routes. As climbing is as much a mental challenge as a physical one, this became a major stumbling block in my attempts to progress to steeper, harder climbs. Where friends would be comfortable pushing on into the unknown, high above their protective gear, I would be racked with self doubt. At the time, I had no idea why this was. I simply couldn't understand why my mental state was so incompatible with the rigours of the sport.

As time went on, this unfathomable mental weakness meant a gap gradually opened up between my climbing aspirations and my ability to achieve them. A series of close calls dented my confidence further; abseiling off a mountain in the Alps during a hail storm with lightning crashing into the rocks all around, and being cartwheeled down an icy route in Scotland by a rogue avalanche. The gap became a chasm as I accepted that my personality wasn't a good match for the bold climbing to which I aspired, and while a few of my friends kept pushing the limits, undertaking ever more audacious routes on ever larger mountains, I drifted more and more into an obscure, stress-free niche tucked away within the broad church of climbing. An activity called bouldering.

Bouldering is climbing distilled; a strand of the sport focused on technically difficult climbs which take place close enough to the ground that the danger is minimal, freeing the climber from the mental aspect of the sport and allowing them to instead focus on the physical and technical challenges at hand. As my lack of self confidence prevented me from climbing big, bold routes in the mountains, bouldering beckoned as the perfect way for me to still push myself as a climber in a safe environment which my mind could cope with. Bouldering was – and still is – a great activity which offers both mental and physical gymnastics in abundance. What it doesn't necessarily offer however, is an outlet for one's sense of adventure.

However, that doesn't mean that a bouldering trip can't lead to adventure.

It was the end of another perfect day's climbing on the sandstone boulders which litter Fontainebleau Forest, near Paris.   The campfire was already roaring away and its smoke rose vertically upwards into the still air, where it drifted among the trees which flickered orange in the light of the flames.   Laughter echoed all around as everyone settled in for a relaxed evening of red wine and Kronenbourg stubbies.

As I reclined by the fire, my phone rang unexpectedly.

'Ben, it's Chris.'

There was a hint of nervous stress in his voice.

'Hi Chris, how's it going? We thought you'd be here by now.'

'I'm about twenty miles away. But I've rolled my car,' came the reply.

'Oh crap,' I said. 'Where are you? Are you okay; do you need some help?'

'I'm just north of Font. The car skidded on a roundabout, hit the curb and rolled onto its side. My stuff went everywhere. Some French guys helped me get it back on its wheels and told me to get going before anyone noticed that I'd taken out a road sign, but the car is a right mess. Where are you camped again?'

'It's La Musardiere, near Milly la Forêt. Can you make it to Font? I'll come and meet you there and guide you to the campsite.'

'Probably, I'll give it at try,' replied Chris.

I jumped into my car and headed off into town where I found Chris, still visibly shaken by the accident. Even in the darkness, it was clear that his car – a miniature Mitsubishi Pinin 4x4 – was very much the worse for wear after its ordeal. Although liberally dented, it was roughly the right shape below the window line; however everything above this level was twisted to the left, where it had impacted the road. The windscreen was smashed, as were some of the side windows. But since being tipped back onto its wheels, it had managed to cover the few miles to Fontainebleau and seemed to drive as it should, so we decided to head to the campsite for the night, and figure out what to do with it over a few campfire beers.

The following day we headed off to Bar le Bacchus – our usual haunt in the neighbouring village – to see what could be done, and before the day was through we'd found a couple of guys who worked at a nearby garage who were interested in buying the twisted remains of the Mitsubishi. 450 rather dubious-looking Euros later, a deal was done and the mangled motor was towed away, much to everyone's relief. That evening with the crisis over, we decided to cram ourselves into the remaining two cars and head to the local Irish bar to celebrate. However, our troubles were really just beginning.

On the way to the bar, I coasted up behind my friend Lee's old Ford Escort at a T-junction, looking forward to our imminent arrival. It was dark but there were still plenty of vehicles about, and so Lee was forced to wait patiently for a gap before he could accelerate across the oncoming traffic. Unfortunately, the word 'accelerate' doesn't accurately describe what happens when a fully loaded, geriatric Ford bogs down under load, and hence they only made it halfway across the road before a speeding people carrier slammed into them with an almighty bang. Metal crumpled and tyres squealed as Lee's hapless Escort spun across the tarmac onto the far side of the road, while the people carrier juddered to a halt in front of me. And then, other than the apologetic sound of a few idling engines, there was silence.

The Escort had been hit in the rear corner, so I headed over to see if everyone was okay. In the passenger seat, Lee's girlfriend Mel was reacting rather hysterically while behind her, the three rear-seat passengers all seemed to be shaken but okay.

Lee and I looked the car over as we waited for the police to arrive. There was a hefty dent behind the rear wheel, the light cluster was shattered and the bodywork was rubbing on the tyre, but everyone in the car was lucky that the impact hadn't been a bit further forward, where people were sitting. Things could have been a lot worse.

Two police cars and an ambulance arrived, and while the police took statements, the Escort's back seat occupants were taken away to hospital for a check up. Meanwhile, I shuttled everyone else to the Irish bar, where the Escort's uninjured occupants met us an hour later. All three of our cars were booked onto a ferry back to the UK the following day, but only one of them was still roadworthy. A plan was needed, and later that evening in the darkened cabin of my Peugeot, Lee and I discussed what to do as I shuttled people back to the campsite.

'So the damage to the Escort isn't too bad, then?' I said to Lee. 'I mean, you managed to drive it back to the campsite.'

'Yeah, it's okay with just me in it. The wheel arch rubs on the wheel as soon as anyone gets in the back, though.'

'Yeah, you can't drive back to England four-up then,' I said.

'We can if we bend the metal arch away from the wheel,' said Lee. 'We can try to find a new light cluster in the morning too, to replace the smashed one.'

As we chatted, a plan gradually formed which would possibly get us all back to the UK. However, in some quarters it wasn't going down too well.

On this particular shuttle run, the back seat of the Peugeot was occupied by two friends of a friend – Laura and Gina. I was meeting them both for the first time on this trip, and while adventure-loving Laura was generally unphased by the ridiculous situation the car crashes had left us in and seemingly enjoyed the uncertainty, Gina wasn't nearly so comfortable with things, and the questions came thick and fast.

'If you bend the metal out of the way, how will you know it's safe?' She fired forward at Lee.

'We'll be able to see whether it's still rubbing when we load the car,' he replied.

'But you don't work at a garage, how can you know?'

'It's common sense,' I replied. 'You can tell just by looking. And besides, Lee knows his way around cars and I have an engineering degree. Between us, we'll figure it out.'

'But how do you know there's not some other damage? You're not qualified to say it's safe.'

'The impact wasn't on the suspension,' said Lee. 'It's purely body damage.'

'You can't say that for certain,' came the answer. 'You could end up killing everyone in the car.'

This conversation bounced to and fro for several minutes, with every suggestion and reassurance we made being batted down from behind a wall of increasingly stubborn negativity. We were working to find a way to get everyone back to the UK on time, but despite knowing nothing about cars, Gina seemed intent on finding a problem for every solution. Eventually, I'd had enough.

'Gina,' I said. 'Are you a Ford mechanic?'

'No.'

'Well shut the fuck up then.'

The car fell silent. And in the rear view mirror, I could just make out Laura holding her hand over her mouth as she tried not to laugh, her face lit up with a mischievous smile which seemed to flicker with the passing streetlights.

The next morning we were up early, trying to bodge the Escort sufficiently to make it home, in a plan which also involved cramming five people into my rather dreary Peugeot 406 saloon. 'Cram' was the operative word, as getting the people home was just the start – we also had the various piles of camping gear and three large climbing crash mats to wedge in somehow. The camping gear was easy – road trip rules clearly state that back seat passengers can be used as an extension of the boot if required, and so a smorgasbord of tents and campsite paraphernalia was wedged in around the car's occupants for the twelve hour drive home. The crash pads required slightly more lateral thinking however, and were eventually lashed to the roof with tent guy lines and what few pieces of rope we had. Lee's Escort had its rear body panel hammered out so it was no longer scuffing the tyre and so, already late, we set off for the ferry port.

Things weren't going too badly until we were about an hour from the port, and the blustery coastal weather started to pick up, buffeting the cars and spraying us with rain. The gusty wind found its way under the three suitcase-sized crash pads strapped to the roof, stretching the ropes and slowly working them loose. But we were running late for the ferry and couldn't afford to stop and readjust the ropes, and so we took the only logical course of action available. We opened all four of the Peugeot's windows, and flew down the road into the storm-strafed sunset at 80 miles per hour, with four very wind-chilled arms reaching up onto the roof and physically holding the flapping crash pads in place. Highway to Hell was blasting out of the stereo as we understeered our way into the ferry port, skidded to a halt at the ticket booth and handed over our reservation.

'Just the four of you in there?' said the ticket man as he handed us our boarding passes.

'Yep, bye,' replied Brummy, from the front seat passenger seat, as he grabbed the pieces of paper and we raced down to board the ferry with only a few minutes to spare. And with Jenny, our fifth passenger, hidden under a pile of coats on the back seat, trying not to laugh.

*   *   *

Bouldering trips to Fontainebleau never ceased to be fun and every trip there was a blur of climbing, laughter and campfires. But by its very definition, bouldering can't be an adventure, and it says a lot that sometimes the most adventurous aspect of a bouldering trip turned out to be the driving aspect. I will always cherish the memories of my climbing holidays and I still look forward to every future outing, but it was clear back then, on that drive home from Fontainebleau, that my desire for adventure would never be satisfied by bouldering alone, however big a role it ended up playing in my life. I'd found a great hobby, but not the calling I was searching for, and bouldering was to become a cul-de-sac from which I had to drive out of to find true adventure.

FIVE

DÉJÀ VU

28th March 2013
Plymouth, UK

Just as the drive home from Fontainebleau isn't always as simple as it should be, so the journey there often doesn't go as smoothly as it could. For the V8Nam Expedition's departure to the continent, there was the small issue of our passports, which only managed to complete the return journey from the Kazakh Embassy 28 hours before our departure. Then there was that perennial issue which plays on the mind of every indefatigable adventurer who attempts the uncertain journey from Britain to France – the ubiquitous ferry strike. This one kept us in limbo until the morning on which we hit the road, but eventually blew over a couple of hours before we set off.

With the obstacles cleared, I swung the Corvette down off Dartmoor, the sweeping country roads taking me into the city of Plymouth where my co-driver was waiting. As I drove I thought back to the trauma which occurred the last time I'd set off on such a big trip, when I'd left for Africa in the Porsche. This time, our departure had been much less fraught. There had been no catastrophic failure of the trip car just before we'd left, and no wars had flared up along our planned route. However, there was one similarity to my departure nearly five years previously which cast its cloud across the crisp march air: co-driver complications.

I pulled up in the terraced street and shut down the engine. The silence was broken only by the wailing of a car alarm and the residual drone of the Corvette's exhaust, which was still ringing in my ears. I wandered over to the front door of the terraced house and rang the bell. The tinker of footsteps drew closer.

'I'm still packing,' Kim announced with an apologetic smile as the door swung open.

It was a strange moment. Just as had happened in the build up to the Africa trip which I'd shared with Laura five years before, the months before we'd set off on V8Nam had been complicated by my co-driver choosing another guy a few months earlier. By the time this had happened, Kim and I had already agreed to team up for the first part of the trip, but our differences meant we'd barely spoken in the preceding month and now we were setting off across Europe together. Or at least we would be, when Kim finished packing.

It was a struggle to fit Kim's suitcase and backpack into the already jam-packed Corvette, but we managed it after a fashion and then set off to catch the ferry to France, already running a little later than planned.

If there's one thing which looks conspicuous cruising down a high street in the UK, it's a bright red Corvette covered in stickers and announcing its arrival via a soundtrack which does a pretty good impression of a warzone. Kim felt decidedly self-conscious and found herself trying to hide in the passenger seat, declaring the newly stickered and roof-racked Corvette to be 'the most ridiculous thing I've ever sat in'. She wasn't the only one feeling self conscious of course; the awkward atmosphere between us made me feel self-conscious too. The situation felt completely unnatural, given how well we'd been getting on a few months before.

'Still', I thought to myself. 'At least it's not as bad as Africa was – we have a working car, for a start.'

Leaving town revealed the first flaw in my plan to drive to Asia – the hastily-installed roof rack started flapping about rather violently when we exceeded 55mph. We pulled over and fixed the problem by removing the spare wheel from the roof – increasing the cabin overcrowding to a near critical level – and tightening the rack supports. This is the sort of issue you can expect when you throw together a roof rack over a few beers using whatever bits of wood and metal you have lying around, and attach it to the car with ratchet straps, just before you leave.

We cruised onward towards Dover, catching up on what had happened over the past few months, when we'd not really been communicating. It was uncanny how similar the situation was to when I'd set off on the African Porsche Expedition with Laura five years before. Still, at least this time we'd only be on the road for two weeks together, as Kim was all set to fly home from Kiev. And anyway, my time in Africa with Laura hadn't ended so badly after all.

This time however, I knew that things would be different. Rather than leading to anything more, our two weeks together would be more of a long goodbye. As if to emphasize the fact, Kim received a message from her boyfriend as we headed through the night towards Dover.

'That's Zack,' she said. 'They're making good time and it looks like they'll be on the same ferry as us.'

Yes, for the first few days of the trip, during which we'd be camping in Fontainebleau, Kim's boyfriend – 'the other guy' – would be joining us. To say I wasn't particularly excited at the prospect would be putting it mildly.

'Great,' I replied. 'I might slow right down in that case. In fact, maybe we should head to somewhere else for the weekend. Like Snowdonia, maybe?'

'Oh shut up,' said Kim. 'You guys will get on great. I know it.'

'I'm not holding my breath.'

*   *   *

For the last few hours of the journey to Dover, I let Kim get behind the wheel. As the Corvette was the first left hand drive car she'd driven, it took her some time to get used to the lane positioning. However, the near-death experiences which resulted from our close encounters with other traffic at least distracted me from ruminating on the situation which I'd once again found myself in, and eventually we were rolling onto the ferry to France, somehow still in one piece.

We found Zack in the vessel's aft restaurant with some friends, who he was travelling to Font with. While Kim was thrilled at their reunion, I immediately felt an uneasy awkwardness come over me. I wanted to escape the situation, but for the next 90 minutes, we'd be trapped on the ship together. Trapped at the same table, in fact. I tried not to show my awkwardness by hiding it behind a wall of bravado, but I doubt I fooled anyone. I'm not exactly prone to such confidence in social situations and putting on such a front doesn't come naturally. Escape was all I wished for, and during the 90 minutes in which I was on the ferry, all I wanted to do was hit the road on the other side, to fire up that big, ground-shaking V8 and roar off through the night to the magical Fontainebleau Forest. Trapped behind my wall of bravado, I counted down the minutes as the English Channel passed beneath us.

*   *   *

The week-long Easter pilgrimage to Fontainebleau Forest had been a tradition for most of my adult life and this was the tenth year on the trot in which it had taken place. Many of my old university friends join the exodus and most years, around twenty of us would pitch our tents and make our homes among the trees, climbing and hiking the days away, before spending the evenings sat around the camp fire. It's something I always looked forward to; a retreat to one of my favourite places in the world, and if this year's trip may have had an unwanted spin to it, at least the large size of our group meant the time I had to spend with Kim and Zack would be minimised. For three days, I made a conscious effort to keep my distance. If they went hiking in one part of the forest, I'd make a point of going climbing in some other area. If they went into town, I'd head for the supermarket. The place was certainly big enough for us all, except in the evenings, when the campfire would call and everyone would come together to share banter and beer into the night. This made the game of avoidance impossible and I'd fall silent, hoping to disappear into the shadows, wondering why life always seemed to pan out like this for me. As the air flickered with flames and laughter, I'd find myself sitting alone in the crowd, wishing that the time to hit the road out of there would hurry up and arrive.

Eventually, on one bright Tuesday morning with birdsong ringing out through the familiar forest canopy, that moment came. It was time to achieve a dream; to drive to the far side of Asia. Despite the emotional battering of the previous days, the thought made me smile, as it wasn't the first time I'd set out on a long drive east across Asia. No, eight years earlier a chance conversation had sewn the seed which led to my first Asian adventure and after that conversation, life had never been the same again.

SIX

A NEW BEGINNING

19th July 2005
Sharpness Docks, Gloucestershire, UK

I watched as the crane loaded the jagged pieces of scrap metal into the cargo ship's open hold. In a cycle which lasted exactly one minute, it would fill its grab from the pile on the quay then rotate, positioning the grab directly above the vessel's hold. The operator would then release the load, which crashed down in an explosion of noise. A plume of dust would rise up into the dry air as the crane swung back shore side to collect another load, and then repeat the cycle. One cycle every minute. Sixty cycles per hour. A whole day spent between shore and vessel, rotating left and right, picking up cargo, sending it crashing down. When the pile on the shore began to drop too low and it appeared that the monotony might be interrupted, a bulldozer would replenish it. When the crane driver needed a cuppa and a bacon sandwich to break the stuporing cycle, another worker would come and take his place. Pick up the cargo and swing left, drop the cargo then swing back to the right. Repeat ad infinitum, cycle after cycle, hour after hour, day after day. The sun arced overhead, marking the passing hours as I watched the ship gradually sink deeper, waiting for the water to reach the load line, at which point it would be fully loaded and the cycle would stop for as long as it took for the loaded vessel to make ready and sail, and the next ship to come alongside.

I was at work. And I'd rather have been anywhere else.

Back in those days, work for me entailed being a marine surveyor. When the crane finally stopped loading the ship, my job was to work out how much cargo had been loaded, by calculating how much water the vessel was displacing, along with the weights of everything else onboard – a pretty unchallenging task, given the marine engineering degree I'd gained in Plymouth years before. I'd been doing the job for several years, ever since leaving the graduate training scheme at the naval dockyard in Devonport – another place I hadn't wanted to be, a workplace which had worn me down with an overexposure to the colour grey. Grey buildings, grey ships, grey skies, grey people; there was only so long I could endure the blandness, so I'd quit and had become a surveyor instead. And that's how I found myself stood next to a Dutch cargo ship, waiting for the stevedores to to finish loading it. But I didn't want to be there, either. I was a square peg in a round hole, and my mind was far away, still invigorated by a world of soaring mountains, thin air and alpenglow.

A few days earlier I'd been lying in my tent, which was pitched on a glacier in the shadow of the Aguille Verte, high in the Alps. A blood-red sunset had given way to an uneasy night and shortly after midnight a storm had broken. Lightning crashed into the granite outcrops nearby, sending flashes of light strobing through the thin fabric shell on which our lives depended. Propelled by a hurricane wind, waves of hail blasted the tent, coming so thick that it sometimes flowed down the glacier like water. The night seemed to go on forever and the storm meant we'd failed to complete the route to the summit our chosen mountain, but it didn't seem to matter. Memories had been made, rich memories of time spent truly living, away from the torpor of the everyday. And despite failing to climb the mountain, the trip could be considered a success, as we'd had an adventure and made it back to the UK in time for our respective jobs. But to find myself back there, standing on the dockside as the crane swung left and right and the dust hung like a haze in the warm air, was all too much.

Wanting to be anywhere else, I jumped into the tatty old Porsche 944 which passed for my somewhat ill-advised daily driver and headed over to the shipping agent's offices in search of a coffee and a break from the mind-numbing, minute-long cycle of grab and drop, grab and drop. John the agent greeted me at the door, his pony tail and Doc Marten boots marking him out as another person who, like me, didn't exactly slot comfortably into the career life.

'Hi Ben, welcome back,' he said. 'How were the Alps?'

'Well, it was a nice enough break, but we didn't get up much. The weather was terrible. We seemed to spend half the trip hiding from storms in the valley.'

'With a beer in hand, no doubt?' he asked.

'Of course. We had to pass the time somehow,' I replied.

John set about making the coffee as we chatted about the previous few weeks and then we walked into his office. He never looked comfortable or at home in an office. He was an individualist, caught in a space which was defined by bland functionality. Like me, he would often exude an impression of restlessness, of being sustained through the mundane everyday by thoughts of something more, somewhere beyond the whitewashed walls, cheap carpet and the view across the docks which the window offered. And on that day, his mind was clearly elsewhere, as he opened up the web browser on his computer.

'Ben, you like stupid adventurous stuff,' he said. 'I bet this is right up your street.'

On the computer screen was the website for an event called the Mongol Rally. I'd never heard of it.

'So, what's that then?' I asked.

'It's brilliant,' he said. 'Basically, you get the worst car you can find and then try to drive it to Mongolia. I'd love to do it if I could find the time.'

'I can definitely see the appeal,' I replied.

I still had an hour to wait until the ship finished loading and I could get to work, and so for that hour my focus was on this new form of adventuring which I'd never heard of before. The Mongol Rally had launched a year earlier, with six vehicles attempting the 10,000 mile slog across

Asia, and as the hour we spent chatting about it progressed, my mind became more and more made up. Stepping out of John's office into the fresh air, I resolved that the following year, instead of spending another summer in the Alps, getting scared, dodging the weather and failing to climb anything, I was going to make it happen. I was going to drive to Mongolia.

My next thought was, 'where the hell is Mongolia?'

Honestly, I didn't really know, other than that it was a long way away, somewhere on the far side of Asia. I think I had a hunch that it was just past a few countries whose names ended in 'stan', but beyond that, I wasn't really sure. My knowledge of Central Asia's geography was pretty terrible.

Despite always having had this determination to experience adventure, in many ways my knowledge of the world had been held back by the nature of those adventures. My climbing had taken me to the Alps and many beautiful corners of the UK but really, it hadn't given me much real knowledge of lesser-climbed places further afield. I was so untraveled that I'd never so much as gotten a stamp in my passport, and the world seemed a very vague place. To this climber of limited ability, the Himalaya represented a blur of lofty remoteness, somewhere over the horizon. The Andes? That was where Joe Simpson fell down a crevasse, broke his leg then wrote a book about it – nothing more. Up until that moment when I thought 'where the hell is Mongolia', my knowledge of the world was pretty limited. I just didn't really have any idea of quite how limited, as life had never exposed my lack of knowledge by drawing me to look closer.

But the human mind is like a gas – it will expand itself to fill the available space. And as I started to look beyond my own limited horizons, my mind broadened in response to this new world which I was only now discovering. As these new expanses of potential adventure revealed themselves to me for the first time, a fascination in the varied world beyond the crags and mountains began to develop. From hiding my lack of knowledge behind casual dismissal – because after all, why the hell would you want to visit somewhere like Uzbekistan anyway? – I delved deeper and deeper, populating these empty spaces in my head where previously, not even my imagination had roamed. Because if I was to drive to Mongolia, I was going to have to pass through these places, and to do that, I needed to understand them. It was that process of delving deeper which transformed my world view. The easily ignored became the uniquely appealing, and the knee-jerk dismissal of the 'stans was quickly replaced with dreams of desert adventures, remote wild-camps and unseen relics of the Silk Road.

Through the promise of offbeat automotive adventure, the world was opening up to me for the first time. The vaguely imagined emptiness of the map began to be replaced with a researched reality; blankness was replaced by richness and craving, all thanks to the unique freedom offered by the automobile.

Ah yes, the automobile. That was another thing I'd have to master, for despite taking great pleasure in driving, I was far from a competent mechanic. I didn't own so much as a socket set, had never even carried out an oil change and probably thought a multimeter was probably some obscure unit of measurement. Looking after cars was another challenge I'd have to confront.

During the chat with John, I'd decided that the classic Mini would be the perfect vehicle to drive to Mongolia. This decision was based purely on my appreciation of the absurd – the idea of crossing the vastness of the planet in something so tiny struck a chord with me. Back then, you could pick up an old Mini for a few hundred pounds and while I didn't really know how to keep a Mini running, they were simple enough that I felt they weighed the mechanical odds in my favour, while still promising to look rather cool out on the Kazakh Steppe. A few months after that pivotal chat with John, I tracked down a 1991 Mini City with less than 40,000 miles on the clock, owned by that mythical old lady which every second-hand car buyer dreams about – you know, the one who only ever drove it to the shops once a week. It was a dark and drizzling evening in South Wales when I viewed it and my torch picked out a few patches of rust, but it ran and drove well enough to justify the asking price of £450, and so it was quickly mine.

When I got it home, I was able to look around my purchase properly for the first time and I saw that on the numberplate where a garage name sometimes lurks, a previous owner had added a sticker which read 'My name is Daisy.' I had my first ever trip car, and now she had a name too.

By this stage, my friend Lee had already bought a Mini for the trip. I'd always known he would. From the moment I'd heard about the Mongol Rally, I knew Lee would be coming along, so perfectly did the event match his finely tuned appreciation of the absurd. Small in stature and thin of hair, Lee's face was often punctuated by a manic grin whose size was directly proportional to the peril of the situation he found himself in. For him, ultimate happiness lay in dangerously loose sea cliff climbs off the Cornish coast, or out-of-condition snow gullies in Scotland. In fact, he was about the only person who was genuinely jealous of my avalanche-assisted descent of a Scottish mountain a few years before – a fact which tells you all you need to know about Lee's love of life's mad and ragged edge.

The Mongol Rally could have been designed specifically for him.

The same wasn't true of the other close friend who joined the trip, though. No, when I first heard about the idea, I didn't think my friend Brummy would be interested at all.

I knew Brummy through the University of Plymouth's climbing club – not so much through actually climbing together, but because at the end of the club social evenings, the two of us were invariably the last ones left propping up the bar. For years our friendship had been thus. While Lee and I would head to the mountains with dreams of challenging routes, Brummy would stay at home and be waiting for us in the pub with a round in when we returned. When it came to climbing, a bit of shared banter at the local climbing wall and a yearly stroll up something like Snowdon would suffice for Brummy, as his reasons for being in the club were very different to ours. He had never projected an air of someone who craved adventure and his appearance was the reciprocal opposite of the anarchic, dirt-bagging climbers we aspired to be. Always impeccably shaved, with neatly cropped hair gelled down onto his forehead and a friendly, rounded face balanced atop a figure built for comfort rather than speed, for all the world he looked like an office-bound IT consultant. Which was rather apt, given that's exactly what he did for a job.

Between Lee and Brummy, only one of them projected an aura of being someone who would consider being broken down on the Kazakh Steppe with an explosively upset stomach to be a crowning moment in their life. However, I'd clearly misjudged Brummy, as he jumped at the suggestion of coming along. With a girl called Tiffany recruited from the climbing club as a fourth member and two Minis bought and ready for the off, the summer of 2006 couldn't come soon enough. The unknown landscapes of Eastern Europe, Russia and Central Asia were waiting for us over the horizon, with all the adventures they'd entail. Very soon, they'd no longer be beckoning to us from afar – we'd be there upon their roads and tracks, bouncing along in our Minis, living the adventure for real.

SEVEN

EAST AGAIN

April 02nd 2013
Fontainebleau Forest, France

We could feel the vistas of Eastern Europe and Asia calling us from beyond the horizon as we took down our tents and loaded up the Corvette, ready to begin our journey across the world in earnest. It was a beautiful morning. The just-risen sun was shining low through the forest, its shafts of light diffused by a soft haze. Songbirds flitted between the trees, and a few early risers were leaving their tents to make coffee.

It had been almost seven years since I'd set off across Asia in the Mini and now here I was, about to do it all again. But how different so many things were! Instead of Daisy the Mini, there was the shock and awe Corvette and instead of clueless naivety, I now carried a quiet confidence born of experience. I'd come so far in those intervening years. Hell, I'd even figured out how to do an oil change, and had gained a basic level of car-fixing competence. But for all that had changed, some things were just the same. The anticipation for the adventure. The lure of the open road, the draw of a magnetic line on an unknown map. Over the previous seven years, road tripping adventures had become something I defined myself by, but familiarity hadn't lessened the joy they gave. The magic was still there.

Such were the thoughts which occupied my idle mind as I struck camp and prepared for a day on the road. Rose-tinted nostalgia and thoughts of simpler times were far more appealing than dwelling on certain aspects of the present.

Since reaching the campsite, I'd managed to avoid Kim pretty successfully, but the act of loading the car brought us into proximity once again and for the coming weeks there would be no escaping each other. We tried to create an air of normality through small talk and teamwork, but our efforts seemed only to emphasize the gulf between us. It had the potential to be a long few weeks before she flew home from Kiev and I was glad we wouldn't be making the trip alone, as when we'd arrived on the campsite, we'd met up with V8Nam's second car, with which we'd be convoying across Asia. And what a car it was.

*   *   *

Our trip's other vehicle had rather fittingly come into my life at ten minutes to midnight on the previous Halloween. The sky had been storming all day, but the raging weather had yielded to an ominous, uneasy silence, through which a far-off rumble had begun to echo through Dartmoor's spooky darkness. Flashes of light had flickered through the trees as it drew closer, the bass-laden noise building to a deep growl as the acrid smell of tortured oil began to fill the air.

Our adventure's second car had arrived, and what a sight it was to behold.

'So, it made it all the way from Southampton, then?' I said to Brummy as he parked the behemoth.

'Of course it did. It's a *Rolls-Royce*, the best car on the planet,' he replied, emphasizing the brand of his latest acquisition with a smug grin.

I joined Brummy in the spacious cabin of the newly-purchased 1978 Rolls-Royce Silver Shadow II and poured us each an Ardbeg whisky as he ran me through its gloriously over-engineered controls, while trying not to think about the laughable fuel economy. Having never been in a Rolls-Royce before, the bespoke, heavyweight feeling which each component exuded was as novel as it was impressive and even through the darkness, the spaciousness and comfort was so apparent that I almost regretted opting for the cocoon-like Corvette as my V8Nam car. Brummy told me about the drive home as we sipped our drams of whisky.

'It never missed a beat. The gauges all stayed where they're supposed to, and it drives brilliantly. It's not silent. You can just about hear the engine in the background as you're cruising along, but the ticking clock is definitely louder. And the ride is great, really smooth and comfortable.'

'And you can make some money on the side doing unimaginative weddings, too,' I suggested.

'You're just jealous because you've got to drive all the way to Vietnam in that tasteless piece of American crap, while I waft there gloriously in a Rolls-Royce,' he replied. 'It's a *Rolls-Royce*. The best car in the world. Nothing you can say can change that.'

'The number of times it breaks down en-route will change that,' I suggested.

'It won't break down,' was the reply. 'Which bit of *best car in the world* don't you understand?'

'I'll remind you of that when it catches fire in Kazakhstan and becomes the best bonfire in the world.'

*　　*　　*

So that was the convoy with which we'd be setting out to travel to Vietnam – an old-world aristocrat of a Rolls-Royce and an all-American 'vette. And in the months leading up to our departure, my quips about the Rolls' reliability had unfortunately proven to not be entirely unfounded. To put it mildly, it had a few problems. A visit to the rarefied world of a Rolls-Royce specialist garage near Exeter showed up a dodgy carburettor, below-par fuel pump, worn-out rear suspension, a broken heater control module, binding brakes, leaking exhaust manifolds and brake accumulators, and a fine collection of rust. And of course, the biggest problem in my eyes – it wasn't a sports car.

However despite this rather daunting list, a chat with the garage owner resulted in the conclusion that it was only the carburettor and brake issues which would stop the old behemoth making it through the 12,000-or-so miles to South East Asia, and with these fixed, the Rolls was ready for its adventure, and in its defence it had made it from the UK to the campsite in France without a hitch. As Kim and I loaded up the Corvette, Brummy and Team Rolls were doing the same a few metres away. The expedition was about to hit the road to the East in earnest.

But first, we had to make it out of Fontainebleau Forest. And having been waved off the campsite by our friends – Team Corvette naturally wearing matching red ear defenders against the small block Chevy V8's unholy noise – we attempted to do just that and made it a grand total of two miles from the campsite before the Rolls ground to a halt by the side of the road. I pulled over behind and wandered over to Brummy's window.

'Only two miles, that's gotta be a record. Even your Fiat 126 made it fifty miles before it exploded.' I said.

'Aren't you forgetting your Porsche?' he replied. 'That didn't even make it to the start line without a new engine.'

'It still got to Cape Town though,' I replied. 'But isn't this supposed to be the best car in the world? What's wrong with the crass piece of crap?'

'There's a weird rubbing sound coming from the back. I don't think it likes being four-up with a boot full of stuff.'

Following a thorough investigation in which it was decided that the rubbing wasn't that bad and the best solution was to just ignore it and hope it went away, we re-boarded our steeds and continued our indefatigable drive eastwards. Or we would have, if the Rolls' engine had started when the key was turned.

'What's up?' I shouted over.

'It won't start,' Brummy replied. 'Flat battery I think.'

'Ah yes. Exactly what you'd expect from the best car in the world,' I replied.

'Even broken down, it's still better than that American dick of yours,' he replied.

'Keep telling yourself that,' I said. 'Do you want me to jump start the worst car in the world, or not?'

'Yes please,' came the reply.

We made it as far as the countryside around Dijon that day, with the Rolls-Royce celebrating its status as the best car in the world by continuing to rub its rear tyres and letting out a puff of oil smoke from the exhaust every few miles. But at least it was still going, even though as we pitched camp, we discovered that it had picked up one more means to torment its crew.

'Does anyone else's stuff absolutely stink of petrol?' asked Brummy, to no-one in particular.

'Yeah, mine does,' replied Fred, who was hitching a lift to Vienna in the Rolls, with the ironic purpose of attending a conference on climate change. 'My sleeping bag in particular. What do you think is causing that, then?'

'Well, the fuel tank is under the boot floor. It must be seeping up somehow,' said Jon, another member of team Rolls who, with nothing better to do for a few weeks, had spontaneously decided to join us as far as the Ukraine.

'Ah crap,' said Brummy. 'We'd better do something about that.'

By this time the tents were pitched and the air was getting chillier by the minute, so we decided to ignore the issue for the moment and head off to the local bar instead, where taxidermied animals and pictures of rally cars jostled for space on the overcrowded walls.

Despite it being April, spring was elusive. The trees were still skeletal and bare and a hard frost had formed overnight, meaning that we awoke to the heavy stillness of a winter's morning, in which down jackets were de rigueur. The roar of our camping stoves broke the silence and as the coffee was prepared, the petrol-soaked Team Rolls kept a safe distance from the flames, while Kim and I crowded in to warm our hands by the burner. And then, with camp struck, we carried on east.

We rolled on into Switzerland, pulling over in a place where the chill air tumbled down from snow-capped peaks, chasing around us as we gazed upwards. The mountains were magnificent and years ago my excitement would have bubbled over as my eyes covetously scanned their features, with every ridge and gulley drawing my attention as a potential route to an unknown summit, but not anymore. I still loved the mountains, but my life had changed and I knew I'd never climb these ones. They were other peoples' adventures now.

We carried on, the Corvette's thunderous exhaust note ricocheting amongst the ridges and gullies, my fading dreams of snowy summits silent beneath the soundtrack of my new direction.

The snow lay thick on the ground as we rolled into Bavaria, our irrational convoy heading to possibly the world's most famous monument to insanity – Neuschwanstein Castle, built by King Ludwig II in an effort to bring to life his dreams of a more romantic age of knights and chivalry. Neuschwanstein was one of Europe's biggest tourist attractions and the sort of place which years before, as an anarchic climber, I would have gone to great lengths to avoid. But I was different now, and my desire to understand the world which made up the backdrop to my adventures now brought me to these places. On climbing trips, the only big old buildings I'd enter were churches which had been converted into climbing walls and offered sanctuary when rain dampened the rock, but I now found myself joining the crowds to wander the Romanesque halls painted with depictions of Wagner's operas, and not wishing I was somewhere else.

I still found myself eyeing up the gaps in the brickwork and imagining them as handholds though, my mind linking them together into climbing routes upon the castle's dazzling walls – thanks to my continued bouldering, that was one part of being a climber which hadn't left me.

*   *   *

Days rolled on into one other, accompanied by the drone of the tyres and the exhausts, and the happy chatter which filled the Corvette's cabin as Kim and I put our differences aside and remembered why we'd got on so well months earlier. It all felt so easy, so routine, and so normal. Seven years since the Mongol Rally, drives like this had become something through which I defined myself. They were part of my identity; they were what I did. And by virtue of that, they'd become normalised in my mind. The very act of driving across country after country now felt as commonplace as driving to work at the docks once had. This was a sign that things had changed, of course – not least within me. My years of experience had yielded an unshakable confidence in my ability to complete these drives and I felt an unwavering sense of inevitability about the Corvette reaching the far side of Asia. With this growing confidence came the ever increasing sense of theatre which was applied to our drives, as evidenced by the drift from one-litre Minis to a couple of the biggest V8s available. Whereas once the appeal of these trips was the leap from the comfort zone into the unknown, now I felt just as at home crossing Europe in a Corvette as I did anywhere else. The cabin of the Corvette was already my comfortable place, far away from the stresses of real life.

But just as when we toured the Bavarian castle, we did leave the comfort of the 'vette's interior from time to time.

In Austria for instance, where having parked the Corvette amid a crescendo of car alarms, we spent several days wandering around Vienna, a glorious place rendered untidy by the last of the snows, which were stained to impurity by the dust of the city. Or in Budapest, which for us was an overnight stop in a hostel still proudly bearing bullet scars from the revolution against the Soviets which took place in 1956. The alternating cycle of driving and sightseeing became our world as we rolled onwards through the days, waiting for the sense of the routine to leave the trip as we left behind the familiarity of this world we already knew so well.

It happened after we crossed into Romania and found ourselves leaving the West behind as we manoeuvred the cars around potholes, horse-drawn carts and eventually, mountain hairpins, before rolling into the modestly-sized town of Borsa, in the country's north, after dark. Daylight revealed it to be a more appealing place than I'd expected from our nocturnal arrival. Weary though not-totally-worn-out buildings nestled together in a groove between the mountains, and heavy set locals went about their mornings while chickens rummaged in the yard beneath our hotel window. After the predictably thorough intake of caffeine with which every day began, we hit the road at nine, climbing out of the town into a magnificent tree-lined mountainscape; a new-to-us-all winter wonderland hidden far from the beaten track.

The snowbanks towered several feet high at the sides of the road as the Corvette roared its way up the mountain, snaking around hairpins and punching along straights to a summit where a lonely church stood sentinel, over 1,400 metres up. And then the road unravelled as it dropped from on high, sweeping sinuously into the village where the Rolls-Royce suffered its first puncture.

'Whoever did these wheel nuts up should be shot,' Brummy ranted as he set about swapping the tyre. 'They're all so tight they won't budge.'

'Have you tried stamping on the wrench?' I suggested, dragging myself away from making lunch to show some interest.

'Of course,' Brummy replied. 'They're so tight, they're not going anywhere.'

'Are you sure you're turning them the right way,' suggested Kim.

'Of course I am,' said Brummy. 'Look, I'll stamp on the other end of the cross-wrench to prove it.'

As his foot came down, the nut turned. Carefully, he kept going nervous that he might be destroying the threads on the nuts. We watched in silence, trying not to laugh.

'What's that all about?' he asked. 'Why on Earth did Rolls-Royce think it was a good idea to make them turn the other way to every other car on the planet?'

'Maybe it's for security. It certainly outwitted you, for starters,' I said.

'So helpful,' Brummy replied. 'Don't feel like you have to wait for us. Feel free to take that crappy American car of yours and wait for us at the border.'

And so Kim and I left Team Rolls in a tyre repair shop and headed out east alone, enjoying the freedom of not having to convoy with the our slower-driving companions. The mountains gave way to flat plains as we approached the Moldovan border, and we joined the local traffic in the enthusiastic overtaking attempts which had became the norm ever since we left Austria. The roads seemed to inexplicably run out ten miles from the border and we found ourselves bouncing across gravel and puddles in a generally eastern direction, the Corvette parting herds of sheep as we asked directions from their confused shepherds. Eventually, we got our bearings when we arrived at a rail-only border and were forced to crash our way north along another fifteen miles of rutted tracks to the road border, which the better-navigated Rolls-Royce had reached an hour earlier.

A flurry of Corvette-related photo opportunities for the border guards accompanied our exit from the European Union and very soon, we were rolling up to the entry to Moldova. But here, we found the border guards were predictably prickly, immediately denying the Corvette entry due to the lack of an insurance green card, despite having let the Rolls-Royce enter the country in similar circumstances half an hour earlier. After a while, a mixture of negotiation and impasse, threats and persuasion prised the door open, thanks to a promise to buy insurance just up the road, where Team Rolls were waiting. Brummy strolled out of the night as I pulled up alongside their very English vehicle.

'We've been here for half an hour,' he said. 'The saleswoman's been getting so confused trying to enter all the information that she actually punched the keyboard at one stage. If you walk in now and try to buy insurance she'll probably have a fit. You won't believe what we found earlier, by the way.'

'Another car as puncture-prone as your Rolls?'

'You could say that. We were driving to the border and I looked in the rear view mirror and honestly, I thought I was going mad. I was sure I could see the front of my car in the mirror but couldn't for the life of me figure out what was going on. I mean, what are the chances of meeting another identical Rolls-Royce in Eastern Romania?!'

'Really?' I said, suspecting a wind-up.

'Yep, another Silver Shadow. British plates on it, as well. We pulled over for a chat. The Moldovan guy driving it had bought it in London as a present for his dad, shipped it to Romania, and was driving it home from the port.'

'I know that guy,' Kim said. 'I was chatting to him at the border. He's studying in London and is home for the holidays. His dad seems to own half the businesses in Moldova. His Rolls is with the customs guys, and his brother is giving him a lift home from the border.'

Still somewhat amazed by the coincidence of meeting another British-registered Rolls-Royce in Romania, I decided to enter the illuminated portacabin we'd pulled up next to and brave the insurance lady, who'd calmed down a little from the stress generated by her attempts to insure the Rolls. All was going well until a second, rather drunk Moldovan lady started shouting at our stressed saleswoman from just outside the door. Clearly unhappy with the situation, the aggression in her voice gradually built until, unable to contain herself, she burst in and commenced a physical attack, hitting and ripping the glasses off her victim. To say we were somewhat taken back by the rapidity in which we'd found ourselves spectators to a wrestling bout between two elderly Moldovan women would be an understatement but fortunately, the combined strength of our party was sufficient to pull the squabbling babushkas apart. In a blur the police were called, and our Rolls-Royce owning Moldovan friend arrived and pretty much completed the insurance paperwork for us, while repeatedly apologising for his country. Despite being held apart, scuffles between the two women continued until a policeman arrived from the border, and with witness statements taken and insurance documents completed, we hit the road into the Moldovan night, blindly following a Vauxhall Insignia driven by our savour's brother to a hotel in Chisinau, the capital. Being young and local, these guys didn't hang around, and I was glad of my 5.7l V8 as I raced to keep up, the Rolls often falling back into the night as we slalomed around potholes and raced down the straights to the hotel, the chase through the darkness infused with a nostalgic déjà-vu for our first-ever drive east, seven years earlier in our Minis.

EIGHT

FIRST TIME EAST

26ᵗʰ July 2006
Pytalovo, Russia

We raced through the night in our Minis, dodging the potholes which sprung from the darkness like traps as we followed a Russian policeman to the hotel. It wasn't quite how we'd expected our time in Russia to begin, but we'd managed less than an hour in the country before the policeman had flagged us down and insisted we follow him to a certain hotel of his choosing, because 'it's dangerous here.' In no position to argue, we did exactly that, our way lit up by the pulsating blue lights atop the police Lada, which gave a surreal air to proceedings.

We'd left London four days earlier.

The hotel turned out to be a standard ex-Soviet affair, familiar to anyone who has roamed the largest country on earth. An unloved building constructed from pale-coloured bricks, three stories high and with metal grates covering all the ground-floor windows, to guard against break-ins. Ladas, Moskvitches and old German cars dotted the broken tarmac outside, which seemed to lazily give way to grass and weeds at its outer edges. Inside, we found heavily patterned, mildewed carpets and wall coverings which were infused with a musty smell that seemed to reach us from decades ago. A disinterested woman sat behind the front desk, and somewhat more attentive members of staff looked after each floor, even though we were pretty much the only guests. But while the sights and aromas of the hotel may have been familiar to those who had travelled in this part of the world before, to me it was as alien as everything else which had happened since that moment four days earlier, when we'd pulled up to the start line of the rally.

Our journey had begun at Hyde Park in Central London, surrounded by almost 170 other vehicles which were attempting the drive to Mongolia, and all of them were a credit to their owner's imaginations. Pretty much the rally's only rule was that engines of over one litre capacity weren't allowed, and so we lined up amongst legions of Nissan Micras, Fiat Pandas, Volkswagen Polos and other shopping cars, all liberally festooned with roof racks, extra spotlights, stickers and mascots galore. A few teams opted for Suzuki Samurai 4x4s, while others had chosen the perennially reliable Bedford Rascal van for the trip. Some cars were fitted with snorkels to aid river crossings, while others seemed to be carrying more wheels on their roof racks than they had touching the road. There were several other teams of Minis, all with gleaming paint jobs, purposeful modifications and boxes full of spares which made our cheap and tatty entrants look most unprepared in comparison.

Until I'd reached the start line, my lack of comprehension as to what we were taking on had made me confident. As I wandered among the other entrants, seeing their workmanship and overhearing conversations about toughened-up suspension, extensive tool kits and well-thought-out tyre choices, I began to wonder how unfounded that confidence was. After all, not only were our cars woefully unprepared, but we didn't even have our passports.

But at least we weren't alone in that.

The rally organisers had agreed to get us all our visas and in keeping with the endearingly unorganised feel of the event, we showed up to the start line not knowing whether their applications had been successful. In fact, we didn't even get our passports back until an hour before we were due to leave. After collecting mine, I wandered back to the car, smiling to myself as I thumbed through the exotic-looking visas now stuck to the previously blank pages. My first ever visas.   Russia, Kazakhstan, Uzbekistan, Mongolia. As I walked through the crowd, past the lines of ready to roll rally cars and their enthusiastic crews, this surreal undertaking moved another step closer to feeling real.

The dream wasn't merely a dream any longer. Piece by piece, it was slowly coming true.

I climbed aboard Daisy, the £450 Mini which I'd plucked from its sedate lifestyle eight months earlier and with a wave from the organisers and our friends in the Red Mini next to us, the dream became real. Without the slightest idea of what I was getting myself into, I weighted the accelerator, lifted the clutch to its biting point and with nerves balanced against excitement, rolled forwards over the start line, into this brave new world of adventurous road trips.

A few hours later saw us in Calais, sat in our Mini as we waited for the ferry to lower its ramp and release us onto the continent. All around us, other ralliers were waiting in line, their brightly painted, sticker plastered and roof rack laden cars lending the car deck a carnival feel. We were all feeling impatient, eager for the off.

As we waited, a few of the cars started their engines and began to rev them, as if they were on the start line of some low-rent motor race. The noise echoed around the car deck.   Then one of the entrants sounded their horn. Another rallier joined in the beeping, and then another. An airhorn began to sound amid the uproar as a dozen, then two dozen, then three dozen horns joined in the deafening chorus. A Dixie horn punched through the drone as forty cars and almost a hundred people turned the ferry into a frenzied celebration of the anarchic side of road tripping. It was   an   atmosphere   charged   with   excitement   and expectation, and the hairs on the back of my neck stood up as I glanced around at my fellow ralliers, every one of them beaming with excitement, chomping at the bit and ready for the off.   I smiled back at them, waving a fist through Daisy's open window in celebration, as the slither of light at the end of the car deck grew wider with the opening of the bow doors and the first cars disembarked, Mongolia bound.

Naturally I would have joined in the horn tooting too, had I managed to fix the wiring before I'd left, but worryingly, back then such a heady feat of automotive engineering had proven beyond me.

We rolled off the ferry at sunset and drove straight through the night, fuelled by adrenaline. We didn't want to stop. The rally had an energy to it, an urgency which we all felt intensely as it swept our little Minis across Europe. Other rally cars swarmed on the road around us as we drove, and crowded the petrol stations wherever we stopped, making us feel part of something big and unstoppable, surging across the globe. Alone, we would have been daunted by the enormity of what lay ahead but with so many of us taking on the challenge, we were flushed with a sense of invincibility. We couldn't fail, not when we were part of something so big, being carried onwards by the combined momentum of 170 cars. Our Minis were part of a great river of automotive mediocrity which was flowing relentlessly east; propelled upon a wave of inevitability.

Day had become night with us behind the wheel, and we were still there pushing onwards when the sun returned. France fell behind us, then Belgium, then Germany. For ourselves and the other ralliers, the Czech Republic was a night out on the town in Prague, followed by a surprisingly long drive to Poland. Already the journey was becoming our lives, and the ever-changing world sweeping past our windows was the backdrop to the adventure. Vast plains of farmland morphed into forests, mountains came and were left behind, the buildings and signs changed with the hours and our excitement was sustained by the sensation of progress, of existing solely at the centre of this great adventure, on the crest of its wave.

The Mongol Rally wasn't how I'd ever imagined travel could be. As all my previous trips had been climbing related, they'd had a goal - get to the summit, complete the route, climb a certain boulder problem. This narrow perspective had led me to view what most folk referred to as travel – the slow drift from place to place, seeing sights, living out of a backpack – as strangely banal. I was convinced that a lack of excitement would mean I'd quickly get bored of such an experience; that I'd find the lack of a challenging goal to focus on would make the experience feel less than an adventure. Above all else, I thrived on the goal, the against-the-odds pursuit of a summit or route, and without such a clear-cut objective, the lure of the meandering backpacking trails had never grabbed me. But this was a different kind of travel, because in many ways the Mongol Rally had many of the same attributes of a climb. Just like the route to the summit of a challenging mountain, it was a trip into the unknown, sometimes dangerous, and always with the potential for the unexpected to occur. It was a team effort with a time limit and a simple, very arbitrary goal – to get to Mongolia. That was our 'summit'. But for me, there was one aspect of the Mongol Rally which meant it stood apart from hard climbing, and that was the fact the mental pressures of the trip were much less than on a serious climb. As we raced across Europe towards the Russian border, our Mini adventure seemed to offer many of the subtle excitements of a big climb, but without the tension which had prevented me from seriously chasing my mountaineering dreams.

I'd found a life with all of the excitement of climbing, but virtually none of the stress.

We crossed into Poland, then Latvia and Lithuania, driving by day and wild camping next to lakes or rivers at night, and as we did so I could feel my world changing. Not just outside, for while the changes to the landscape were obvious, the changes within me felt so much bigger. I was becoming a Mongol Rallier. It felt like an anarchic badge of honour – the symbol of someone for whom shunning the obvious choice of a 4x4 to instead drive a crap car to the far side of the world was a perfectly normal course of action. Already, I was proud of what I'd achieved with my £450 Mini, and I was growing more so with every milestone which passed us as we skimmed anarchically over the surface of the world.

Often, I found myself smiling to myself as I drove, thinking about where this life of adventures had led me. I liked the direction this new-found world of mine was going more with every extra mile east.

*   *   *

Once we'd made our way through the indecipherable bureaucracy of the Russian border and found ourselves following that police car through the darkness to that unloved hotel with the heavily patterned carpets and mouldy walls, something began to dawn on all of us, however. The rest of Europe had just been the warm-up, and now we were off the metaphorical map. It was here in Russia that the real adventure was going to begin.

NINE

THE CHAMELEON COUNTRY

10th April 2013
Chisinau, Moldova

Tired after the tricky border crossing, the fight at the insurance kiosk and the headlong rush through the night to the hotel, we rose late for our one and only morning in Moldova. The sky was a uniform blue, but there was still a chill in the air, as just like in the rest of Europe, spring seemed in no hurry to arrive.

Despite having been in the country for barely more than twelve hours, we started loading up the cars in order to head to Ukraine. We couldn't hang around, as Kim and several of the occupants of the Rolls-Royce had to catch flights home from Kiev. Moldova would be added to the long list of places I'd passed through, skimming over the surface and never really getting beneath the skin of; never really understanding.

Ever since the Mongol Rally seven years earlier, this rapid progress had always been something I'd loved about these drives – the satisfaction of always pushing on, sweeping through ever-changing landscapes and taking pleasure in advancing dramatically across a map. But as I thought forwards to the coming afternoon's border crossing into Ukraine – our second border crossing in 24 hours – I wondered whether I was missing something. Maybe those who travel slower, sacrificing the thrill of what feels like unstoppable momentum for the satisfaction of a deeper connection with a place, were onto something? Quite possibly, and certainly, since the Mongol Rally every big trip I'd made had been slower paced than the last. As I fired up the 'vette and headed back north, I could feel myself wishing I could stay just a little longer and get to know even a little of what makes Moldova tick. The guidebook talked of endless wine cellars beneath the ground and fine dining above it, and the few locals we'd met had certainly piqued our interest. But the urgency of our progress meant it wasn't to be. Just like so many overnight stops before it, Moldova was added to my list of places to return to for a more thorough exploration in the future, free from the time constraints inherent in a quick drive across the globe. The only problem was that with seven years of road trips having passed since the Mongol Rally, the list was already long enough to fill a lifetime of holidays. As I crossed the border into Ukraine that afternoon, deep down I knew that there was a good chance I'd never return to experience Moldova properly. I'd probably never be back, and the thought infused me with a slight emptiness.

*　　*　　*

The potholes started almost as soon as we left Moldova, appearing suddenly out of the darkness and pounding the Corvette, whose stiff suspension and low-profile tyres transmitted the impacts directly to Kim and I. We swerved left and right as we drove, attempting to avoid the worst of them, while the Rolls-Royce glided along imperviously, its occupants completely isolated from the broken tarmac and no doubt thinking our erratic progress seemed a tad melodramatic.

The rough roads led us to Vinnytsya – a town which naturally, we'd never heard of – and we checked into a once-opulent hotel in the centre of town, whose decline since its Soviet glory days had left it with no hot water, stinking bathrooms and stubbornly unhelpful staff. Still, at least they'd retained the heavily patterned, musty carpets, the starchy, Breshnev-era bedsheets and the garishly overpowering wallpaper with a sprinkling of mould, and I derived a twisted satisfaction from the resultant atmosphere, which flooded my mind with memories of that Russian hotel we'd stayed in during the Mongol Rally.

Once again, just like that day on the Mongol Rally, Western Europe had been well and truly left behind. The adventure was on.

The following day, potholes continued to be our constant companions as we headed to Kiev, a dull drive across uninspiring farmland, beneath a sky of monotone overcast. On reaching the outskirts of Kiev, our first impressions were of dreary buildings, grey skies, wailing car alarms and a seemingly unsmiling populous, while our first attempt at getting a meal resulted in a serving of uncooked chicken, cunningly concealed within a chicken Kiev while I received possibly the most laughably small attempt at a sandwich ever devised. And all the while, the people seemed to brush unsmilingly past whilst the cold, bland weather did nothing to sell the city's overbearing, Stalinesque architecture to us.

Yes, it's fair to say that after 24 hours in the country, Ukraine hadn't risen very high on our list of favourite places.

But no country I'd visited before had the ability to grow on you as quickly as Ukraine. On our second day there, the melancholy grey gave way to a crisp blue sky, through which uplifting shafts of sunlight speared between the buildings. We spent the morning wandering around Independence Square, the air flush with a buzz of optimism for the coming day and the grandiose architecture no longer dulled by both the previous day's drabness and our own fatigue. Even early in the day, the bars and restaurants were overflowing onto the streets as Kiev's beautiful people sat down to eat, drink and send laughter ringing through the crisp, cool air as they enjoyed the moment. As much as the weather, it was they who brought a positive air to the city, a cheery human side which defied a sad history.

For few countries have had a more unlucky recent history than Ukraine. In the 1930s, Stalin used the nation as a testbed for his unique brand of internal policies, the most destructive being collectivisation – the confiscation of land from farmers, to be amalgamated into large, state-managed farms. These farms were set unachievable quotas for production and were forced to run in a way which ignored everything the generations of farmers had learned up to that point – because obviously, the state knew best. Except in this instance, the state's assertion that it knew best, when combined with export quotas which left insufficient food for the general population, resulted in a famine in which over three million Ukrainians died. This famine was followed up a few years later by Stalin's Great Terror, a series of purges which indiscriminately hollowed out the general population by firing squad or expulsion to the gulags. If you think the country deserved some respite after all this, you'd be right. However unfortunately, Hitler had other ideas, and for the next few years two of the largest armies ever assembled fought each other, sweeping back and forth over the still-reeling lands, slaying combatants and civilians alike, destroying cities and adopting scorched-earth tactics which meant that by the time the dust settled and Ukraine found itself once again part of the USSR, another six million of its people lay dead. So it's fair to say that in living memory, Ukraine has had more than its fair share of pain. And that's before you remember that as you sip your coffee in a Kiev café, one of the more infamous places in recent history lies abandoned just over the horizon, 70 miles to the north.

Chernobyl, that symbol of catastrophe, where 27 years before our visit a bungled safety test had combined with a series of design flaws to send one of the reactors spiralling out of control. The resulting steam explosion blew the reactor apart and sent nine tonnes of super-hot radioactive material billowing into the atmosphere. Hundreds of the gallant and selfless people who worked to bring the situation under control received fatal doses of radiation and died from burns or radiation-related illnesses in the weeks and months after the explosion. Tens of thousands more people were forced to permanently leave their homes, and the legacy of the accident still lives on through increased rates of cancer among those affected. It will be 20,000 years before the immediately affected area will be safe for humans to live in again.

And speaking of disasters, for me the time in Kiev saw an altogether more personal disaster being brought to a close – it was time for Kim to return home. She left my life on our second morning in the city, shuttled to the airport in the Rolls-Royce along with the other folks for whom The Ukraine marked the end of their time on the trip.

Kim and I had got on well on the drive across Europe, but it was definitely time to go our separate ways. Before the trip, we'd not really talked as it would have been inappropriate to, and now our journey together was over, it was time to revert to how things had been before. I'd faced a similar situation years before, when I'd set off across Africa with Laura, but I knew this time it would be different. There would be no happy ending. The evening before she left, we talked things over.

'I just wish I could date Zack and have you as my adventure buddy,' she'd told me.

'You know that can't happen,' I'd replied.

'It's just not fair though,' she'd said. 'I wish we could just be friends.'

'That boat sailed last year when you didn't tell me about you and Zack,' I'd replied. 'With all that's happened, it wouldn't be fair on Zack for us to keep hanging out. That's why this has to be goodbye.'

'I guess,' she'd replied as she wiped a tear from her eye, and we'd chatted on for another hour with a false casualness, taking what awkward enjoyment we could from what I was sure would be the last time we'd meet.

The following morning, she'd messaged me from the airport, asking me not to walk out of her life. I hadn't replied.

*   *   *

We drove south out of Kiev, and alone in the Corvette, music blaring as I dodged potholes, I felt as if a weight had

73

been lifted from my shoulders. I'd miss Kim, but I'd done what needed to be done in order to avoid things escalating into a painful mess in the future. Well meaning friends told me that I'd dodged a bullet where Kim was concerned and as I drove, I hoped I'd dodged a bullet emotionally too, by getting away from the messy situation at the first possible opportunity. As the complications of having Kim in my life were left in the past I rolled onwards, my world distilled to just me, my Corvette and the 10,000 miles of road which stretched ahead to the South China Sea.

Our first stop after leaving Kiev was a relic from Ukraine's past, when Moscow's mutual animosity with The West called the shots. As we approached the site, which lay amid a flat sweep of farmland, there was nothing to hint at the power once contained behind the flimsy-looking fencing which surrounded it. However, appearances can be deceptive and we were actually on what was once the front line of the Cold War, a missile silo and command centre which, if hostilities commenced, was tasked with the destruction of much of Central Europe – not that you'd know it, as the smells of agriculture drifted to us from across the fields, and a few birds drifted peacefully overhead with the breeze. Nuclear Armageddon, hidden in plain sight.

The base of the 46th division of the 43rd Rocket Army of the Soviet Union consisted of a series of underground launch silos, one of which contained a control centre from which in the event of war, orders from Moscow would be received and carried out; orders which could, given the power of the tactical nuclear missiles housed in silos in this part of Ukraine, wipe large swathes of Europe off the map. When the Soviet Union collapsed and Ukraine finally became an independent state once again, it found itself in possession of the third-largest arsenal of nuclear weapons on the planet. Still reeling from the continuing impact of the Chernobyl disaster and facing an uncertain future financially, one of the first acts of the new government was to abolish this inherited nuclear capability, with all weapons being either destroyed or transferred trustingly to Russia. Over two decades on, this base and the museum it houses is all that's left of the nuclear capability which, for almost 40 years, existed beneath Ukrainian soil.

Our guide for the visit was an old soldier, his fatigues still bearing the insignia of his former unit. Once, he was the keeper of missiles aimed in our direction, but by the time of our visit he had become the custodian of a piece of history, preserved as a warning to the future. He led us through tunnels lined with cables and ducting, and we ducked under pipework and glanced at unidentifiable pieces of equipment. Deeper and deeper we went, eventually reaching a tiny elevator which sent us thirteen stories underground to the living quarters, and the control room. Here, our guide and his comrades would be sealed in for two weeks at a time, their world a cylinder just over 3m wide, resting at the bottom of a missile launch tube, ready to defend the Soviet Union. Banks of dials and controls lined the turquoise-painted, circular room, all focussed on ensuring that when the one button which mattered above all others was pressed, a missile would rise from the sleepy farmland of The Ukraine and arc through hundreds of miles of air to fall to its target, obliterating it with fire, shockwave and radiation.

Now the missiles are gone, and the launch button no longer has the power to change the world, except through the very act of its preservation, which in its own small way serves to guide the world in a brighter, less futile direction.

Unless you're Brummy, that is. Then it gives you something to press while shouting 'Fuck you, Paris!' with a worrying amount of glee.

*   *   *

The roads continued to take us east, and were far worse than I'd expected the Ukrainian tarmac to be. Rashes of potholes appeared without warning, and the Corvette's alloy wheels were dented, it's laughably low underside was repeatedly scraped across the fractured tarmac, and we almost ran out of fuel on several occasions as we crossed the less populated swathes of what is one of Europe's largest countries. I hadn't expected such difficulties at this stage of the trip, but I wasn't troubled by the heavier-than-expected going. I still had the confidence which came from being in my element, and I was also feeling positive thanks to having said goodbye to Kim. At that moment in 2013, my own personal present seemed to mirror Ukraine's – the future seemed brighter than the past.

For several days, it was an austere world through which we passed. Winter's grip remained powerful. The trees were yet to gain the luxury of foliage and the landscape's bleakness presented a world still missing the saturation of light and colour which spring would soon bring. The towns were austere too, their outer reaches marked by low-rise relics of wood or concrete tucked untrustingly behind tall fences, and their centres still a Soviet dream of concrete apartment blocks, rising above unlovely open spaces where weeds pushed up through concrete, windows were concealed behind iron bars and paint flaked into the wind.

Since independence, Ukraine hasn't had an easy ride. In the '90s, inflation had hit a peak of over 10,000%, and millions of people had left the country in search of a better life. Meanwhile, political manoeuvrings between those leaning towards a future closely aligned with Europe and those who were more comfortable in the Russian sphere of influence had paralysed the country's sense of direction. The seemingly starved-of-investment world we were driving across reflected this, and after several days alone in the Corvette, taking it all in, I thought I had long-suffering Ukraine all figured out.

But then we arrived at Donets'k.

Now, Donets'k is a fairly unhyped city of just under a million people. It's in the part of Ukraine which looks east to Russia, rather than west to the European Union, and as its claims to fame are concerned, being surrounded by coal mines is about as good as it gets. Donets'k is also not exactly short of heavy industry, but there is one thing it rather lacks - tourist attractions. Generally when the best-known sights a place has to offer are the main street and a six metre tall statue of a Soviet politician from 100 years ago, you don't rock up with particularly high expectations.

We'd planned on Donets'k being an overnight stop during our drive and after finding a cheap hotel, we popped out to find a bite to eat. Walking the main street, our city-du-jour wasn't exactly selling itself to us. The blandly soviet-styled buildings, while not completely run down, weren't exactly inspiring, and the more open spaces were equally predictable, right down to the T-34 tank mounted on a plinth in the centre of one of them, a monument to what is known in these parts as the Great Patriotic War. After a few miles of aimless strolling, we already felt like we'd seen it all before, and so we dropped into a bar to eat.

From the rather low-key entrance, the stairs dropped down into the building's basement, where the view opening up to reveal a large, high ceilinged room. Against the wall, the glittering bar was lined with all manner of glamorous bottles of spirit, and the well-attired bar staff were flamboyantly making obscure cocktails to order. Tables were packed with customers tucking into pizzas, the beer was flowing freely and the walls were lined with a surf bar decor inspired by the far-off worlds of Hawaii and Tahiti. But at first none of this drew our eye, as all our eyes were turned upwards, to the World War Two fighter plane hanging from the ceiling, with surfboards slung beneath the wings and squadron insignia seemingly inspired by a Beach Boys song.

Of all the things we expected to find in this obscure corner of the Ukraine, a replica P-51 Mustang hanging from the roof of a bar with surfboards on the bomb racks was pretty low on the list.

We were beginning to like this place. And we'd only just scratched the surface.

After dinner, we wandered down to the John James Hughes Brewery, which was named after the Welsh mining tycoon who'd founded the city back in 1869. Beneath the portrait of this Victorian titan of Imperial Russian Industry we found a bar and micro-brewery worthy of the most fashionable corners of London. Near the entrance, a highly polished, brass-and-copper vat bubbled away, making the beer which was served either from the bar, or from the bar taps which were plumbed directly into each and every table and enabled you to refill your glass without even standing up. And the beer was good too, hoppy and characterful in a way which had been rare in the previous week on the road. As we drank, Grant – who'd joined us in Kiev – perused a map of the city.

'You won't believe this,' he said, looking up, 'but the Liverpool Hotel is just around the corner.'

Obviously, we had to wander over and take a look, and when we heard piped Beetles music drifting through the Ukrainian night, we knew we were there – an impression which was confirmed by the life-size brass statue of the band which stood by the entrance, with a mosaic-tiled Union Jack as a backdrop, just to emphasize the Anglophile atmosphere. Not that this was necessary, of course - the red London phone box which stood opposite did that job just fine. We wandered down the stairs into the bar, where an overload of neon signs jostled for attention, and our eyes were drawn to another red phone box, and a technical drawing of HMS Vanguard which hung on the far wall – exactly what you'd expect to find in the former Soviet Union. One thing you wouldn't expect, however, was the telephone located on each and every table in the place. Why? Well, if you'd like table service, you can simply call the bar. Fancy saying hello to the folks on the table across the way? No problem, just call them up. What a quirky feature to find in the basement of a hotel named for Liverpool, tucked away in Eastern Ukraine!

We stayed in Donets'k for several days, and further explorations revealed an inch-perfect replica of an Irish bar, a German bar whose centrepiece was a couple of backlit, eight-foot-high steiners, and a café which was attached to the Liverpool Hotel and did a fine full English breakfast. We also heard rumours of a bar which was fitted out to look like the interior of Captain Nemo's submarine on the other side of town, but never made it over to check it out. And all the time as we wandered this unspectacular city with the best theme-bar scene this side of Vegas, we found ourselves wondering, 'why?'

The nearest we could get to an answer was that we were enjoying the result of a spot of out-of-control one-upmanship. Donets'k is surrounded by mines and factories, which mean there are some very wealthy business owners scattered around the place, and that's before you consider the area's mafia presence, which also results in a few people getting very rich. But once you've built yourself a mildly fortified mansion and bought a fleet of bulletproof Range Rovers, what other ways are there to show off your fat stacks of cash in somewhere like Donets'k? The simple answer is to out-awesome your rich friends' theme bars by building your own – hence the surreal world we found ourselves in when we stopped in this corner of the Ukraine.

Often in travel, it's the unexpected places which make the biggest impression and stay with you the longest. A much-hyped tourist destination is already on a pedestal when you visit, meaning it has much to do simply to meet expectations, let alone exceed them. But when you have minimal expectations, the scene is set for them to be exceeded by the greatest of margins. For us, this was what happened in Donets'k. And so, when we finally pulled ourselves away and headed onwards to the Russian border, we did so already talking about returning to Donets'k someday in the future.

TEN

NEW WORLDS

29th July 2006
Samara Oblast, Russia

One week after we'd crossed the Mongol Rally's start line in London, our Minis were carrying us deeper and deeper into this exciting new world which we were experiencing for the first time. The familiarity of the Latin alphabet was left behind as signs and documents switched to an indecipherable Cyrillic. Around us, the other drivers became ever more frenzied and aggressive and police checkpoints multiplied to become an hourly occurrence, with rotund officers disinterestedly scanning our paperwork and dreaming of bribes. But it wasn't just our physical world which was changing. Our own personal worlds were also continuing to change, as we settled into life on the road.

With every new day, our existence gained a greater simplicity. From that moment when we'd left the start line in London, the frenzied activity of the weeks before our departure had given way to a sense of freedom and calm; the myriad of tasks which were jostling for attention giving way to a life where all that was required of us each day was to rise and drive onwards to the next point on the map. After a few days of this, it became an almost therapeutic existence. The stresses of our old lives were forgotten, replaced by a world where the only goal was to keep moving forwards. It was a life of crystalline simplicity, far from the worries and demands of the everyday.

This uncluttered, almost trance-like state into which we descended offered a great vantage point from which to view the world through which we were travelling. And every day brought new experiences far removed from our lives back home. Experiences seemingly from another world.

In Moscow, we visited St Basel's Cathedral, an explosion of jauntily tuliped domes, unfamiliar proportions and confident colours which bore no resemblance to the more sombre cathedrals of back home. We were in Russia's capital city, but we may as well have been on the set of a Star Wars movie, given how unaccustomed we were to buildings of such flair and exuberance. Near the Kazakh border, we found ourselves driving through seas of sunflowers and brooding forests, and in the evenings we'd roll through poor villages of single story shacks topped haphazardly with tin roofs, in which every property had a smouldering barbeque out front, tended by the village wives and billowing smoke as the working men drifted back from the fields and roads for dinner. We flashed through these charcoal-scented domains in seconds, but these briefest of glances meant they became a part of us. A glimpse of a world we'd remember forever more, the lives of those who lived there made real to us through the medium of the road trip. And with every new country, the sense of adventure kept on building. Crossing from Estonia into Russia had seemed huge, but it was dwarfed in our minds as the Kazakh border loomed.

Kazakhstan. Who in their right minds ever goes to Kazakhstan? And more to the point, who even drives there?

The sense of being off the edge of the map grew greater; the satisfaction which we gained from doing something hardly anyone else did increased. Organised event or not, there was no question in our minds that it was a real adventure in which we were living.

And we were living it from behind the wheels of a couple of tatty old Minis which we'd bought for peanuts, and which so many people had confidently declared had no chance of making it out of Europe. Alongside the feeling of adventure, a sense of satisfaction was building too, born of achieving something which had been declared impossible. The sense of fulfilment grew with every mile further east that we travelled, along with a huge respect for Daisy and Babs, the two Minis which were now our homes.

Until we reached Kazakhstan, the driving had been easier than we'd expected. Other road users were at times erratic or aggressive, but not dauntingly so. The roads were generally tarmaced, but as they weren't outrageously broken and potholed, our Minis took the conditions in their stride. But Kazakhstan promised to be where things would get a lot more serious, being a country the size of Western Europe which was mostly desert, and in which many of the main roads had fallen into disrepair. Added to that, the heat, remoteness, dust and harsh conditions promised to push our Minis to the limit. We were confident though. We'd been on the road for ten days when we reached the border, and we already felt like we'd been doing this for our whole lives. We were Mongol Ralliers, and proud ones at that. Going forward day after day and beating the odds along the way was now simply what we did, and with so much already achieved, there was no way the rough roads of Kazakhstan were going to dull our momentum. We swung intrepidly away from the border post – stopping a few hundred metres further on to look over a grumbling wheel bearing on our red Mini – and faced down the latest leg of the adventure.

The biggest challenge was the 200 mile stretch from Aqtobe to Aralsk. On our map, it was simply another road; a solid red line which confidently spanned the desert, as if passage would be a mere formality. But we knew better. From what we'd gathered from the previous year's ralliers, the map lied, and that comforting red line actually represented a strip of decades-old tarmac which had been completely destroyed by repeated cycles of extreme temperatures, overloaded trucks and negligible maintenance. We knew that the year before, people had failed here. That knowledge excited us, as finally we had an opportunity to prove our adventuring credentials, and those of our Minis, to those who had doubted us. The fact that others had failed here gave this most challenging part of the drive an irrational allure. But we weren't worried. We wouldn't fail. We were better than those guys – at least, that's what we told ourselves.

As we headed into the desert and the tarmac deteriorated beneath us, the beginning of this next stage of the adventure was marked by our first camel sightings. Punctuating the featureless horizon of the steppe, several of the aloof beasts stood back from the road, chewing tufts of dry yellow grass and roundly ignoring us. Clearly we were nothing of note to them.

But the feeling wasn't mutual - we'd just driven from sleepy old England to a place where camels roam free! With the empty landscape around us, the shattered road beneath us and the two-humped Bactrian beasts dotting the horizon, we'd driven our Minis to the heart of the adventure. What a place to be!

We pushed on confidently into the desert. The potholes gradually increased in density until they were the norm, meaning that any smooth tarmac was greeted with surprise and celebration. The temperature rose into the forties and the tussocky semi-desert of the Kazakh Steppe stretched away in every direction as we powered onwards towards the horizon, determined that nothing would stop us. When the road conditions broke the red Mini's exhaust mounts, we simply tied the pipework and silencers back on with speaker wire and continued. When the tarmac fractured towards the impassable and it seemed we might not be able to continue, we took to the desert, revelling in the adventure as we surfed our little cars along sandy tracks with vigour. And when the sun dropped to the horizon and darkness overtook us, we drove off the road into the empty steppe and camped beneath a million stars, our lives once again crossing over into another world which was new to us all.

It took two days for us to cover the two hundred miles of shattered tarmac and sandy track, and in those two days we proved to ourselves that we could do this. As the road surface began to improve we revelled in the fact that we'd faced up to the crux of our drive, the pinnacle of our challenge, and succeeded. Rolling into the town of Aralsk, our steeds dust-stained and battered but still riding high, we held a new-found confidence that we'd get to Mongolia. We now knew we were equal to the challenge.

But the poignant, dustbowl town of Aralsk is not a place to dwell on glory, for it owes its very existence to the Aral Sea, and the history of this body of water makes it a place of rare sadness.

In the 1950s, the Aral Sea was the fourth largest lake in the world and Aralsk was a vibrant waterside town, looking out across its shimmering surface. Its harbour supported a fine fishing fleet and for longer than anyone could remember, its economy had been dominated by the natural harvest offered by the omnipresent waters. But mankind thought he knew best, and Soviet planners diverted the rivers which flowed into the lake to irrigate cotton fields further south and entirely predictably, the fourth largest lake in the world began to dry up. Gradually, the water receded from the town and whilst an extensive dredging operation kept the harbour connected to the inland sea for a while, eventually the channels silted up, the waters disappeared over the horizon, and Aralsk quickly became a forlorn dustbowl, its raisin d'être gone. When we arrived in town, grimy from our days out in the desert, the nearest water was eight miles away and was so salty that fish could no longer live there. Forty-five years of irrigation and neglect had left the Aral Sea less than a tenth of its former size, and despite being one of the world's worst environmental disasters, nothing had really changed, and it was still shrinking at the time of our visit.

In Arals'k, the harbour infrastructure was still in place, but where water once sparkled, now there was only sand. Cranes which would once have been used to unload the day's catch hung silently, rusting in the salty air. A few preserved fishing boats stood on the quay, but it had been decades since the waters had disappeared over the horizon.

I walked to the far end of the harbour, where a few more boats lay in sand which was once beneath the sea. They were a sad sight which spoke of boredom and frustration, vandalised and patina'd with decades of neglect. As I walked, my feet kicked up the salty dust from what was once the seabed, and amid the dun-coloured sand, everywhere I looked I saw countless white fragments glittering in the sun. I reached down and picked up one of the larger fragments, and recognised that it was part of a shell. I was walking on the graveyard of an ecosystem, sacrificed to irrigate the cotton cash-crops which were making a quick buck further south, and doing further damage by leaching swathes of productive land back to windblown, polluted desert in the process. And all so a few rich people could keep the money rolling in.

The experience brought us back down to earth from the heady high of conquering the steppe, and it was a pretty morose group of Mongol Ralliers which left Aralsk that day, continuing the drive across the empty desert.

*   *   *

Every adventure needs a moment when things don't go to plan and the obstacles seem insurmountable. A moment of reckoning. For our Mongol Rally experience, that moment happened in Uzbekistan. Before our fateful visit to the spectacular Silk Road city of Samarkand, everything had felt reasonably in hand. By the time we left to continue the journey, our adventure had acquired an edgy, out-of-control feeling which suggested that anything could happen, at any moment – and it generally did. The first inkling that change was in the air was when Brummy disappeared. It was a glorious evening, and we were all set to head out to view the mosques and madrasas in the golden light. But one quarter of our team was no-where to be seen. Eventually, Lee found him.

'So, where is he?' I asked.

'He's barricaded himself in the toilet of the hotel room,' Lee replied. 'I think he's gonna be there for a while. He says to just go on without him.'

So with one team member struck down by the cuisine of Central Asia, we headed out to the incomparable Registan, one of the best preserved complexes of buildings on the whole Silk Road. And when we returned a few hours later, Brummy was still locked in that tiny room. In fact, he ended up answering the angry call of nature for so long that by the time he emerged, the bulb had blown.

Unfortunately, writing off a light bulb was the least of our worries, as on our return, we found that my passport had been written off in the washing machine. I'd sensibly left it in the pocket of my trousers, and handed said trousers in for washing without checking said pocket.

Oops.

It was at that moment the adventure became real. Until things started going wrong, there was a feeling of inevitability to our progress but suddenly, one team member and one passport down in the corrupt police state of Uzbekistan, we knew we'd have to dig deep if we were to make it to the finish.

Early the following day, I hit the road to the British embassy and was amazed when the staff there managed to keep a straight face as they sorted me out with a replacement passport and a printout of the Mini's V5, which had also been a casualty of the washing machine. We then headed back into Kazakhstan, making it across the border a grand total of two hours before what was left of our visas expired, and pushed on. Meanwhile, the red Mini had gone through the Fergana Valley into Kyrgyzstan, and we were eventually reunited near the nuclear testing area of Semeipalatinsk, where during the cold war, a grand total of 456 nuclear bomb tests were carried out, scattering fallout over nearby villages and permanently polluting the steppe.

Yeah, from ruined ecosystems to nuclear fallout, our time in Kazakhstan wasn't exactly a good advert for the Soviet Union's environmental conscience.

Once we were reunited with our friends in the red Mini, we grabbed a few beers and they filled us in on what we'd missed.

'Well, you could say it's been eventful,' explained Brummy. 'Firstly, there was the time near Almaty when we were driving along and Lee – who was driving - turned to me and said, 'I need to stop'.'

'I did need to stop,' confirmed Lee. 'It was an emergency.'

'Quite,' said Brummy. 'So Lee coasts to a stop by the side of the road, calmly gets out and strolls away behind a bush as if nothing was up. The next thing I see is a pair of pants arcing through the air from behind the bush. Lee had shat himself while driving along and hadn't so much as blinked at the fact. Total English reserve, just 'I need to stop', and the next thing I know pants are flying through the air.'

'Well, in that situation you want to get them as far away as possible,' said Lee. 'And anyway, what about that time we stopped by the stream in Kyrgyzstan?'

'Yeah, that was funny.'

'So we were up in the mountains,' explained Lee. 'And the car was overheating, so we stopped by a bridge over a stream so I could top up the radiator. Brummy went to the other side of the bridge, threw up into the water and decided not to tell me. So, I'm there filling water bottles to top up the radiator and twenty feet upstream, Brummy's chundering into the very same water.'

'I shouldn't have told you that,' Brummy said, not showing a hint of shame.

'I even drank some of the water, too,' said Lee.

'Well, that's up to you.' replied Brummy.

'So at least the car is still going okay, even if you guys aren't?' I asked.

'Oh no,' replied Lee. 'Don't be ridiculous. You know when the wheel bearing went in Turkistan, and we bodged in a Lada one, using bits of a coke can as spacers? Well, the CV joint followed suit a few miles south of here, just as it was getting dark.'

'I told you that you should have brought a white Mini,' I said.

'So there we were, stuck out in the middle of the steppe at dusk,' continued Lee. 'Fortunately, another Mongol Rally team came along and they gave us a tow to Semey, and dropped us outside a hotel.'

'Not a hotel exactly,' said Brummy.

'Okay, they dropped us outside a brothel.'

'Better,' said Brummy. 'And it turns out, it's the only brothel in the whole of Asia that's run by a deaf person. All we wanted was a couple of beds for the night, but you try to explain that to someone who can't hear you, and doesn't understand English, when you're two guys who have just walked into their brothel.'

'So you got more than you intended to?'

'No, we got two beds for the night, and then we got the car towed to a garage which pinned the CV joint back together, and then we came here.' Lee said. 'How about you guys?'

'Well it's all been plain sailing for us in comparison. My temporary passport and the visas out of the old passport seem to be working at border crossings so far, though I did have to throw the confetti-like remains of the V5 at a particularly grumpy insurance guy earlier, who kept insisting on seeing the original. Daisy is still going strong, but the rear suspension has collapsed on one side, so I've used a ratchet strap tensioned from the front subframe to the rear cone, to bring it level again. No biggie really, after all, it'd be a shame to finish the rally without having to make at least one bodge, so yeah, things could be worse.'

'I guess Tiff doesn't agree?' said Brummy, nodding his head knowingly in a direction away from our camp.

'Probably not,' I replied.

For the whole conversation, she'd been off in the woods living her own version of Lee and Brummy's story, but at least dignity appeared to have been maintained in this instance.   No pants had flown parabolically upwards through the warm Russian air as we chatted into the night, and the next morning we rose early, for the vast expanses of Siberia still lay between us and the end of the drive.

ELEVEN

THE STEPPE

18th April 2013
Izarino, Ukrainian/Russian border

Just beyond the Corvette's steeply raked windscreen, the Russian border post shone bright beneath fluorescent lighting, an island of clinical white light in the darkness. From the large, petrol station-style awning which covered it, to the prefabricated buildings from which the guards peered out, everything was jarringly new, and the whole crossing had the air of having only been built the week before. But the procedures and paperwork required to cross into Russia hadn't changed and I remembered it all vividly from those unforgettable days seven years earlier, when we'd nervously taken our Minis through a border post to the north. Back then, I was crossing such a border for the first time and so the experience had been infused with the thrill of the unknown, as if I were grappling with a puzzle to gain access to a forbidden world. That crossing had resulted in the first-ever stamp in my passport, on the page opposite my first ever visa. But what had once been new and exciting to me now felt normal - the customs declaration, the nonchalant thumbing of visas by the guards, the temporary import permit for whatever strange vehicle I happened to be driving and the final, tension-dissipating thud of a rubber stamp hitting a passport. I'd been through it all so many times before, and our journey through this latest border felt routine. Or at least it did until I rolled away from the checkpoint and parked the Corvette next to the kiosk where we'd be buying insurance.

I glanced up the road and saw the headlights of an old Lada growing brighter as they approached, before slowing to a sudden stop once the driver of the little Russian saloon spotted the Corvette. Our newfound friend was clearly a petrolhead. His spotlessly clean, dark blue Lada was lowered and sported a set of Minilite-style alloy wheels, while the license plates were offset for further boy racer kudos. And he was simply blown away by the Corvette which had just rolled across the border from Ukraine. Sadly, the language barrier prevented much conversation with the jeans-and-T-shirt attired Russian or his impossibly slim girlfriend, and so instead he welcomed us into his country in a manner which I imagine is universally appreciated by car enthusiasts.

Doughnuts.

Revving up the little Lada's engine to a frenzy, he lit up the rear wheels and sent it spinning like a top, headlights swinging round and round like drunken searchlights. The squeal of hard rubber on gripless tarmac filled the air as his little car rotated in greeting, only 100 metres from the police at the border post. Because of the hard rubber, tyre smoke was minimal but even so, it seemed certain that one of his rear wheels must explode at any moment. However, somehow they remained intact and after several minutes of gratuitous hooliganism and contagious laughter he stopped, shook our hands through his open driver's window and then wheelspun off into the night, the smell of hot oil and rubber still hanging in the air.

We'd been in the country for less than five minutes, but purely on first impressions, we decided we rather liked this bit of Russia.

*   *   *

Our first morning in Russia brought sunshine, and we launched into what promised to be one of those classic, unforgettable days on the road. The sky burned blue over an endless rippling plain of grasslands, whose all-encompassing sameness was disturbed only by the tarmac beneath us. The road ran unrelentingly straight and was smooth enough for me to relax, which made for a nice change from having to be continuously alert for potholes, as the roads in the Ukraine had demanded. The Corvette was up for the drive, droning along behind the Rolls quite happily, but coming alive in those moments when it was called on to use all of its 5.7 litres to overtake a lorry. Or simply to keep me entertained, for at the end of the day I am a person of simple needs, and a charismatic V8 fills most of them. The Corvette's bespoke engine was growing on me more with every day. I was sold on its addictive combination of low down torque that give way to a cammy surge of acceleration as the revs rose, all accompanied by a soundtrack which wouldn't be out of place on a quarter-mile drag strip.

We raced across the landscape for hour after hour, loving the experience and feeling completely liberated from the worries of everyday life as we counted down the kilometres to the day's destination. As is usual when things are going smoothly on any big road trip, life had distilled down to a beautiful simplicity, in which all outside stresses had become so distant as to be irrelevant. All that mattered was the drive, keeping the car going and getting to the evening's destination. But as the signs counted down to our destination; as we burst from the rolling grasslands into the tattered outskirts of the city, everything about our journey began to feel more than a little frivolous. For we had just driven into Volgograd; a town which today sits somewhat off the radar of the world, but on which the future of the planet once hung. For in 1942, the town was known by a much more evocative name. Back then, it was named Stalingrad, and a million people laid down their lives in the battle between the Soviet and Axis forces to control it.

As I cruised into the city with my thoughts bogged down in history, I tried to turn my mind back to those days over 70 years ago, when the ground beneath the Corvette's wheels played host to the biggest battle the planet has ever seen.

From how Volgograd looks today, it's almost impossible to imagine it as the burning crucible within which the direction of world history was decided, for the original city was almost totally destroyed in the artillery barrages, the bombing, the tank skirmishes and the hand-to-hand fighting which once made it the most important front line on the planet. As reconstructed in the post war period, the new city is a work of dated Soviet optimism; a maze of ugly high-rises and crumbling tarmac, crowded around a centre which drips with predictable Stalinesque grandeur.

After entering Volgograd, we parked the cars and walked over to a memorial garden which is dedicated to the 1,150,000 Soviet conscripts and civilians who were killed or injured in the defence of the city; a sacrifice which was pivotal in saving the Soviet Union from defeat by the Nazis. It was almost deserted, but a few locals were there, wandering slow and unsmiling amid their history. Towering over the memorial garden, an 87 metre tall sculpture stands defiant and proud, dramatically silhouetted by the setting sun. It is a statue which represents Mother Russia, brandishing a sword as she calls upon her citizens to defend the Motherland. Massive and imposing, yet reassuringly human in its alarmed expression, the statue convincingly manages to tread a fine line between the glorification of Soviet might and the sacrifice of its most vulnerable citizens, and leaves you in little doubt as to the momentousness of the events which had taken place on the very same spot, 70 years earlier.

Later, as I drove through Volgograd, the memorial statue dominating the view through the Corvette's windscreen, I tried to picture just how many people had been killed in the battle for this city – almost all of them simply unlucky enough to have been caught up in the biggest battle of the biggest war the world has ever known. From both sides, the total came to over a million people. That's equal to the city's total current population. The only way I could imagine that number was to picture twelve Wembley Stadiums, all packed to capacity. And then imagine that each and every person in each of those twelve cheering crowds was snuffed out in their prime by events they had almost no control over.

War.

What a fucking waste.

*   *   *

Other than the telegraph poles which shadow the road, nothing rises above the horizon. Our world is a sweep of parched sand, scattered apologetically with tufts of grass and sliced in two by a strip of weary asphalt. Waves of dust sweep across the road as we drive, ducking and diving before the chill April wind. No longer satisfied with existing only in the background, the sky has taken centre stage, dominating the vista with its sheer size.

We'd been in Kazakhstan for less than an hour, and already the empty drama of the steppe had left us in no doubt that Russia, this was not.

The shores of the Caspian Sea lay a few miles to our south, but such was the flatness of our world and the unsuitability of our vehicles for roaming the raw desert, that we never saw it. We drove on, our attention being drawn to whatever objects rose above the sweeping horizon. First there were camels, grazing disinterestedly in the dusk. They brought a smile to my tired face. Once again, I had driven to a place where camels roam free, and the thought still made me smile. A bit further on, we found the desert scattered with the distinctive symbols of the oil industry, their slow nodding motion drawing the black gold to the surface. But these were mere outliers. A hundred miles to our south, challengingly located beneath desert and sea, lay some of the largest oilfields in the world.

We arrived in the oil-town of Atyrau long after dark. Flushed with the money which flows wherever black gold is struck, hotel prices were high, but amid the wailing car alarms we found a room in the main railway station which we could afford. In it, three hard, lumpy mattresses lay on beds with broken slats. An ill-fitting window looked out onto the station platform, and mosquitoes worked their way in through the gaps. Reluctantly we settled down for the night, our senses bombarded by the station tannoy as it made loud announcements in Kazakh, the rumbling noise and shaking walls caused by trains passing a few metres away, and the high-pitched whine of blood-sucking insects circling in for a meal.

We barely slept a wink, and morning seemed to take forever to arrive as the trains, the mosquitoes and the tannoy kept up their assaults on our senses right through the night. At 7am, Grant's alarm went off.

'Let's get out of here,' sighed Brummy.

'Yes, let's,' I replied.

By ten past seven, we were with our cars in the car park, Grant and I looking terminally in need of a caffeine, and Brummy looking deeply amused.

'What's up?' Grant asked.

'I just went down to the toilet,' Brummy said. 'There was a lady cleaning them, when this fat Kazakh guy came in. He took one look at her cleaning the urinals, and then just started pissing in her cleaning bucket instead.'

'Classy,' I replied. 'Let's get as far away from this place as possible. But first, coffee.'

*   *   *

The map promised us an easy day on the road. The yellow line which indicated the 200 mile road to Aqtobe ran easily across the steppe, as if our passage would be a formality.

But just as it had on the Mongol Rally seven years earlier, the map lied.

After leaving Atyrau, the road quickly deteriorated into nothing but a dirt track, which had been gouged into an endless succession of peaks, troughs and ridges and then hardened by the harsh dry climate. With hundreds of miles of empty steppe stretching ahead, we were forced to crawl along this undulating mess, the Corvette's total lack of both ground clearance and suspension travel meaning that often, when cresting a bulge, it would be reduced to three points of contact with the ground, as one of its rear wheels flailed anything up to half a metre in the air.

I would have been loving it, if it wasn't for the thought that there could be two hundred miles of similarly slow progress ahead. The Corvette may have been tough, but there was no way it could take two hundred miles of this punishment.

Luckily for me however, it wasn't the Corvette which broke. Rather, it was the dignified refinement of the Rolls-Royce which failed, its politely puttering exhaust suddenly adopting a tank like drone after about five miles of this treatment.

Grant jumped out and lay on the hard desert, inspecting the many metres of piping which passed beneath the car.

'It looks okay down here,' he shouted up.

'Well it's definitely broken somewhere,' replied Brummy. 'Are you sure?'

'I'm sure,' said Grant. 'Open the bonnet, maybe we can see the problem there.'

And sure enough, the problem revealed itself – the exhaust manifold on the left bank of the mighty six-and-three-quarter litre V8 motor had cracked in two, resulting in a Rolls-Royce which rivalled the Corvette in the aural uncouthness stakes. It had only been half an hour since we'd left tarmac for the first time on the trip, but already we were beating a retreat back to firmer ground.

In the dusty town of Maqat, the Rolls-Royce was bounced onto some oversized ramps to give us a better view of the broken exhaust, and we promptly decided that the thought of trying to remove the manifold to make a repair was rather terrifying – the car was 35 years old and the bolts holding the manifold to the head had probably never been undone in that time, so shearing one off was a real possibility. With this in mind, we found a local welder and had the two parts of the manifold tack welded back together while in situ, a tricky task which involved working with cast metal in a very tight space, but eventually the two halves of the manifold were reconnected. With the Rolls now returned to its whispering ways we hit the road again, and found that the repair lasted all of 50 miles before the welds failed, the din returned, and we elected to ignore it and push on anyway.

To avoid the bad road which had done for the Roll's exhaust, locals had recommended that we take a 300 mile detour to the north, via the imaginatively named town of Oral. And so we set about the longest detour of our lives, crossing empty steppe on smooth tarmac, beneath a cumulus-dappled sky. It all sounds rather boring, doesn't it? Well it would have been, were it not for the efforts of the Kazakh police, who hounded us all the way with endless checks of our paperwork, questions about the cars and attempts to extract money from us. In one particularly busy hour, we were stopped seven times, sometimes by police cars, on other occasions by the checkpoints which dot the main roads in a throwback to the paranoid Soviet times.

As we drove, we found ourselves back on our old Mongol Rally route, and so I began to scan the landscape for anything which I might recognise from our passage seven years earlier, but it was futile. While everything about the landscape was familiar, its sameness left nothing which stood proud from the endless steppe, and so I never knew for sure if I was genuinely revisiting a memory, or simply moulding a memory to fit. Was that the row of trees outside Aqtobe which we camped behind with the Minis? I couldn't be sure. Is this the police checkpoint where they pulled Lee into the office for speeding, and he collapsed in fits of laughter when the policeman starting thumbing the paperwork while repeating the words 'durka durka' - a line straight out of the Team America movie? Maybe, but then again, maybe not. I was moving through a familiar world, but without the heightened appreciation which recognition would bring. Had I now spent too many months on the roads of the world and lost the sense of wonder and excitement from my road tripping? Perhaps to some extent, as crossing Kazakhstan was certainly feeling almost routine to me.

That evening, we checked into a truck stop a few hundred miles north of Aralsk and ate borscht to the sound of 'Gangnam Style', the Korean pop song *du jour* which had been following us ever since we left the UK. The light faded from the landscape and soon, out of the windows there was nothing but a uniform blackness. But once again sleep came slowly, as the following morning, we would be getting to grips with our old Mongol Rally crux – the rough and ready road to Aralsk.

*   *   *

It was the smoothest tarmac I'd ever seen. It ran dead-straight to the horizon and we sped along it in perfect comfort, with even the Corvette's ride proving silky smooth, despite its rock-hard suspension. In the Rolls – where all enthusiasm for rough roads had evaporated with the broken exhaust – a state of celebration prevailed. After about half an hour, they pulled over and Brummy jumped out and lay on the tarmac, stroking it.

'It's so smooth,' he said. 'Can you believe how smooth it is?'

'Bastards,' I replied, not remotely seriously. 'They knew I was looking forward to 200 miles of off-roading in the 'vette, so they do this. I bet they tarmacked it on purpose, just to piss me off.'

'Only you would wish for bad roads,' said Brummy.

'I'll take that as a compliment,' I replied. 'This is about as interesting as the M5.'

We drove on, covering in three hours what had taken us two days in the Minis seven years before. Traffic was quiet, with only a few trucks droning the other way and in doing so, providing the freshly-laid tarmac with purpose. For we were driving along what is sometimes referred to as 'The New Silk Road', a smooth-flowing artery linking China and Europe, along which trade can flow. The flawless asphalt beneath us was paid for with Chinese money and laid by Chinese workers, all for the benefit of the Chinese economy.

Meanwhile, out in the desert to our left, the old Soviet-era road along which we'd driven our Minis lay broken and forgotten, an abandoned relic from a world which had been left behind. At one stage, we stopped our cars and walked over to it, the silence of the steppe ringing in our ears even more loudly than the V8s ever could. Brummy and I wandered the broken surface of the now abandoned track, silent and alone in our thoughts. It was like stumbling upon a mirror to our past, and I pictured our Minis battling their way along this ribbon of possibility through the austere desert, and thought back to the people we were back then - clueless and naive, but propelled forwards by the excitement of the unknown. This was where it had begun, all those years ago, at the heart of our Mongol Rally experience. But progress had left it behind. What was once so important to us was now slowly being reclaimed by the desert, and we too had changed, our confidence now being solidly built upon years of experience, rather than the burning exuberance of youth. In the seven years which had passed since we'd last visited this remote spot, the world had moved on. And so had we.

Unlike the road conditions out in the steppe, Aralsk hadn't changed much since our last visit. The old fishing boats displayed on the quay had been given a new lick of paint and a small museum had sprung up in a glorified shed next to them, but the melancholy air of sadness remained. The salty dust was still carried on the wind, the shell fragments still glittered sadly in the sands which were once the seabed, and the occasional camel still wandered the streets. It was a town frozen in decay, a place without a purpose and what was worse, a place without a hope. Landlocked among sands and polluted by pesticides washed down from the water-stealing irrigation schemes which had destroyed its future, it felt frozen in time, as if nothing had really changed since we were last here. But we knew this wasn't strictly true. Over the horizon, of the four main bodies of water which remained when we visited in 2006, one had now completely disappeared – what was then known as the Eastern Basin was now the Aralkum Desert. The combined surface area of the waters had continued to plummet and the only glimmer of hope came from a damming project in what remained of the North Aral Sea, which had succeeded in raising water levels there. But overall, the outlook remained bleak. To the south, cotton remained Uzbekistan's biggest cash crop and there, the dried up sea bed was suffering its latest indignity, with prospecting for oil and gas being well underway, a much easier task now the waters had gone.

*   *   *

The road flowed onwards, leaving behind Aralsk's moroseness to cross a landscape so empty that even the smallest undulations seemed to acquire the gravitas of mountains. The yellow steppe dominated, its parched, stubbly grasses rising to the infinite blueness of the big sky. A chill wind played upon the empty landscape and cut sharply at our skin when we left the shelter of the cars.

Laid upon a landscape so devoid of focal points, man's intrusion seemed akin to a desecration. Power lines rose unwelcome into the pure sky, aesthetically coarse and jarringly visible from miles away. Satellite dishes topped a few of the hillocks that rose from the horizon, providing communications to the Baykonur Cosmodrome which lay secretively to the north of our route. Litter dotted the roadside, sometimes rising to play with the dust upon the eddying wind, and occasionally a pipeline or railway track would sweep in to split the landscape in two, as if attempting to reduce its unimaginable vastness to something easier for the mind to comprehend. Kazakhstan's steppe is a landscape defined by its very nothingness and against this, the grim functionality of man's detritus has nowhere to hide. Very few structures could be considered a welcome addition to such a place, but that doesn't mean none existed, as we discovered at our next stop.

The small university town of Turkistan was smothered by a police presence which was an order of magnitude greater than anything else we'd encountered so far on the trip. Every intersection seemed to sport a bored officer lazing by a blue-lighted Lada patrol car, and every few miles we'd be stopped a checkpoint, where our papers would be checked. However, after running the gauntlet of authority in our rather conspicuous cars we eventually arrived at the town's – and Kazakhstan's – greatest architectural jewel. The Kozha Akhmed Yasaui Mausoleum.

It rose sheer to a height of almost 40 metres, a façade of dun-coloured history, bookended with turret-like towers and split by a covered arch. Replacing an earlier structure on the site, the mausoleum had been thrown skyward on the orders of Tamerlane himself, with workers toiling on the project for sixteen years, striving for perfection. Dedicated to the memory of Sheikh Akhmed Yasaui, a twelfth century mystic who founded the Sufi order, it was – and still is – Islam's second most holy site of pilgrimage, with only Mecca offering a greater cachet.

But it was never finished.

When Tamerlane died in 1405, work ended abruptly, leaving the building tantalisingly close to completion. As we approached, centuries-old wooden beams still jutted from within the soaring arch, the scaffolding they once held long gone. The structure's dun colour was unintentional – the glazed brickwork which was to have jewelled its surface was never completed. The mausoleum's imposing front stood like a question mark, a blank canvas for your mind to fill with dreams of what might have been.

As you begin to walk around the structure, those dreams morph to reality, for it is then that you realise that it was only the front whose completion was cut shorts by events. From other angles, the mausoleum glitters with glazed tiles of sand and lapis blue, which pattern the walls and arches with intricate precision. Above the walls, your eyes are drawn to the towering dome, measuring over eighteen metres across and matching the sky with its shimmering blueness. This is largest brick-built dome currently standing in all of Central Asia, and proof that Kazakhstan has more to offer than steppe and sadness.

We left town under the gaze of the ever present police, and as we headed back towards the open steppe, we were promptly run clean off the road by a convoy of a dozen black limousines, with blue lights flashing and police outriders on motorbikes shadowing them.

Later, we heard that the president of Turkey was paying a visit, and that it was his secret service entourage that had ran us off the road. Suddenly the heavy police presence made perfect sense.

*   *   *

The days merged into one another as we rolled on through Kazakhstan's more populated south. The flat wilderness of the steppe, which for days had been our world, gave way to a land of gentle gradients, and the first shimmering glimpses of the Tian Shan Mountains started to flicker in the distance. The cars were in their stride now, nonchalantly battering their way through the endless roadworks, and we were in our stride too – living with their acquired foibles had become second nature to us. Following several unsuccessful attempts at a repair, the Rolls' broken exhaust no longer bothered Brummy to distraction, and so it droned on routinely, day after day, like some luxurious Sherman tank. The Corvette, meanwhile, had worn through its rear brake pads and begun to score its rear discs. With no replacement pads to hand, I continued with only the powerful front brakes by disconnecting the hydraulic brake line to the rear wheels, making sure there was an air bubble in the line and then reconnecting it loosely, so it looked fine to any inquisitive policeman who insisted on looking under the hood at the tremendously foreign 5.7l V8.

Police continued to be a regular feature in our lives, though despite the reputation of people in uniform in this part of the world they were generally benign, and usually took a real interest in our cars after a brief, uncomprehending glance at our papers. Requests to have photos taken in the driver's seats or to look under the long bonnets were regular, as were suggestions that the Corvette should wheelspin away when we continued on our way. And even when we were in the wrong, the Police weren't too difficult to cope with. When a speed trap clocked me doing 38 in a 30 zone, I escaped a fine simply by telling the policeman that I was English, and hence I went to the pub with David Beckham – definitely a white lie to remember if you ever find yourself being pulled over in southern Kazakhstan.

After our days on the Steppe, Kazakhstan's south seems gloriously populous, and at the end of every day on the road, a city awaited. The night after we'd roamed Turkistan's UNESCO ruins, it was the turn of Shymkent – a city which bears the honour of being twinned with Stevenage. Years before, we'd spent a night in town at the imaginatively named Hotel Shymkent, as Lee struggled to wedge a Lada wheel bearing into his Mini's front wheel hub, using pieces of sliced up coke can as spacers. This time however, the hotel was fully booked when we arrived, due to a wedding which was in full swing, and so following a half-hearted attempt to rent our wedding-spec Rolls to the groom, we found accommodation down the street.

Shymkent hadn't changed much. The kitschy children's fairground which was spread out in a park opposite the Hotel Shymkent was still doing good business, and remained a pleasant place to find a café, order a cold coke and relax in the dappled spring sunshine. The Independence Park still offered a trippy experience as the sun went down, the curious steel sculptures shimmering in the reddening light. However on this visit, we added another experience to our list of Shymkent memories – a visit to a nightclub.

Inside, the only lighting was from series of strobes, meaning the whole room went from a brilliant light to pitch darkness several times a second. Next to the bar stood a heavy-set guard with a shotgun, while a similarly tooled-up guy stood by the entrance. Dancing with any of the girls present seemed to trigger a cry of 'no no, very dangerous', from our local friends with whom we'd gone to the club, and the general atmosphere was one of machismo, malice, mafia and guns. Lots of guns. A quaint Dartmoor pub, it certainly wasn't.

*   *   *

The mountains drew closer and closer, their monochrome bulk rising into the sea of clouds which boiled from their summits, but which occasionally parted for long enough to catch a glimpse of the eternal snows which crown this westernmost extent of the mighty Himalaya. After so long in the featureless steppe, we were drawn to them like landsick sailors sighting the shore, enticed onwards as the contours beneath us began to increase and the border with Kyrgyzstan loomed, first in our minds, and then in our windscreens.

The border was marked by the fact that I managed to cross it with more money than I had reached it with. This was thanks in part to Kyrgyzstan's anarchically simple procedures – no insurance is required, for instance – which meant that reasons to hand over money were minimal, and partly due to a curious transaction which took place in no-man's land. The guy in the Lada which had rolled up behind the Corvette – a short, round sort of guy, with a spacehopper of a stomach squirming out from beneath his check shirt – was eager to buy something. Anything. He saw we were English, and being from The West, we simply must have some of the finer items from our capitalist world for sale.

107

He thought wrong. But this didn't stop him, and having refused to sell him my clothes and my Lonely Planet guidebook, I yielded when his attention fell upon the dixie horn, strapped to the Corvette's somewhat pointless roof rack. 'Thirty dollars,' said I, by typing out the figure on my phone's screen. 'Deal,' said he, through the universal symbol of a raised thumb and a handshake. 'Stop that,' said the nearby customs officer, conscious that No-Man's-Land isn't really the place for black market deals. However, when I went away to get my passport stamped, I left the Dixie horn on the Corvette's rear wing. And when I returned, it had been replaced by a pile of well-thumbed local currency. The deal was done, and so into Kyrgyzstan we went.

*   *   *

For mile after mile, the road just kept on rising, but the mountains which hemmed it into its valley rose faster, reaching for the sky with a craggy chaos that energised us. It had been thousands of miles since we'd last encountered anything which could even be called a hill, but now we were heading upwards into another world. The range which forms the spine of Kyrgyzstan is called the Tian Shan, which translates as the Mountains of Heaven. As we breathed in the pure, chilled air which rolled down from the snowfields still far above us, the name certainly felt apt.

At an altitude of around 3,000 metres, there stood a fairly modern tourist hotel, its steep-sided pyramidal form designed to shed the winter snows. Next to the hotel, a few traditional yurts were dotted, squat and strong and looking far more appealing than the Kyrgyz take on a ski lodge. Being one of the few Rolls-Royce owners in this part of Kyrgyzstan, Brummy elected for a pricey room in the hotel. Grant and I took the cheaper option and pitched our tents further up the valley, next to a river of meltwater which flowed past the boulders and fir trees towards the world of desert and steppe below; a world which already felt so far away.

The morning broke with the cool freshness and clarity that only a mountain range can bring. It reminded me of those days when climbing was my life, and I'd emerge from my tent into such a morning, soak up the views of the Alps or the Scottish Highlands, and be sure I'd found my calling in life. Anything seemed possible in those crisp wilderness mornings spent beneath mountain or crag - even me overcoming my lack of a strong head-game to achieve my climbing dreams. Back then, there was no way I could conceive of the path my adventures would follow, which would see me leaving the world of bold climbing behind to drive the world. But I still missed these perfect moments in nature, and as I sat next to my tent and packed my rucksack, I looked forwards to the day's hike up the Ala-Archa Valley.

The path drifted gradually up the hillside, the dense forest of firs giving way to a world of rock and hardy grasses as the treeline fell below us and the panorama of the valley opened up. A cirque of tall and serious mountains was revealed. Peaks of rock and ice over 4,000 metres tall, with snow-choked gulleys and alpine ridges offering challenging routes to their summits. Thickening wisps of cloud swirled upon their heights, as an interplay of sunlight and shadow brought their flanks to life. We hiked onwards towards Peak Korona, all the while being alternately warmed by the suns warmth and cooled by the chill breeze, and feeling brought to life by the exercise and our surroundings.

There's only so long you can sit in a car before you need a break, and a good hike in the mountains is pretty much the ideal way to blow away the cobwebs. Or at least that's what Grant and I thought. Brummy was happy enough to stay in the valley with his feet up – gazing lovingly through his expensive hotel window at his Rolls-Royce, no doubt.

We were around 4,000 metres up when the clouds swept down to dance around us and we found our way blocked by a steep snowfield, our world reduced to shades of white. Hiking in trainers and without either ice axes or crampons, we decided that pushing on would probably result in rather more of an adventure than we'd planned for, and so we headed down. The shadows were already sweeping across the valley when we made it back to camp, and in the failing light, the air had regained its chilly embrace. Some nearby Russian campers had both a campfire and a bottle of vodka going, and they beckoned us over to join them, and share in the warmth of both.

There were five of them – four guys and a girl – and without wishing to pander to stereotypes, they were already on their second bottle of vodka by 5pm. Or at least the guys were. The girl wasn't drinking.

'When I was young, I drank too much,' she told me, in heavily accented English. 'And something went wrong inside me. Now, if I drink, I die.'

She was barely into her twenties, but her gaunt features spoke of stresses beyond her years.

The group had headed up into the mountains from Kyrgyzstan's capital city of Bishkek for a few days, and their primary goal appearing to be to drink as much vodka as possible. Despite being one person down due to their lingering risk of death, they were doing a pretty good job of it, and insisted we join in the toasts.

And if there's one thing these guys were passionate about, it was toasts. There were toasts to the mountains, to our respective countries, to adventure, to the non-toasting member of the group, even toasts to toasts, all knocked back in the decisive manner which seems to define Russian machismo. The second bottle of vodka was emptied, and a third opened. The pace of Russian being spoken around the campfire increased, the translations being offered to us by the only sober person present became ever more surreal. The world began to sway as the flames of the campfire adopted a hypnotic air, and it felt that if I only gazed into them for long enough, the answers to all the world's problems could be found. And still the evening went on.

Brummy was the first to flag, standing up unsurely and announcing that he was calling it a night, before meandering off into the darkness.

He reappeared about fifteen minutes later.

'Okay,' he said. 'I give up. Where's the hotel?'

'You went the right way. Just keep following the river and you'll get there.'

'I did!' he said. 'I followed the river and I ended up back here. It happened twice.'

'You think the river flows in a circle?' Grant asked. 'Just keep the noise from river on your left and you'll get there.'

'I did, I'm telling you. There's something wrong with this bloody country,' he slurred, before once again wandered back into the night, muttering something about how no Rolls-Royce owner should ever have to go through this. Meanwhile around the campfire, we placed bets on, and toasted to, his survival.

It was late now, and Grant and I had slowed our vodka consumption considerably, but the Russians had responded to our weakness by increasing the urgency of their drinking. Soon, it was gone midnight and the forth bottle of vodka was gone. Time for sleep? You'd think so, but if you do, you're clearly not a Russian in the Tian Shan.

'We shall drive to the town and find another bottle,' announced one of them. 'And you shall come with us as our guests.'

It wasn't a suggestion. It was a statement.

Four of us piled into their little 4x4, and we pottered down towards the nearest village. Fortunately, the road was sufficiently bad that the Russians were forced to drive slowly, meaning the risk to our lives was minimal. On reaching the village, our host pulled up next to one of the first houses, jumped out and confidently strode up to the front door. The rest of us lingered by the car, hoping the darkness meant we would go un-noticed.

'It's the doctor's house. He will have vodka,' we were told.

The statement was half true. It may have even been completely true, in fact, as it was the doctor's house, and he may well have had vodka, but the shower of abuse which was triggered by the request for it left our enthusiastic leader in no doubt that he wouldn't be getting any. Not deflated in the slightest, he drove us on to a boarded up shop, and began pounding on the door.

As he did so, I glanced around the group, and just as earlier, by the doctor's house, something didn't quite add up. There were four seats in the 4x4, and four of us were occupying them during this drunken hunt. But every time we stopped, there were six of us. Definitely six – despite my occasional double vision, I must have counted six times.

Even as our chauffeur returned triumphant with a bottle of vodka, having got the shop owner to sell it to him at one in the morning, I couldn't figure it out. Four of us drove back to the campfire, and six of us once again took up our seats and toasted the very existence of vodka, as the evening began to wind down with the dying of the flames.

The following morning, I asked Grant how there could have been six of us each time we stopped.

'Didn't you notice?' he replied. 'Every time we got into the car, two of the Russians climbed up onto the roof, and then climbed back down when we stopped.'

I hadn't noticed at all. I'm blaming the vodka.

* * *

The following morning dawned just as full of mountain promise as the day before, but my reaction to it couldn't have been more different. To put it mildly, I was hung over. And it wasn't just any hangover. No, it was one of those hangovers where everything seems muffled and distant and you're trapped alone in your own world, raked by dehydration, headaches and a feeling of nausea. All you want to do is stay still for as long as it takes to go away, but unfortunately, that wasn't an option. We had 150 miles to drive that day, including the border crossing back into Kazakhstan. At that moment, the kitsch, loud interior of a Corvette could scarcely have been any less appealing.

I followed the Rolls as we drove down out of the mountains, and became ensnared by the chaotic roads of Bishkek's outskirts. As we drove, the Corvette's electronic brain detected some problem with its mighty motor, and put it into limp mode, causing a big reduction in engine power and throttle response, and triggering a deeply unpleasant, droning engine note in the process, which seemed to resonate in my skull. This onslaught scaled up what was a full-on hangover into something which felt more like a medical emergency, as I cursed the wandering navigation of team Rolls and willed the day's drive to be over.

After an hour or so we reached the border and immediately the car was surrounded with a bustling crowd of people. Money changers, people selling bottled water, those claiming to be fixers, eager to help us make the crossing – for a fee, of course. The backdrop to the chaos was provided by the dulcet tones of Gangnam Style, which echoed across the border post. I wanted nothing more than to simply crawl into the footwell and disappear, but that wasn't really an option given the conspicuousness of a British-registered 'vette in Central Asia. Or the size of a Corvette's footwell, come to think of it. Wearily, and without making any eye contact with my accosters, I climbed out of the car. Ahead, Brummy and Grant were encountering a similar melee as they left the sanctuary of the Rolls' interior.

'Kill me now,' I shouted over to them.

'Worse than the hangover you had in Calcutta?' asked Brummy.

'Calcutta was a picnic compared to this,' I replied. 'Seriously, kill me now.'

'With pleasure,' replied Brummy. 'But let's get this border done first.'

It took hours. We went from queue to queue, from customs to immigration, from police to passport control. It was purgatory. The day had built up to become the first truly hot day of the trip, and clouds of smothering dust were floating around the border post, kicked up by the heavy flow of people trying to cross it. For half an hour I was denied entry because the computer system at the border didn't recognise the existence of the UK, and my will to live drifted away with the minutes. But then we were free again, rolling back into Kazakhstan for the three hour drive to our hotel in Almaty, with the sun beating through the Corvette's glass roof and baking my day from bad to worse – a situation which wasn't even lifted by the fact that the car's temporary lapse into limp mode seemed to have fixed itself at the border.

In Almaty, I parked the Corvette as the warbling note of car alarms echoed across the city, and lowered the window as the Rolls-Royce pulled up alongside.

'What is it with the world these days,' I shouted through Brummy's open window over the ground-shaking rumble of the idling Corvette. 'Everywhere we stop there's a car alarm going off. They really should do something about this global crime wave. I wonder what's causing it?'

'Yes. I wonder,' replied Brummy, as I silenced the Corvette and the ground stopped shaking. 'So anyway, how are you feeling? Did you enjoy the drive?'

'Worst day on the road ever,' I replied.

'Worse than that day in Ethiopia, when you'd shat yourself thin the day before?' asked Brummy.

'Definitely,' I replied. 'Next time I suggest one of these road trips, just remind me of today and tell me to shut up. This is going to stay with me for a long time. Let it be known that May 11th 2013 is the day that Ben decided he can't be bothered with road trips anymore.'

'Sure,' said Grant. 'Like you're ever gonna stop.'

He was right of course, and my aversion to road trips wore off with the hangover, but for Grant, it really was the end – this time, anyway. The day after our arrival in Almaty, I ferried him to the airport late one evening, and dropped him off ready for his flight home. Six hours later, I was back again to collect his replacement for the next leg of the trip – a friend from my climbing days, called Ian.

We ended up spending five days in Almaty, enjoying the city's abundant shops and restaurants, its many tree-lined avenues and its prime location beneath the snowcapped mountains of the Tian Shan. While there, we made another attempt at having the Rolls-Royce's exhaust welded back together, which proved as futile as not only the previous attempt, but also the time we'd tried to fix it with a tin can and some exhaust sealant while out on the steppe. We also decided to sort out the Corvette's lack of rear brakes, and in a workshop stacked to the rafters with different pads, we found that the brake pads from a Toyota Camry were a good match for the Corvette, and with a bit of sawing and filing, the Japanese parts were made to fit the American callipers, meaning we were good to go again.

So, there's a top tip for you if you have a Corvette C4. Toyota Camry rear brake pads, and a hacksaw. You read it here first.

Eventually, we left Almaty and drove the last few hundred miles to the next border crossing. Up to this moment, everything about the trip had felt routine, as it hadn't really deviated from ground we already knew. That was about to change though. As we drove, the signs next to the road counted down the kilometres to the line on the earth's surface where we were to leave Kazakhstan behind, and begin our Chinese adventure.

116

TWELVE

SIBERIA

14th August 2006
Veseloyarsk, Russia

Behind us, a mile back down the road, a line stretched across the map - the Kazakh border, which we'd crossed in our Minis the previous afternoon. But the border wasn't all that was behind us. Our rear view mirrors also framed three weeks of the kind of adventures which most people would consider the highlights of a lifetime. We'd covered 7,500 miles across eleven countries. In our tiny cars, we'd overcame borders, breakdowns, bureaucracy and bad roads to make it this far. Even the small matter of my destroyed passport hadn't stopped us. And through all the obstacles we'd gained in confidence and experience, to the point where we were allowing ourselves to dream of the finish line.

But the finish line was still 2,500 miles away, and those miles stretched away from us across the biggest landscape of all.

Siberia.

The name hung in my mind like a void. It was the greatest nothing on earth. An empty, malevolently brooding sweep of land defined by its unfathomable size and legendary cold; cold in terms of both the air temperature, and the welcome I'd grown up to expect there. All my life, it had existed on the edge of my comprehension, separate from the world I felt I knew. It wasn't somewhere people went to voluntarily. People disappeared there.

We dropped our tents, repacked the tiny Minis, finished our morning coffees and set forth across its vastness.

The mottled, sometimes broken tarmac went on forever. Outside of the well-spaced cities there was no getting lost, as there was only one road. It shadowed the Trans-Siberian Railway for much of the way, as if afraid to break out into the wilderness alone. Our Minis crawled through the landscape, feeling insignificant in comparison to the other road users, which seemed to primarily be trucks, serving the Russian Far East.

Often, it felt like a miracle that we were still moving at all. Not only had my passport issues failed to stop us but by rights, Lee's Mini's journey should also have ended long before. Its engine sounded like a bag of bolts, and the repair to its damaged CV joint seemed eager to cause issues every few hundred miles, when the bodge would shear and needed to be pinned back together. This was a problem, as we weren't exactly overburdened with things with which to make such a repair. In desperation, when we were in Novosibirsk, Lee popped into a hardware store and bought a hacksaw so he could chop up the jack handle, turning it into a supply of pins which would hopefully coax the long-suffering car across the finish line.

But as we crawled onwards, we found that the time we were losing to each repair meant that Brummy was looking increasingly likely to miss his pre-booked flight home from Mongolia, and so he joined me in the more reliable Daisy for a dash to get across the Mongolian border before it closed for the weekend. We knew we'd have to average at least 37 miles per hour for almost two days to do this, on Siberia's broken tarmac, but the challenge didn't faze us. We were Mongol Ralliers now. Against the odds, thousand-mile dashes across Siberia were just what we did.

Looking back, my memories of this forced drive have been smothered into a hazy blur of fatigue being balanced against willpower, but a few things still stand out. I remember rolling into the sodium glow of Krasnoyarsk at three in the morning where, hopelessly lost, a policeman in a Lada led us onto the correct road out of town. I remember being overtaken by a convoy of French 4x4s on a guided trip, a long line of muscled up Toyota Land Cruisers and Humvees, and seeing in their midst a modified

Citroen 2CV, sponsored by a French magazine and making its overblown travelling companions look rather silly as it bounced along in the rough Siberian roads. 'One of us', I thought to myself as we exchanged a smile and a wave. I remember the lightning flashes strobing through the night and the heavy raindrops which hit the windscreen as we skirted around Lake Baikal in the early hours of the morning, its colossal mass of water remaining unseen. The endless forests stayed with me too, lining the road for hour after hour without a break, but above all, it is the tiredness which dominates my hindsight, and a vague recollection of once having to swerve around a set of headlights which appeared out of nowhere in the early hours, only to think back to the event five minutes later and not be sure whether it had been real, or a hallucination. The only real sleep of the drive happened a few minutes later, 40 minutes snatched with the car parked by the road, the engine still idling away as the battery was too weak to restart it. And then it was back to the marathon grind across the never-ending landscape, which at night was barely visible in the pale glow of our dimming headlights.

We reached the Mongolian border shortly before it closed for the weekend, and were across it with a few hours to spare. We felt on top of the world – we'd just driven to Mongolia! As we cruised along the surprisingly smooth tarmac towards Ulan Bataar, with yurts dotting the empty landscape and a fire-red sunset adding drama to our passage, we felt invincible. With only two hours to go to get to the finish line, and a third of the world behind us, we thought we could finally relax. We'd done it.

Ahead of us, the hazard lights and warning triangles burned bright in the dusk. Skid marks on the road showed the last moments before the collision, and a few shattered pieces of bodywork lay where the cars had touched. A Nissan Micra sat battered on the tarmac, its front suspension collapsed and its Mongol Rally stickers now seeming vaguely frivolous. Nearby, a local's somewhat dented Toyota had left the road, skidding a short distance into the steppe. The occupants of both cars were wandering around the scene, looking understandably shocked, and rather at a loss as to what to do.

A drive across a third of the world, only to crash almost within sight of the finish line. I couldn't believe the bad luck which had befallen this group of Mongol Ralliers.

The occupants of the Micra were American, and they couldn't leave the scene until the police arrived. They looked nervous. Mongolia isn't exactly near the top of the list of countries in which you'd want to end up in police custody. And there was almost nothing we could do to help. We hung around for about an hour, but when the police arrived it was decided that we should carry on, rather than risk becoming embroiled in the situation. We loaded the American's luggage into the Mini and drove to Ulan Bataar, crossing the finish line late at night, and heading straight to a hotel.

Five hours later, an exhausted Brummy was on his way to the airport to catch his flight home, as the weak Mongolian sunshine began to trickle through the window of my hotel room.

*   *   *

The Americans were released from Police custody a few days later, after paying a bill for the repairs to the local's car, and what was left of their Micra crossed the finish line shortly afterwards, lashed ingloriously to a low loader. Given how the badly their situation could have gone, they'd gotten off lightly. They were $1,500 down, but they had come away with a story which they'd be able to dine off for the rest of their lives.

As I lingered at the finish line – a British-owned pub called 'Dave's Place', which sat incongruously in the centre of town – I came to realise that experiences like the accident were what the event was all about. The Mongol

Rally wasn't about finishing. Rather, it was about the adventures which one had along the way.

Once I was over the finish line, I enjoyed spending the afternoon at the pub, joining other ralliers in having a few beers on the open air terrace which overlooked the car park and sharing stories from the road as we watched the new arrivals roll in. Anyone who crossed the finish line looking fresh, their car undamaged and their journey having gone to plan, would get a cheer for sure, but the real enthusiasm was reserved for those who'd been forced to battle on against the odds. For instance, the team whose Fiat Panda's engine mounts had failed, only for them to get a plank of wood long enough to span the car's front wings and then dangle the engine from this beam, enabling them to complete the last five hundred miles, got a roar of appreciation and many pats on the back, and were bought drinks for the rest of the night.

In the anarchic world of the Mongol Rally, being overly prepared just isn't cricket; it's simply a miscalculation which smothers the adventure out of the journey. If nothing goes wrong, then everything has gone wrong, because without problems, there is no adventure. And if there's no adventure, then what's the point of even leaving home? The destruction of my passport in that washing machine, while thoroughly regrettable at the time, had come to define my journey. I'd screwed up, but had battled my way out of the situation to reach the finish anyway. When I told people that I was the guy who'd made this particular error, my fellow ralliers gushed with respect. On the Mongol Rally grapevine, which spanned half of Asia via the event's website, it was widely assumed I'd flown home from Uzbekistan, but no. Fuelled by the rally's spirit of daft perseverance, I'd kept pushing on and made it to the finish. I took pride in this, and appreciated the rally's twisted nature, where being stupid enough to destroy your passport is completely forgivable, but being well organised and efficient certainly isn't.

As I rested at the finish line, proud that I'd earned my Mongol Rally spurs, the world seemed to have opened itself up to me, becoming a blank canvas criss-crossed by unknown dusty roads and full of possibilities for adventure. But I knew that whatever the future held, those adventures would be undertaken the Mongol Rally way. Not for me was the reassurance of a well prepared 4x4, or the well-trodden paths of the gap-year backpacking circuit. No, there was a whole world out there, and if I was going to see it, it would be through the grimy windscreen of the least suitable car possible. And speaking of unsuitable cars, we'd left the UK as a team of two, and one of those was still missing. Several days after I'd crossed the finish line, Tiff, Lee and the red Mini were still somewhere in deepest Siberia.

After three days in Ulan Bataar, basking in the warm glow that comes with beer, steak and success, I received a phone call from Lee telling me they were close, and so I had Daisy's tired engine jumpstarted by another team, before heading back up towards the Russian border to offer up any assistance their faltering car might need to cross the finish line. As it turned out, it was just as well that I did.

We were reunited 100 miles north of Ulan Bataar, and I shadowed the tired red Mini as we counted down the miles to the finish. It was amazing it had got this far at all. Five further temporary repairs to the CV joint had been needed to get the car across Siberia, and the engine was sounding even more like a schrapnel-filled washing machine than usual. But it was still soldiering on. With around 10,000 miles completed and less than 100 still to go, the end was virtually in sight.

Eighty miles from the finish, the engine noise took a turn for the worse, with the shrapnel washing machine seemingly going to a spin cycle. We stopped, checked the oil, and decided to push on. What's 80 miles when you've already done 10,000?

Everything, it turns out.

From my vantage point behind the red Mini, I saw the whole car shake like a warship hit by a fatal broadside. A waterfall of oil a foot wide burst from the sump, leaving a black line of finality on the tarmac which drifted to the right as Lee guided the stricken car over to the side of the road. The acrid smell of burning hung in the air. It smelled like death. The death of a Mini.

Deep within the engine, a conrod had fractured, punching a hole in the motor and allowing its vital fluids to gush out as it self-destructed. A catastrophic failure with only 70 miles to go, after Lee has spent an entire month dragging the thing across Asia – luck doesn't get much worse than that.

If the motor had lasted another 70 miles, and self destructed as it rolled over the finish line before the crowd of perma-drunk ralliers at Dave's Place – preferably catching fire as it did so – then Lee would have had the perfect rally. Sadly, he had the misfortune to have suffered a catastrophic engine failure with less than one percent of the total distance still to go. However, despite being covered in grime and looking exhausted from the effort it had taken to get this far, Lee was remarkably stoical about it:

'Well, it made it to Mongolia, and that was always the goal. To drive to Mongolia. Given all the problems en-route, I'm calling that a win.'

We strung a rope from the back of my Mini to the front of Lee's and towed it to Ulan Bataar, where the sight of the two Minis struggling into Dave's Place, joined by ten feet of frayed blue chord, sent a cheer rippling through the crowd. And then it was time for beer.

*   *   *

We spent a week in Ulan Bataar before flying home, and my memories are a kaleidoscope of the random and the insane. Firstly, like virtually all of the other ralliers, we donated the cars to charity, to be auctioned to raise money for local street children. To do this, we had to deliver them to a compound just out of town, an operation made challenging by the fact that on the night he'd arrived, Lee had swapped his dead Mini's brake master cylinder for a round of beers, meaning that not only would it not go, it now wouldn't stop either. Eventually, we elected to drive out of town with the two long-suffering cars connected by half a foot of rope, and the red mini crashing into the back of my beloved Daisy every time we needed to stop – a fitting way to end to an amazing adventure, albeit an end tinged with sadness. I'd become rather attached to Daisy, my surprisingly dependable £450 Mini, and I was very sad to see it go. It had been a fantastic companion on the road, and had looked after me in such a way that even my total lack of mechanical competence hadn't been a bar to reaching the finish. But now the car which I'd bonded with more than any other was being consigned to memory. It didn't seem fair, even though there was no other choice.

With the cars gone, we spent a few days getting to know the city before flying home, an experience which was bookended by the powers of good and evil. We encountered the power for good first. While exploring the city one day, we found ourselves being passed by all manner of locals, hurrying towards the city's sports stadium with an urgency which could only be described as religious. Curious, we followed them and on entering the stadium, we were presented with prayer scarves by the Buddhist monks who were lining the entrance.

Inside the stadium, a happy air of anticipation and celebration prevailed. Families sat on the grass, picnicking, and groups of friends laughed and joked together, waving their prayer scarves aloft while others sat in silence, lost in themselves. And then suddenly, a fission of excitement swept through the crowd, and all attention turned to the makeshift stage, high in one of the stands.

Because that was the moment when no other than the Dalai Lama made his entrance, taking a seat in the centre of the stage.

We looked at each other in disbelief – we'd just accidently gatecrashed a prayer recital by the Dalai Lama himself. No wonder the devout Buddhists around us were rather excited – without believing our own luck, we settled in to listen to the prayers of one of modern history's great people, in a language we couldn't hope to understand. But it didn't matter. That was the Dalai Lama, just there, talking to us. An audience with one of the most revered people in history. It was almost worth the 10,000 mile drive.

The following evening, we stumbled upon something which celebrated a rather different piece of history. From a distance, it looked like just any other bar, tucked a little way back from the tarmac on Peace Avenue. But as we approached, the whole experience acquired an air of unreality, on which Lee commented first.

'Is that what I think it is?' he asked.

'Yes. Yes it is,' I replied.

'I guess the rumours were true then,' replied Lee.

We were approaching the bar's entrance on an exquisite marble walkway, and embedded into the last marble block before the door, there was a swastika.

Inside, among the bar's surprisingly expensive and trendy décor, the Nazi references came thick and fast. The brushed aluminium bar for instance, wouldn't have looked out of place in a Notting Hill club, were it not for the line of Luftwaffe emblems embossed into it. Some of the rooms contained mannequins of German soldiers in army uniforms clutching machine guns while in the toilets, recruitment posters for the Wehrmacht hung with pride. We headed into a finely wood-panelled room next to the bar, opted for a table beneath a framed portrait of Hitler, and Lee went to get us a few beers. When he came back, he was in fits of giggles.

'You won't believe this,' he said. 'There's a sign on the bar, saying they're doing a special offer this week. Two for one on gas chambers.'

'Oh dear Lord,' I said. 'No way is that true.'

'It totally is,' replied Lee. And he wasn't lying.

If the Mongol Rally was showing me one thing, it's that it is most definitely a strange world we live in. The following day, I asked Dave – of Dave's Place fame – about the bar.

'Oh, that place,' he said. 'That opened a few years ago. Apparently the guys behind it had noticed that we get a lot of German tourists here, so they decided to open a German theme bar. They googled German history, and that's what they came up with.'

A day later, I was heading for Heathrow onboard an elderly Korean Air Boeing 747. As I glanced out of the window at the world we'd just driven across, my mind flashed back through 10,000 miles of adventures, and left me with an overwhelming feeling that my life had just changed forever.

* * *

After the highs of the rally, a return to everyday life beckoned. I went back to surveying cargo ships, and got stuck into climbing again. But something had changed. My eyes had been opened to a whole new world of adventure, and unlike climbing, it was a form of adventure which I felt fitted my skill set. The biggest climbs were still far beyond me, and probably always would be, but the biggest drives? These, I now knew I could do. As the events of the Mongol Rally sank in, the automobile's potential as a facilitator of adventure was cemented in my mind, and even started to colour my climbing trips.

The first of these happened only two weeks after I'd got back from Mongolia. Some friends had shot off to Fontainebleau for a late-summer week on the boulders, and as work was quiet, I decided to join them. Usually, I would have loaded up my sensible Peugeot saloon for the drive out, but not this time. No, the white Porsche 944 which was sat on my drive would be going, trading off space for climbing gear against the fun of the journey. A friend and I loaded it up and headed out for a week, during which time spent climbing was interspersed with stories from Siberia and the steppes of Asia. As I relived the trip next to the campfire, anecdote by anecdote, while sat with my back against the old Porsche which I'd never so much as driven out of the country before, I became certain I'd found a new calling. My friends were suitably taken by the stories – in particular a girl called Laura, who I'd only met once before, during that climbing trip a year earlier when we'd crashed most of the cars and discovered that Gina was not, in fact, a Ford mechanic.

This trip to Fontainebleau marked another diversion from the norm. Rather than maximising time on the boulders by climbing right up to the moment the ferry home was calling, I actually decided to leave a day early, heading home via Germany, and my first laps of the Nurburgring. A day of climbing was given up for a day of automotive adventure, in the only car at the race track loaded to the roof with camping kit, climbing gear and duty-free. The change in my priorities was happening quickly.

* * *

It was a typical Friday evening, five days after I'd got back from the Nurburgring. Brummy, Lee and I were sat in the Seymour Arms unwinding after a long week, and the conversation had predictably came around to road trip ideas. The beer didn't seem to be producing much in the way of inspiration though, and most of the suggestions were pretty forgettable.

'How about Mondeos to Mexico?' suggested Brummy.

'I wouldn't even want to drive to Macclesfield in a Mondeo,' I replied. 'And anyway, how would you get it across the Atlantic?'

'I have no idea,' said Brummy.

127

'Me neither,' I said.   'How about the Soviet Six? Straight across the old Soviet Union, with a straight-six engine?'

'Haven't we just got back from basically driving across the Soviet Union?'

'Well yeah, I guess.'

As we chatted away about these uninspiring ideas, Lee was silent, staring at his pint of Jail Ale with a look on his face which combined concentration and inebriation in equal measure, the sum of which was to make him look mildly constipated.   Eventually however, his trademark smirk spread across his face, and he spoke.

'V8Nam.'

'What?' I said.

'V8Nam. Get a V8, drive it to Vietnam,' replied Lee.

For a moment we were silent, glancing at each other with appreciative grins on our face, before someone broke the silence.

'Lee, you're a genius.'

'I know,' he said. 'But thank the Jail Ale, not me.'

We ordered another round, and the conversation gained a new level of energy as we talked about what cars might be eligible, and what routes might be possible. And an hour later, at the end of that night, we chinked our glasses in agreement. It was happening; one day, we would drive V8s to Vietnam.

We'd only been back from Mongolia for a month, and already, seeds were being sown. Future plans were in the offing.

*   *   *

The well lubricated bravado of a Friday night and the cold light of day are two very different things, and it would be many years before we finally made the V8Nam idea into a reality. However from that moment, the idea was part of us, a long-term ambition to work towards. First however, we had a somewhat more humble road trip to dream up.

The vehicle? A Fiat 126, which for a few years in the '70s and '80s, was Italy's boxy little answer to the Mini.

I'd became the 'proud' owner of the Fiat on my return from Mongolia. Before I'd left, I'd been chatting to my family, and had mentioned in passing that I'd enjoyed having the Mini as an around-town runabout, and I fancied getting another Mini, or maybe a Fiat 500, on my return. My family took this onboard, and found the Fiat 126 for less than £200, when I was unable to protest due to being somewhere out on the Kazakh steppe. On my return, the little car was presented to me as a late birthday present and so one day in late September I took the train up to South Wales, and set out to drive it the 140 miles back to Plymouth. But within a few miles, I came to the conclusion that I rather disliked it. I'd just completed the adventure of a lifetime in my beloved Daisy, the toughest and most charismatic car I had ever owned, and to my very biased mind the Fiat felt tinny and rather rubbish in comparison. It took two and a half hours to get the Fiat home and by the time I parked it, the dislike had turned to hate. It was the worst car I'd ever driven. In fact it was so bad, I needed a beer to dampen the memories.

I called Brummy: 'Seymour Arms? Fifteen minutes?'

'See you there,' was the reply.

I explained the predicament over a pint.

'It's bonfire night soon. We could just set it on fire?' Brummy suggested.

'Tempting, but it's generally frowned upon to torch your birthday presents without at least getting some use from them first.'

'So you think we should take the piece of crap on a road trip?'

'I guess we have to,' I replied.

'But you hate it,' said Brummy. 'Just driving it to Plymouth has turned you into an alcoholic.'

'I know, but we've gotta do something with it. It's basically a Mongol Rally car, so doing something ridiculous with it would be the right thing to do. It would be both rude and disrespectful not to, in fact.'

'Okay, but can we burn it after the road trip?' said Brummy.

'Maybe,' I replied. 'But you're right. I do hate it.'

'Where's your least favourite place in the world? We could drive it there?'

'Newport docks? Hmmm, I'm not convinced.'

'Where then?' asked Brummy.

'Well,' I replied. 'It is the car from Hell, so maybe we should drive it to Hell.'

'Where the hell is Hell?' Brummy asked.

'I'm not sure,' I replied. 'But I think there's a Hell in Norway somewhere.'

'We could burn it in Hell when we get there,' suggested Brummy. 'It definitely needs to burn in Hell.'

'How about we do it at New Year?' I suggested. 'Hell should be frozen over by then.'

And so, over a few beers in the pub, our next adventure was dreamed up – a New Year's trip through the Scandinavian winter to a village we still weren't 100% sure even existed, in a £200 Fiat.

It was to be the first automotive adventure we'd undertake which we'd dreamed up ourselves, battling through the snow and ice of the Deep North. And as much as I hated that shitbox car, already I couldn't wait.

THIRTEEN

COUNTRY UNDER CONSTRUCTION

07th May 2013
Korgas, Xinjiang Autonomous Region, China

The Chinese border grew large in the Corvette's windscreen as we rolled across No-Man's-Land. Ahead of us, the tallest flagpole of the trip thrust far into the cloudless sky and from it, a huge, blood-red Chinese flag flew solemnly in the breeze. Beneath this symbol of the nation, four immaculately turned out young soldiers stood unflinchingly to attention, as if they'd not moved for days. Each of them was exactly matched in height and build, their ceremonial uniforms were perfect in fit and their rifles rose plumb-vertically against their shoulders with such accuracy, it was as if a superior officer had aligned them with a set-square. As we awaited our turn to enter the border post we watched the trucks in front of us roll past the resolute guards, who maintained their rigid stance as if their lives depended on it. It was a display of discipline every bit as impressive as a London Beefeater.

Then it was our turn to pass.

The motionless guards began to twitch as the V8 rumble reached their ears, and they desperately tried not to turn their heads. Then into their field of vision there inched a Rolls-Royce and a Corvette, their big engines being revved in greeting by the grinning Westerners at their wheels. For a few moments the soldiers remained motionless, as their curiosity was smothered by the potentially career-limiting consequences of breaking rank. However it quickly became all too much, and the steely-eyed order and discipline of the Korgas border post rapidly fell apart as we drove beyond their field of vision, with drillsquare uniformity suddenly being replaced with dropping jaws, blinking eyes and a general aura of confusion. We were well past the guards before they finally gave up any remaining pretence of order and left the enormous flag unguarded, scrambling after us in a most disorderly fashion, to find out who the hell we were.

And so began our time at the Chinese border.

Even without being chased across the frontier by confused soldiers, China is a rather awkward place to take a car into, and our preparations for this leg of the journey had begun a full five months earlier when we'd put together a detailed itinerary of our proposed route and timings for the perusal of the Chinese Government. This rather hefty document included details of which roads we'd be using, when we'd be driving them, where our overnight stops would take place and what points of interest we intended to visit. To this dossier was added information on who we were and what cars we'd be driving, and the whole lot was presented to the government via a fixing company called NAVO Tour, which specialises in making the more esoteric and left-field tourist visits to China possible.

With no easy way for us to drive around China, this excursion across the huge country had been the crux of the whole V8Nam plan, and so it was with great relief that we'd heard that our intentions had been green-lighted, a few months after they'd been presented to the government. Our plan to cross China from Kazakhstan to Laos was go, and as a result, the entire V8Nam Expedition could go ahead.

But that didn't mean that crossing China would be remotely straightforward, and even the outwardly simple act of getting the cars across the border took four days, such was the weight of bureaucracy involved, and we found that our experiences at the Chinese border were quite unlike any other borders we'd ever crossed. For instance, the cars needed to go through the Chinese equivalent of an MOT test before they'd be allowed on the road there, with a test centre having been built near the border for exactly this purpose – a factor which had caused us a fair amount of stress as we'd approached the border, because quite frankly, the cars were already suffering. Every attempt to fix the Rolls-Royce's exhaust manifold had failed, meaning it still sounded rather tank-like as it inched its way across Asia. Meanwhile in the Corvette, bodged rear brakes were the least of our worries, given the faulty cooling fans and the gradual increase in engine temperatures we'd been seeing, along with its annoying habit of randomly going into limp mode, a faux-pas which was fixed in the time-honoured manner of turning it off and on again. However our final issue was perhaps the most pressing - the state of the rear tyres, which were already almost bald, thanks to a degree of over-exuberance in both Europe and Central Asia. These tyres were a worry as the chances of getting hold of 275/35R17 rubber in the course of our dash across China were vanishingly slim, and the car's newfound tail-happiness was already making itself known. Despite these faults, surprisingly it was only the Rolls-Royce which presented any issues at the MOT test, further relinquishing its title of 'best car in the world' by failing thanks to its laughably ineffective handbrake. However in any frontier bureaucracy like this, there's always some wriggle room, and some off-the-record negotiations eventually got it a clean bill of health.

With the cars now deemed acceptable for the Chinese road network, they also needed Chinese license plates, and we needed to get ourselves Chinese driving licenses – an interesting document to secure since it hinged on an eye test which required us to read Chinese characters at various distances. Now, as the only Chinese symbol I know is the one for 'dog' – useful for when you're trying to avoid restaurants which specialise in canine main courses – it's a test I would have failed, were it not for the assistance of our guide.

The guide is another area in which driving in China is unlike anywhere else – not only do you have to have your entire itinerary checked by the government, but foreigners also have to have someone approved by the authorities with them at all times, mainly for assistance, but no doubt partly to keep an eye on us as well. Our guide hailed from Chengdu, went by the adopted Western name of Shannon and was most helpful when it came to getting the cars across the border, being able to brush under the table such things as our apparent blindness when faced with Chinese symbols, or the utter uselessness of the Rolls' handbrake. Or even the sudden increase in customs deposit the authorities demanded when they saw that it was indeed a real-life Rolls-Royce which had just rolled across the border – albeit the scruffiest and loudest Rolls on the Eurasian landmass.

For the four days it took our guide to assemble the inch thick dossier of paperwork necessary to bring the cars into the country, we lived in a hotel a few hundred metres into China and took in our first taste of this enigmatic nation of over a billion people. Ironically, given China's huge population, our first impression was that the place seemed deserted. The border city of Korgas, complete with its broad avenues and jarringly new apartment blocks, was empty. Few cars prowled the new tarmac, and the pavements were barely peopled. The Korgas International Trade Centre was conspicuous by its lack of traders and only the steady flow of trucks across the border gave any sense of purpose to this shiny new ghost town.

But despite this, a frenzy of construction work was still in progress. The Chinese Government was clearly taking a 'build it, and they will come' approach to the development of this strategically important border city, which forms another piece of the jigsaw that had resulted in us driving perfect Chinese tarmac on the road to Aralsk – China's desire for easy access to its export markets. More apartment blocks were going up, warehouses were spreading across the city's outskirts and a glorious future was being promoted on the billboards. From nothing, this empty desert outpost was being dragged into playing its part in the 21st century Chinese dream, whether it liked it or not.

But in some ways, Korgas didn't feel like a Chinese city at all. Many of the people seemed little different to those in Kazakhstan, and their tones, features and beliefs still looked west to the mosques and markets of Central Asia, rather than east to far-off Beijing. These people were the Uighur Muslims, and they carried with them a frontier confidence, altogether grittier and more swaggering than the Han Chinese immigrants whose arrival from the east was giving purpose to the rash of new tower blocks all around.

At night, the feeling that we weren't yet in China became more profound. The customs of Central Asia still seemed to hold sway here. The rich smell of lamb shashlik kebabs roasting over hot coals filled the dry desert air, while groups of men sat together, raising cups of tea to their bearded mouths as their laughter rippled through the night, in response to jokes told in a Turkic dialect far removed from Mandarin Chinese. Among these larger-than-life Uighurs, the pale-faced Han Chinese arrivals from the east seemed to float anodynely in the background, like ghosts. They faded away to inhabit the shadows, uncertain strangers in someone else's country.

But sometimes, appearances can be deceptive.

We had just crossed into the Xinjiang Uighur Autonomous Region, but despite the name, we were in a region where it was the Uighurs who were outnumbered and dominated by the Han Chinese. Due to the influx of migrants from the east, the Uighurs had become strangers in their own land, outnumbered by the Han who had been flooding in for decades, drawn by government incentives such as lower taxes and a relaxation of the one-child policy.

Separated by religion, traditions and a mutual distrust, the two populations exist alongside one another, but live completely separately. Decades of division has driven a deep wedge between them, leaving each side of the invisible barrier proud of their distinct ways, and suspicious of the motives of their neighbours. The Han Chinese see themselves as bringing wealth, infrastructure, education and health to the disadvantaged peoples living on China's frontiers, and find it difficult to understand why the Uighur people are so ungrateful for their apparently selfless efforts. But the Uighurs view things rather differently, as they find themselves strangers in their own lands, their customs and religions being oppressed and their very identity being diluted by the influx.

This was brought home to us a few days into our enforced stay at the border, when after a long day of attempting to batter our way through the heavy bureaucracy, we returned to the hotel to find a Uighur wedding party arriving at the same time. Despite the wedding-spec Rolls still being stuck at the border, the party were most welcoming of the rather under-dressed Brits they found in their midst, insisting on having their photos taken with us before inviting us to the wedding reception. And of course, that's not exactly something we were going to turn down.

The reception was held in the hotel's darkened function room, which was brought to life by the shafts of light which swept across from the dance floor. We sat at a circular table and were plied with various fruit juices, the couple's Muslim beliefs meaning alcohol was officially off the menu. The music was loud and hypnotic, being defined by a fast-paced, flowing rhythm to which the Uighurs danced with abandon. Often, the dancers would glance over to us, making sure that their Western guests were being looked after, and one of the guys who could speak some English elected to spend the evening with us, speaking guardedly and occasionally falling silent before glancing across to Shannon, the only Han Chinese in the room.

The swirling music, unfamiliar dances and the fruit-juice buffet were all just as foreign to Shannon as they were to us, and the only time the wedding goers spoke any Chinese was when Shannon addressed them in Mandarin. Some couldn't understand Chinese at all; Uighur was their language, and this was their country, their day. They gave off a superior air which implied that Shannon, and in fact the whole of the Han Chinese, had no place in their celebrations. And every time someone glanced towards us from the dance floor, there was no language barrier. Their glances said silently what they couldn't say in public: *'this is who we are. Remember us. We are Uighur, and we're not like them.'*

When I finally went to bed that night, the music was still blaring, and it easily found its way up through the floor of my hotel room. I didn't resent it though; our inclusion in this most closed of Uighur events meant I found it almost welcoming. And besides, it was better than yet another pummelling by Gangnam Style.

*   *   *

After four days of having our enthusiasm for international travel gradually eroded at the border, we were finally free to continue – that is, if you define 'free' as having permission to follow an officially approved route across a country, while the government peruses the inch-thick dossier which they've assembled about you and your trip. Yes, China was certainly setting new records for paranoia as well as paperwork, and the paranoia continued once we were rolling. Seemingly every few kilometres, an overhead gantry spanned the smooth new road which we were following, and camera flashes from the gantry would mark our passage. For the next month, we – along with every other car on the highway – would be tracked across China with intimidating accuracy. Any thoughts of drifting off our agreed route didn't even make it an hour out of the border town. If you take a car into China, be prepared to wave goodbye to the romantic traveller's notion of drifting vaguely through the landscape, with no fixed intentions other than satisfying your curiosity. No, in China curiosity is officially discouraged.

But what would we find if we did drift curiously from our route, out in this desert province 1,500 miles from

Beijing? Our research had turned up a vast desert, where the empty sands are punctuated with all manner of curiosities, from ancient ruins to alleged forced labour camps; from nuclear test areas to colossal mines. Seemingly, what Kazakhstan had been to the Soviet Union fifty years earlier, so Xinjiang has become to China in more recent times. An expanse of emptiness, where the abundant resources can be extracted, and the dirty side of a superpower's development can take place, far from prying eyes. But as we rolled away from the border, our Corvette and Rolls-Royce setting off the cameras every few kilometres and, no doubt, confusing the hell out of someone in a traffic monitoring centre elsewhere in the country, we saw none of this. Instead, it was an unexpected mountainscape which held our attention. From a landscape seemingly dominated by nothing – neither desert nor farmland – the terrain rose and we were swept along a valley on smooth tarmac with clean slopes of grass and fir trees rising above us, and a rocky creek burbling below. We kept on climbing and the highest summits began to retain a trace of the winter snows, while the air acquired a cutting chill. But as dramatic as it was, the landscape was seemingly inconsequential to the Chinese engineers who'd built the road, and the smooth surface continued to sweep us effortlessly upwards. It was a road built for efficiency, not thrills; a highway which seemed to take no pleasure in its surroundings but rather saw them as an unfortunate inconvenience to be crossed as efficiently as possible. And it succeeded, tunnelling through mountains and sweeping over drops with a bold confidence. At one particularly memorable point we passed beneath a soaring suspension bridge, after which the road curved around in a big circle, gaining sufficient altitude for the roadway to pass onto the bridge, allowing us to soar over our previous path, a few hundred metres higher in the sky. And then we came across something you don't really expect to find when you're over 2,000 metres up. A huge lake, stretching away to the distant mountains which formed its far shore. We pulled over to stretch our legs.

The wind was cold now, unexpectedly so after the warmth of the border town, whose desert setting suddenly felt so far away. The gusts threatened to pull our car doors from their hinges, and cut through us until we found our warm coats, which were buried deep in our luggage. A few Kazakh-style yurts stood nearby, completely unruffled by the breeze and with horses grazing next to them, oblivious to everything. It was a vista of alpine paradise, made accessible by the coincidence of the highway's route, but as so often happens when paradise is paved through, it felt vulnerable. Already, a tourist hotel had been built at the lake's eastern end and further development seemed inevitable as China's domestic tourist market grows. The G30 Linhao Expressway's journey through these foothills of the Altai Mountains may have been routed purely to follow the path of least resistance, but if there was money to be made from the shimmering beauty of its surroundings, then of course the possibility would be exploited. Such is the way of modern China.

The road swept down from the mountains in the same way in which it had risen up to meet them – with an air of permanency which challenged the nature through which it travelled. It made no attempt to blend in. It was simply laid across the landscape like a statement – *we are here to stay*.

Given that it could be argued that one of the purposes of the road is to bind the country's Muslim West ever closer to the East, such a statement may not be purely accidental.

After a few hours of driving in which the combination of smooth yet strangely gripless tarmac and ruined rear tyres made the Corvette a sideways liability on anything over half throttle, the road had flowed down from the alpine heights and once again entered a desert, whose unrelenting dryness was broken only by those towns with sufficient irrigation to bring a rare patch of green to the landscape. But mankind's presence was always felt, and with it, his determination to benefit from these wild lands. Even out here, in small towns on the fringes of the Gobi, tower blocks were being thrown up by the dozen, their stark concrete structures already dusty from the blown sands, as cranes worked day and night to complete them. We passed factories and power stations being built with war-like urgency, while those already completed belched black smoke into the dusty air, visible for miles around. For day after day our surroundings were like this, the artery of smooth tarmac being fleshed out with the structures of a country under construction; structures which will facilitate further migration from the crowded east, speed up the harvesting of the region's abundant raw materials and bind the nation together ever more tightly through infrastructure and development. It was an unattractive process. All the natural beauty was being sacrificed from the landscape through which we were driving, day after day, as the temperature rose ever higher. And amid the change, the Uighurs looked even more like strangers in a world which was no longer theirs; a world that kept on racing into the future at a breakneck speed, leaving them stranded like relics of a rose-tinted past, the romance of their camel trains and caravanserais lost forever in the dust.

The settlements which rose so infrequently from the sands continued to turn their backs on that past. In the shadow of the mountains, the city of Urumqi – whose main claim to fame is that it is the furthest city from an ocean anywhere on the planet – rose concrete and unlovely, a regional centre with its eyes so firmly fixed on generating money that Uighur sentimentality no longer has a place there. Further down the road, the sprawling buildings of Turpan baked in the depression which gives it its name, 80 metres below sea level and 40°C above freezing. The following day, our stay in Hami was memorable only for a chance meeting with some Swiss overlanders in a couple of Land Rover Defenders which were having far more reliability issues than our ill-advised steeds, with failing head gaskets and worn suspension having punctuated their

142

long journey from Zurich. Not that we were fairing much better, with the Corvette now overheating whenever our progress was slowed by traffic, and its rear tyres completely devoid of tread. We rolled onwards, overnighting in the towns, and spending our days amid the nothingness which separated these nodes of life, around which there was only desert. The endless desert. Tamed by a smooth tarmac road and watched by the gantries of cameras which flashed at us without fail as the sands rolled past the windows for hour after hour, the romance of the past erased by the steady flow of development sweeping in from the east.

But there are still places in which the past has been allowed to live on. Places such as the Mogao Caves, where we stepped into the darkness from the glare of the day, and the years were instantly swept away. Years, centuries, even millennia. The first caves were dug here by monks around 1,600 years ago as a place in which to meditate, far from their modern world.

But from these simple beginnings the site grew, with more caves being carved into the conglomerate rock, paid for by rich donors and fitted out gloriously as shrines, until an entire valley wall had been converted into a honeycomb of worship. Inside, the caves were decorated with paintings and murals from floor to ceiling and statues of Buddha, some of which were so large they need a four-story tall subterranean cavern to house them, while others were small enough to fit into your pocket, should you be in a pilfering mood. At one stage the rock here was pockmarked with thousands of caves; today, almost five hundred are preserved, and a few of these are open for the public to tour.

To protect the artworks, no lighting is allowed in the caves and so it takes some time for your eyes to adjust as you enter, the bright sunshine of the outside world being replaced with a cool darkness, through which the grotto's features slowly become visible. From the proportions which define them to the sculptures and murals which bring

143

them to life, every cave is unique, and during tours the guide uses a faint torch to illuminate the features of interest – a fairly straightforward task given the caves tend to be covered in curiosity from floor to ceiling.

Once we'd toured a few of the more run-of-the-mill caves which are open to the public, we were inevitably led to cave seventeen – the library cave, which has became a lodestar for how unfairly China has been treated by the wider world.

This particular cave was sealed up around the year 1000AD and went undiscovered for almost a millennium, before the Mugao Cave's self appointed caretaker – Abbot Wang Yuanlu – discovered its concealed entrance around the start of the 20th century. Behind the entrance, the intrepid abbot stumbled upon a veritable treasure trove of ancient manuscripts, stacked from floor to ceiling and packing out almost all of the not inconsiderably-sized space. Word spread, a few years passed, and then the Hungarian born archaeologist Aurel Stein arrived, on assignment from the British Museum. Aurel, a heavyweight of Central Asian archaeology, was well aware of the significance of the discovery, and over time he set about winning the trust of Wang sufficiently to convince him to sell many of the documents to him, for the rather token sum of £130. On his return to London with his haul, its true significance became apparent. Amongst the haul was the oldest printed text in existence – the Diamond Sutra, dating to 868AD – and many other items of unparalleled historical significance. And this was just the beginning. Aurel's discovery opened the floodgates, with archaeologists from France, Japan, Russia and America all making a beeline to the caves and leaving with anything of significance which they could strap to a camel. The humiliation continued on the slow-burn, with China powerless to stop it.

Cave seventeen is empty now, and the airy space speaks more loudly than any of the other caves. It speaks of China as a victim, a country which has been disrespected and humiliated by foreign powers for too long, and in doing so, it provides an insight into the nation's determination to re-attain its greatness which has characterised its leadership ever since Chairman Mao seized power.

Much of this determination is centred on a united China, as the all powerful Communist Party see the minority living in the nation's west, such as the Uighurs and Tibetans – along with their strategically important and mineral rich lands – as being inarguably Chinese, hence the efforts which are being put into tying the nation together through infrastructure and migration. To the Han Chinese, this is the most natural thing in the world, and the lack of thanks they receive from the minority populations is met with considerable bemusement. As we drove away from the Mugao Caves, I chatted to Shannon about the lands we'd been crossing for the previous few days.

'We've given them so much,' she said. 'We've built schools, hospitals, and railways. They pay lower taxes than we do, and they can have more children, yet they still seem to resent it.'

'But they didn't ask for any of this,' I said, my mind flashing back to a certain Monty Python sketch about the Romans.

'And still we gave it to them. We've done everything we can for the Uighurs, and yet they're still ungrateful.'

'I guess it's like my people's experience in India,' I said. 'We built roads, railways and schools there too. We gave them a legal system and introduced the basics of democracy. But they were never happy with the situation, because our being there hurt their pride. Nobody likes to be ruled by an outsider.'

'But we're not outsiders ruling Xinjiang. It's part of China.'

'Did anyone ask the Uighurs if they want to be part of China?' I said. 'Or, the Tibetans?'

'That's all in the past. Right now we're doing everything we can for these people, and they just don't seem to care. They hate us.'

'They're strangers in the land they see as theirs, being ruled from Beijing. However much you do for them, that will still hurt their pride, and so they'll still resent you. Like I said, it's like the British experience in India. You'll never win their acceptance, neither with carrot or stick.'

In many ways, Shannon was typical of the well-educated Chinese middle class which is driving China's domestic economy forwards. She lived in Chengdu with her husband and single child, had been to Europe and was great company with a ready smile and a fine sense of humour. We talked about many things in the course of our month together crossing China, and generally found agreement or common ground. But on this one subject – the relationship between the Han Chinese and the country's 56 different minority groups – we never reached a mutual understanding. The Western appreciation of the underdog butted up against the apparently unquestionable facts handed down by the Chinese Communist Party, and a void was left between us.

But had these outlying regions, such as Xinjiang and Tibet, always been part of a greater China, as the country's current leadership insists? Or is a united China, with a history stretching back through the millennia, a modern fabrication which fulfils the needs of the Chinese Communist Party? The truth sits somewhere between the two extremes. Over the centuries, the ebb and flow of China's fortunes have caused the outermost regions of what constitutes modern China to drift in and out of the various dynasties' spheres of influence in an endless interplay of conquest and withdrawal, meaning that sometimes these outlying regions came under the direct control of Beijing, and sometimes not. But to the Han Chinese, a historic boundary exists which, until recently, not only defined who they are but also demarked the outlying regions of their lands.

The Great Wall.

For centuries, this triumph of construction represented the farthest extent of Chinese civilisation in the minds of its people.   Within the wall, comfort, culture and enlightenment reigned; beyond it, barbarians lived. To be expelled to a life beyond the wall was the greatest indignity which could befall a resident of Imperial China. It was a physical line on the map which broadcast the differences between what the Chinese saw as their cultured lives within the wall, and the savagery of the Central Asian steppe which existed beyond it. What China now wishes to be one homogeneous nation, the wall once cleaved clean in two. And finally, after over a thousand miles of driving across the Xinjiang desert, we were about to pass through this most famous of barriers, and enter old China. With the Great Wall just over the horizon and the Corvette wagging its tail excitedly on the greasy tarmac, Ian and I pushed on using only the lightest of throttle applications, in the hope that it wouldn't spin us off the road into the scenery before we reached it.

FOURTEEN

THE ROAD TO HELL

01st January 2007
Steinkjer, Norway

Loosened by the polished ice beneath our wheels, the back end of our little Fiat 126 jumped suddenly sideways as we crested the rise. Brummy corrected the slide, but as he did so the rear-engined car fishtailed even more enthusiastically the other way. One more desperate attempt to retain control, and all was lost. Helplessly wedged in the back seat, I looked over my shoulder and watched in horror as we hurtled backwards towards an icy fjord, the moonlight shimmering delicately on its surface.

'Brake!' I yelped helplessly.

'I am fucking breaking!' Brummy replied stoically.

We flew backwards, our speed slowly being scrubbed off as the fjord loomed closer in our vision. Our wheels clipped its bank, nearly spinning us into the depths, and we hurtled off the road onto the only bit of flat grass for miles. Wheels glissading over the soft snow, we slid to a halt less than twenty feet from the water, and a similar distance from the pine trees which had loomed up in our path through the darkness.

After a while sat in silence, my heart rate dropped sufficiently for me to speak again.

'Right, that's it. I'm driving.'

*   *   *

Driving through the Arctic winter to Hell in a Fiat 126 had seemed a far better idea a few months earlier, when we'd come up with the plan over beers in the Seymour Arms, after my drive home from Wales.

149

A week after dreaming up the idea, we'd taken my blue Fiat up to deepest mid-Devon to collect a second 126, which Brummy had found on the internet. It was impossible to miss it as we pulled into the street where it lived. Glaringly yellow and with black flames painted fetchingly down the side, it looked rather out of place in the smothering autumn mist. A previous owner had scrawled 'Bad Boy' on the car's bluff front, and 'no fat chicks' was painted on the wings - clearly, we'd found the perfect vehicle for an inconspicuous trip to the Arctic. At least unlike mine, it was the earlier air-cooled version, and so promised to be perfect for the far-below-zero temperatures we anticipated.

Considering the arduous ordeal awaiting them, the modifications to the cars were most thorough, consisting of fitting winter tyres and, well that's it – such is the way of the Mongol Rally veteran. And so on Christmas Eve I waved Brummy off in his yellow steed, with plans to meet in Dover on the 27th.

My phone rang an hour later. It was Brummy.

'Hi there. I'm at Cullumpton services. The yellow peril caught fire, but don't worry, I've put it out.'

'What happened?'

'Well, the oil filler cap fell off and oil splashed onto the engine. Oh, and the exhaust's fallen off.'

'Need a hand?'

'If you've nothing better to do.'

An hour later, there were two diminutive Fiats at Cullumpton services. Brummy had got the oil topped up and a friendly chap from the AA had replaced the exhaust bolts, so we were good to carry on. We made it another twenty miles up the motorway before my boot flew open, and it had to be held shut by a bungee strap for the rest of the trip. Ten miles further on, the yellow peril started to lose power intermittently, so we pulled in to check it over. Nothing obvious looked to be wrong – a predictable conclusion given that neither of us had much of a clue as to what we were looking for when it came to troubleshooting engines.

'Looks okay to me. Let's push on and see what happens,' Brummy suggested.

And so we did, for half a mile. Then with a loud bang, the little yellow Fiat shot foot-long flames from its tiny exhaust and coasted to a halt at the side of the road.

'I don't think it wants to go to Hell,' said Brummy, as his attempts to restart the engine failed.

So out came the towrope, and the two lashed-together Fiats crawled through the darkness to South Wales at a snail's pace, where following a cup of tea at my parent's house, we had a look at the recalcitrant Fiat. It wouldn't start, a problem which was eventually diagnosed as a faulty condenser. Given that it was Christmas Eve and Santa doesn't typically deliver condensers for 25 year old Fiats, we sadly conceded that its journey was over. With only 100 miles completed, and still another 1,500 to go to reach Hell, we were down to one Fiat.

I left South Wales on Boxing Day evening, and headed through the unwelcoming night towards Birmingham. The temperature was hovering just below zero, and spooky patches of dense fog drifted through the darkness. The plan was to collect Brummy and another friend named Jim from Birmingham, somehow cram the three of us into the tiny car and boldly set course for Hell. However, I was broken down on the hard shoulder within an hour of setting off.

The engine had lost power and begun to splutter and misfire intermittently, gradually becoming worse over a period of a few miles, until I ground to a halt on the hard shoulder. I turned the engine over, but it refused to fire. Pulling my coat on, I readied myself to brave the cold and to take a look at the motor, but then decided to try to start it one more time before leaving the sheltered cabin for the chill night. This time, it spluttered angrily before coming to life from its temporary slumber. We were back in business.

A few miles down the road, the problem repeated itself. Again, waiting a minute was enough to get the engine spluttering into life again. 'Carburettor icing,' I said to myself as I pulled away, thinking back to what I'd learned during my flying lessons all those years before. It made sense. The air was visibly moist and the temperature was hovering around freezing.

As the damp air is drawn through the carburettor, it accelerates, which causes a drop in its temperature and chills the exposed metal inside the carburettor to below zero, enabling a build-up of ice to occur which prevents the engine from running smoothly, or in our case, from running at all. When stopped on the hard shoulder, the heat from the engine would melt the ice, enabling it to clear the motor and let us carry on our way.

Three breakdowns later and revelling in our ridiculous plight, I arrived at Brummy's house in Birmingham. We strapped a couple of bags to the roof, piled the remainder on the back seat, and the three of us climbed aboard and set off to Dover. And broke down again about 20 minutes later. In an attempt to feed warmer air into the engine, we took off the air filter and ducting to the carburettor, enabling it to draw warmer air from within the engine compartment. This improved things a little and we made it to Dover by 7 in the morning, having ended up on the hard shoulder seven times in the first 350 miles of our trip.

Belgium and Holland were just as cold and damp as England, and our number of stops soon reached double figures. Desperate, we toyed with the idea of buying a cigarette-lighter powered hairdryer to feed warm air to the engine, but none of the service stations seemed to sell such tat. And so on we spluttered, to Germany.

We spent our first night on the continent in Dortmund with some German friends, who were deeply confused by our journey.

'Why do you want to drive to Hell? It makes no sense.'

'Because it's funny. And because we can.'

'But there's nothing there. Why drive for days to get to somewhere where there's nothing to do?'

'For fun.'

'Where is the fun in three of you being cramped into that little car for days on end? There is no fun in this.'

'You Germans have absolutely no sense of humour.'

'Well at least we have common sense.'

The next morning we headed north, up the autobahn to Denmark. The weather had improved, warming up enough to prevent the carburettor icing problems from reoccurring. On this leg of the journey, I sampled the Fiat's luxurious rear quarter for the first time. Wedged in by a pile of rucksacks, movement was virtually impossible and deep-vein-thrombosis seemed a certainty. Within minutes of climbing aboard, all feeling in the legs would be unavoidably lost, which wasn't a bad thing as it turned out, as it made the cold less noticeable. It was freezing back there. The trickle of warm air from the heater was only of use to the lucky folk sat up front, and a continuous flood of cold air flowed in through the ill-fitting passenger door, blasting the car's unfortunate back seat passenger. The only way to survive this was to don a down jacket, woolly hat and gloves, snuggle beneath the sleeping bags we'd brought along and think warm thoughts. At least the reactions of other road users provided an entertaining distraction from the hardships, ranging from the unbridled enthusiasm displayed by much of Germany's youth, to an aloofly studied indifference from the more mature members of society.

It was dark when we reached Denmark and following a conference over some very strong, very expensive coffee, we decided to push on through the night to Oslo. This proved somewhat of a blur. A darkened Denmark left no imprint on our memories as we flew past the interestingly named town of Middelfart, and over the grand suspension bridges which provide a link with Sweden.

As we drove further into Scandinavia, the shadowy landscape turned snowy before hiding itself in a dense fog which slowed our progress to walking pace and froze onto our poor car's bodywork. Soon, the bags on the roof were encrusted in ice, as was the front of the car. Fortunately the ice had the decency to stay out of the carburettor this time and so on we inched, passing through the unmanned Norwegian border post at about five in the morning and reaching Oslo shortly afterwards.

Oslo proved to be just as clean and smart as you'd expect, and so after a few hours of attempting to sleep while cooped up in the Fiat, we stretched our aching legs with a stroll before completing the obligatory visit to the Viking museum, and then rejoining the long road to the north. Slushy snow lined the verges and sometimes drifted across the tarmac, but it wasn't thick enough to hinder our progress. The Fiat's attempts to slow us down were more successful, however. As the day went on it lost power, seemingly running on only one cylinder and stalling if the revs dropped below 1,500 RPM. As darkness fell, we pulled into Lillehammer and checked into a hotel before heading out for a much needed drink. The first round came to a then-eyewatering £18 for the three of us, and the evening just got more painfully expensive from there.

With all of our wallets battered by the experience, we ended up in a local bar where Jim and I abandoned Brummy, who was chatting to a rather drunk, patriotic Norwegian ('don't mention the Euro. I mentioned it once, but I think I got away with it') and headed back to the hotel. Which we promptly woke up by firing the Fiat up to keep some heat in the engine. We then disconnected the battery and I drunkenly strolled back to our warm hotel room with it tucked under my arm, much to the confusion of the receptionist. Brummy arrived twenty minutes later and collapsed face down on his bed, while Jim and I polished off a few beers smuggled over from England at about a tenth a price of the Norwegian beers.

Through smothering hangovers, we struggled to the car the following morning and found it cocooned in its own block of ice. After forcing our way in we connected the battery and were amazed when it actually started. We found the cause of the previous days rough running easily – one of the HT leads had melted onto the hot exhaust, causing it to short out and prevent one of the cylinders from firing - quite a problem when you only have two cylinders to begin with. A few quick twists of gaffa tape soon solved the problem, and so after a stroll around the Olympic village, we carried on north towards our date with Hell, and the New Year.

On the last day of 2006, Trondheim was deserted. In Norway the New Year's celebrations are a family affair and so there were no packed bars, no revellers in the streets and little of the raucous atmosphere you get in the UK. We parked the Fiat and wandered the surreally deserted streets until we happened upon a familiar sight. Shaped like a London tube logo, the sign for the 'Kings Cross' English pub beckoned us in from the cold streets. We'd found our venue to see out the old year, at £7 a pint.

New Year's Day began predictably, with all three of us dulled by hangovers. The Fiat was also suffering, and was very reluctant to fire up and complete the remaining ten miles to Hell. But fire up it did and away we went, pulling up next to the village sign five days and 1,600 miles after leaving the UK. Fortunately, the place was just as deserted as Trondheim had been the previous night, which kept the disapproving looks to a minimum as we drove the little car onto the station platform for a photo shoot by the station sign, which read 'Hell – Gods Expedition' – and all because of a drunken conversation in the Seymour Arms a few months earlier.

Then we faced a decision. We had less than four days left in Norway before our ferry left from Bergen, about 400 miles away. We could have drifted down to the port, enjoying the scenery and the extortionately-priced beer at a leisurely pace. However, given the preposterous nature of our journey so far, there was no way we would be going for such a sensible option. We were Mongol Rally veterans now, and that meant that sensible options didn't get a look-in, especially as to our north lay the Arctic Highway, beckoning us to strike out through barren mountains and sinuous fjords, crossing the tundra in search of the Northern lights.

Hell is located at 63.5° north, so the midwinter days are short and cold. Leaving the place we had spent nearly a week driving to on the basis of a silly idea we'd dreamed up in the pub a few months earlier, we chugged on through the drizzle into the night. As darkness set, an Elk watched us disinterestedly from the side of the road, the Scandinavian cliché completed by a backdrop of forest and mountains.

It was a disappointingly cloudy evening, the sky interspersed with snow showers which mocked our foolish plan. As the tarmac road gave way to a ploughed and graded surface of ice, the last vestiges of light lingered long enough to inject a beauty into our surroundings. The ice under our wheels was surprisingly easy to drive on and we were able to plod on at around 40mph, thrilled to be heading north to the Arctic and surprised we'd made it so far. Onwards we went, gaining confidence in the Fiat's ability to reach the Arctic with every mile. And as our confidence increased, so did our cornering speeds, until Brummy flew over that sweeping crest next to the fjord and the Fiat bit back, almost pirouetting us into the icy waters.

Feeling chastened, we continued at a more sedate pace, reaching the town of Mo I Rana – the official start of the Arctic Highway – in time for a predictably expensive dinner. And then back into the Fiat we crammed ourselves, and off to the Arctic we went.

The Arctic Highway crosses the Arctic Circle on a suitably bleak plain, where the graded ice of the road merges almost imperceptibly into the snowy expanse through which it meanders. We stopped at a sign which read 'Polarsirkel-Senteret' and took some photos, lit by the few trickles of moonlight which found their way through the overcast.

'It's not looking good for spotting the Northern Lights,' Jim commented, speaking for all of us.

As we piled back into the Fiat, I spotted the vaguest green twinkle through a tiny gap in the clouds, just above the horizon. It was the aurora, pulsating away behind the overcast. We stood and watched for a few minutes as this tiny patch of sky phased from the infinite rich blue of night, to a green glow as millions of charged ions pummelled the atmosphere hundreds of miles above. My mind extrapolated what it must look like above the clouds, where nature's most ethereal spectacle was being played out. With a mixture of sadness and awe, I climbed back into the Fiat, resigned to the knowledge that the overcast would prevent us from seeing nature's most glorious fireworks properly.

We continued north, through sweeping vistas of plummeting cliffs and perfect mountains, as the cloud thickened above us. The temperature plummeted to -10°C as the night took control of the landscape, and the drifts of snow lining the road became ever higher. And then the clouds were behind us, and the crisp white snows were painted hauntingly by the full moon. But the Aurora Borealis was now nowhere to be seen.

The further north we went, the more beautiful the empty landscape became. Lit by moonlight crystalline in its sharpness, the fjords became more precipitous and foreboding, the mountains reached nearer to perfection and even the star-drenched sky seem to move closer. And then, framed by the long suffering Fiat's windscreen, a faint emerald curtain draped itself over the sky ahead, and began to shimmer.

We pulled over to watch as the aurora built in intensity, hypnotised by its movements. It cascaded across the sky, flickering playfully and then disappearing, before reappearing with the dignified intensity which only nature can produce. Sometimes, rather than sweeping through the skies it would simply hang in the same place for minutes at a time, only to race off to another part of the sky without warning.

After watching for fifteen minutes the cold overcame us, and so we piled back into the Fiat and continued north, stopping every so often when the skies were lit up so stunningly that it seemed disrespectful to drive through the display.

As we carried on into the early hours, Brummy and Jim slept while I pushed onwards in a state of near ecstasy. Hundreds of miles of empty perfection swept past the little Fiat, which a few days earlier had seemed incapable of even leaving the UK. Often, I would stop to photograph yet another flawless mountainscape, or find myself cruising down a perfect valley, the path of the ice-road beneath me being mirrored by the shimmering aurora high above.

Most unexpectedly of all, even the Fiat felt right. From thinking it the car from Hell a few months previously and cursing its stuttering progress at the start of our journey, it had shown itself to be a machine of character. Few other cars could have made the Arctic experience so memorable, and certainly no new car could compare. Its rear engine, rear wheel drive layout was great for traction on the ice while the fast, light steering made sliding the car around on the throttle an easy joy. In the bitter cold of the Arctic night, I warmed to the little Fiat, and its big heart.

Jim took over driving at about five in the morning, and I slept until it got light, buried on the back seat beneath a pile of sleeping bags and down jackets and feeling completely content with the world, as if coaxing the Fiat to the Arctic was the most normal thing in the world to do. It was five months since I'd stepped into my Mini and set course for Mongolia, and such journeys already felt completely natural to me. Buried on the back seat of the Fiat, freezing cold yet happier than I could remember, I had an epiphany. This was now who I was. It was what I did. I'd found my calling in life.

A crisp dawn rose from the horizon as we pulled into Narvik, a remote port over 100 miles beyond the Arctic

Circle. A winter's day this far north is almost apologetic, consisting of a few dim hours of twilight. The sun wouldn't rise again for nearly a month.

Leaving the tired Fiat in the icy streets, we went off in search of coffee. The caffeine break increased our consciousness greatly, but had the opposite effect on the Fiat, which protested at being abandoned in the cold street by stubbornly refusing to re-start.

The battery on a Fiat 126 is located in the front bonnet, just behind the grille. During the previous night's drive, it had been continuously blasted with freezing air, which had left it unable to muster enough charge to start the engine. Fortunately, the solution was obvious. Brummy warmed the battery by placing it on his lap and hugging it ardently beneath his fleece jacket, while I cleaned the electrical contacts on the engine. Ten minutes later, the Fiat spluttered into life and we were on our way north to visit the islands of Lofoten and Vesteralen, which rise jewel-like from the ocean, 130 miles beyond the Arctic Circle.

As the light faded from the bewitching landscape of mountain and fjord, we began to retrace our steps south. We had just over two days to cover the 1,000 or so sheet-ice miles to Bergen, from where a ferry would take us back to England. Darkness became complete as we chugged past the now familiar outlines of spectacular mountains, silhouetted against a thousand stars.

The weather changed as we neared the Arctic Circle, a blizzard sweeping in to demonstrate just how lucky we'd been on the long drive north. The storm-driven snow coated the little Fiat as its flapping wipers struggled to clear the windscreen, while the wind buffeted us alarmingly. Our view of the world was reduced to the hypnotic blur of snowflakes warping past us, painted brightly by our headlights, and a sea of spindrift beneath us, which flooded across the road with the wind. Fortunately, our winter tyres kept us moving and so we crawled onwards through the melee, until we found the road closed by the drifting snow.

Following a half-hour wait, a snowplough arrived to escort us through the blizzard. It cruised along, nonchalantly clearing the snow at about 40 miles per hour and we were forced to use every one of the Fiats 26 horsepower just to keep up. But keep up we did and soon the storm faded, leaving us to cruise down to Trondheim in time for a morning beer at the Kings Cross. The pub's cockney owner was somewhat sceptical of our claimed journey.

'Narvik? Nah. You can't have been all the way to Narvk and back! And you can't have seen the lights either. I live here, and I've never even seen 'em.'

After pacifying him with photographic evidence we carried on south, the car and ourselves now firmly slotted into the routine of cruising slowly through the icy wonderland for hour after hour. Another night in Lillehammer battered our wallets further before we set off on the last section of the trip.

The E-16 snaked through the darkness, its sweeping curves rising and falling at the beck of Norway's never-ending mountains. Maintaining enough traction to keep the overloaded Fiat going on the uphill sections was challenging, often requiring a careful balance of power against clutch, but the hills always seemed to end in the nick of time. The early hours of our last morning in Norway saw us sliding out of the darkness into the otherworldly lighting of the Lærdal Tunnel - the longest in the world. For fifteen miles we sliced through the earth, our progress marked by the rhythmic pulsing of the overhead lighting as we passed. At three points along its length, the tunnel builders had widened it to form a cave which glowed ethereally before blue floodlights. And then we flew back into the night, sweeping towards the towns of Voss and, a few more tunnels later, Bergen.

The 24 hour ferry voyage back to the UK rapidly descended into drunken relief that we'd survived the trip, and it was three weary, hung-over people who pulled up to Newcastle passport control.

'Just the two of you in there?' the policewoman asked.

'Nope, three,' Jim replied, tunnelling out from the cocoon of sleeping bags and rucksacks in the back seat, passport in hand.

'Wow, you must be really good friends!' the Policewoman exclaimed.

'We are now!' Brummy shouted back with a grin and a wink, as we regained our passports and clattered triumphantly back onto English soil.

FIFTEEN

THROUGH THE WALL

14th May 2013
Jiayuguan, Gansu Provence, China

England felt a long way away as we set off along the road
to the Great Wall, and as we drove the tank-like exhaust
note of Brummy's Rolls-Royce combined with my
Corvette's antisocial roar to produce a din unique in all of
China. On leaving the Mugao Caves, it was the shallow
scoop of the Hexi Corridor which offered a path of least
resistance for our passage, the open desert rippling as the
hills rose gently to either side of us, forming a broad valley
through which the smooth tarmac flowed beneath the
camera-gantries and through the toll booths. The landscape
wasn't conventionally dramatic. Rather than crowding in
around us, its crags and hillsides stood far back from the
road, but our surroundings possessed a subtle drama
nonetheless, stemming from a long history which played on
the emotions of those passing through it. Because at the
end of the Hexi Corridor there is the outpost of Jiayuguan,
where for nearly 700 years, the 'Last Gate under Heaven'
had stood.

After almost seven weeks and over 8,000 miles on the
road, we'd reached the fort which marks the end of the
Great Wall of China.

The fort is a substantial affair which rises timelessly
from the dun-coloured desert to dominate the Gansu
Corridor. To its north, the Great Wall stretches away over
the mountains and into the distance, splitting the landscape
for a scarcely imaginable 3,000 miles before it reaches its
opposite terminus, on the shores of the Pacific. However to
the south, the wall seems to lose its sense of purpose,
wandering vaguely into the mountains before quietly
petering out amid the seasonal snows of the Qilian Massif.

Jiayuguan isn't just the last gate under Heaven; it's also the end of the world. An overused phrase? Certainly. But for hundreds of years, to the people of China it was exactly that.

The fortress was built by the Ming Dynasty in the 14th century and for much of China's history, to gaze out from its ramparts was to be gazing out across the unknown. Behind you lay all of China, with its culture, technology, peace and order. But beyond the battlements was the world of the barbarian. A lawless, inhospitable desert, populated by bandits and camel trains. To walk out through any of the Great Wall's fortified gates, such as that at Jiayuguan, was to leave behind the safe world you knew. For hundreds of years, in the minds of the Chinese it was the place where civilisation ended; the place where you abandoned the niceties of the known world and stepped back into prehistory.

We roamed the fort, taking in its bulky guard towers and fortified, boulevard-like walls, which were so wide that the cavalry could ride their horses along the battlements at will. Like many Chinese sites of national interest, in its current state it felt strangely over-restored and sterile, the past polished to meet the needs of the present. The stocky battlements were perfectly smooth and uniform in their tan colour, looking as if the builders had only just left. Above these square-cut fortifications rose three exquisite pagodas, finely detailed and crafted from rich hardwood. The impregnable battlements and delicate craftsmanship formed a surely intentional juxtaposition, which represented the combination of power and civility which the Chinese dynasties wished to be known for.

Few other people were visiting the fort, and the gift sellers who were scattered around the site were doing slow business as a result. Feeling sorry for them, I purchased an original copy of Chairman Mao's 'Little Red Book' from one of them – my first souvenir of the trip. Inside, its original owner had, in their fervour, underlined various sections of Chinese writing, and I asked Shannon to translate one of the highlighted passages.

'Er, it's something like 'Following the thoughts of Chairman Mao is the only way to add to the glory of China,' came the reply, the apparent lack of conviction in Shannon's voice maybe hinting at a slight embarrassment at being asked to read it aloud. I pocketed the book and as my friends continued to wander the fort, I drifted away before strolling up to the battlements alone.

I stopped at the crenulations, ten metres above the desert floor, as an uncertain breeze fluttered past. The sky was clear of clouds, but the sun was yet to acquire its full summer intensity, which made for a comfortable temperature. The mud-brick blocks, from which the seven century-old battlements were made, felt cold as I rested my hands upon them and gazed out over the vista. To the west, the Hexi Corridor stretched back the way we had came, the slopes of the snowcapped Qilian Mountains forming its northern boundary, and mirroring the rise of the Mazong Mountains to the south. As I looked back at our route, my mind's eye extrapolated the path of our progress beyond the few miles which were visible. I thought back to the Taklimakan Desert, the Central Asian Steppe, the endless cornfields of The Ukraine and the rest of Europe beyond, beaming with satisfaction as I did so.

I'd just driven a Corvette to the Great Wall of China, and it had felt effortless. I smiled to myself, savouring the moment. I'd come a long way since my Mongol Rally days, when everything was difficult and new. I'd come of age as an automotive adventurer and in doing so, made that calling my own. It had been a long journey, but the lack of confidence which had plagued me as a pilot or climber had been banished. All I needed was a remote land and an unsuitable car, and I was on top of the world.

Shading my eyes from the sun as I gazed across the bleached brown lands, I felt content. The village on Dartmoor which I called home was eight time zones away, and was separated from me by many different cultures,

165

mountain ranges and deserts, but it mattered not. Wherever I parked the Corvette was now my home, and my life was contained within the thin corridor of the road which I was following. The road to the East. Before I set off on V8Nam, I'd been wondering who I would become when the drive was over, but now it didn't seem to matter. I was the trip now. The challenge and I were one, and my present being floated unresolved in the transition between who I was before, and who I was to become once the drive was over. Not that I really felt connected to the person I was before the trip, as to look back on my life before departure was to look upon a life which could have belonged to anyone. The distance had made me view it from afar, with an absence of emotion. I missed my house and the people I knew, but only vaguely, as though my connection to them was through a different life, whose contrast to this world was so great that they couldn't possibly be linked. Instead of a fixed roof and a daily routine, there was the road and its endless flow of hotels. Instead of Kermit, my perfectly cosseted green TVR, there was the slowly decaying Corvette. Instead of a social life which revolved around my friendship circle, there was an endless line of strangers which stretched back through the hostels, petrol stations and roadside cafes of half of Eurasia. It was a strange existence, transient and superficial on one level, yet deeply intense and satisfying on another, and for now, it was my world.

These thoughts swirled around my mind as I gazed out from the battlements, expressing themselves as a constant interplay between satisfaction and wonder. Who I once was, and who I would become; neither was important now. It was that exact moment which mattered, standing on the ramparts of the Great Wall of China, gazing out into the desert. I attempted to absorb the moment and record it to my memory forever, and with this done I lifted my hands from the ancient brickwork, took a step back and carried on roaming the fort.

It was certainly an impressive structure. The outer walls form a defensive ring more than 700m in circumference, and the passageways which wind their way through the fort change direction suddenly to slow down the progress of any invaders, while providing the defending soldiers on the battlements with a wide field of fire down upon their foes. But despite the fact that it was a serious defensive fortification, in its day its best-known role was as an exit, for it was the place where undesirables, from shamed bureaucrats to petty criminals, would be expelled from the world under Heaven, to spend the rest of their days wandering the barbarian hinterland.

The tunnel through which the expelled would pass was over thirty feet long and of bare stone, devoid of luxury as if to prepare those passing through it for the austere world which awaited them beyond the wall. In a building which had been restored to such a degree that the human connection with the past felt silenced, it was the only place which still spoke loudly. Lowered voices and apologetic footprints echoed in the austere space, their significance gradually reducing to nothing, like the memory of those who'd passed this way in the previous millennia. Once, the tunnel was the point where two incompatible worlds met, and it provided the stage for all the high drama which goes with such a pivotal place. Now, it is a curiosity over a thousand miles from China's western border, and the modern world sprawls across the valley around it.

To the east of the fort, the modern town of Jiayuguan hunkers down in the shadow of the Great Wall. It is typical of the smaller towns out here in China's west, and the contrast between its unloved structures and the polished past was stark. Apartment blocks and tower cranes rose into the blue spring air, while the horizon was scattered with factory chimneys, belching their smoke skyward around the clock. On the streets, the population went about their lives among buildings whose griminess seemed at odds with their relative newness. While past glory was

167

revered and polished, the present day town was a tool; a place which facilitated life without receiving any emotional connection in return. Like Hami or Urumqi, it left little impression, and barely lingered in our minds once we'd left.

Not that leaving was a particularly straightforward process in this instance. Crawling through the slow rush-hour traffic to leave the town, the Corvette's overheating reached new levels. The temperature gauge explored the furthest reaches of the dial with rather more conviction than it had done in the past, the dashboard warning light came on and as if to emphasize the point, steam began to rise from beneath the bonnet. I had no choice but to pull over and investigate.

'Is it supposed to do that?' Brummy asked helpfully, as he emerged from the Rolls.

'Of course it is. Just like your Rolls is supposed to sound like a cement mixer,' I replied.

'The best cement mixer in the world,' he said.

'That's not really something to be proud of,' I replied.

'Neither is an overheating Corvette.'

Down in the Corvette's nose, next to one of the front wheels, the radiator expansion tank was hissing as it boiled over and foaming brown water spurted out from beneath its lid. This was a situation which had been threatening to occur ever since we'd entered China, but as usual I'd hid behind my mantra – 'it'll be fine.' The problem was pretty easy to spot – the cooling fans weren't kicking in as they were supposed to when the motor hit a certain temperature. Maybe a faulty relay was to blame, or perhaps the temperature sensor itself; either way, we didn't have time for a thorough investigation, so I wired one of the fans directly to the car battery, using a fuse holder as a switch. For the rest of the journey, this set-up became part of the morning ritual, as I'd insert the fuse to fire up the fan before each day's drive, and remove it before wandering into the hotel each evening. All in all, the problem, and its solution, were no big deal to me; fixing an overheating sports car in rural China was just kind of what I now did now. I'd come on a long way since the Mongol Rally days, and felt proud of my progress as we got back on the road with only twenty minutes lost.

*　　*　　*

From Jiayuguan we rolled on southeast, the sense of achievement of having driven beyond the Great Wall in our unsuited steeds bubbling up within us. As on most of our trip across China so far, the tarmac was fresh and smooth, the toll booths regular and the camera gantries omnipresent. However, poplar trees lining the road gave our departure from Jiayuguan an almost European feel, which combined with occasional irrigation projects to make us feel we were finally escaping the desert. The change in scenery was a definite bonus, as all of us were keen to put the sweltering, development-scarred sands of China's northwest behind us. Luckily for us, the sensation of leaving the desert behind was about to get greater, as our route was about to soar skyward, up into the cool air and crags of the Tibetan Plateau.

SIXTEEN

THE RICKSHAW RUN

05th April 2007
Bar le Bacchus, Milly la Forêt, France

'Right then folks, I'm heading to the bar. What's everyone having?'

'Really? You're buying a round?' said Brummy. 'This is a new one.'

'Of course not. We settle the bill at the end of the night here, remember? Another Affligem? Does anyone else need a drink?'

Various orders were shouted up and down the table; 'demis' of Pelforth and Affligem, and the occasional glass of wine. I squeezed over to the bar of the Bar le Bacchus. This wasn't exactly a long commute, as the place was so small that our group of about a dozen Brits had totally packed out. Patrice was there serving as always, and in our five years of climbing trips to Fontainebleau Forest we'd never failed to visit, and so had got to know him pretty well.

'Bonjour Patrice, trois demis de Affligem, un vin rouge et un Pelforth pour moi. sil vous plait'

Patrice began to pour the beers with his usual élan, first rinsing the glasses with a blast of water, before angling them beneath the bar tap and filling them to the brim, finishing with a swipe of a knife to remove the foam from the top of the glass, his rounded Gaelic face beaming from beneath his gradually greying hair as he did so. He always looked happy when we walked in, probably because we never left without running up a healthy, three-figure bar bill. As he worked through the order, I glanced around. The dim lighting and dark wood of the shelving behind the bar were familiar now, the backdrop to happy memories which stretched back for years. Our group were the only people in the place and the air was filled with the voices of friends, excited for a week of climbs, campfires and nights under canvas.

I carried the first few drinks back and sat back down at the table.

'What time is it?' asked Brummy.

I glanced at my watch. 'It's just coming up to eight,' I replied. 'Are we doing this, then?'

'Definitely,' said Brummy.

We'd been watching the clock all evening, as at eight o'clock that evening, entry to the Mongol Rally's follow up event opened – a tuk-tuk based, 2,000 mile journey across the Indian Subcontinent, catchily named The Rickshaw Run. While sat around the campfire the night before, Brummy and I had decided to see whether we could secure a place. By ten past eight that evening, via the primitive web browser on my Motorola flip phone, we'd done just that.

Smiling at each other, we chinked our glasses of beer together, our thoughts already racing towards the future.

'To India,' I said.

'India,' was the one-word reply, and so with two months to go, the clock began to count down towards our journey from Kolkata to a place called Manali, at the helm of an eight horsepower auto-rickshaw.

*   *   *

It had been a long flight from England, and my body was aching and stiff as I retrieved my bag from the overhead locker and joined the awkward queue of people waiting to disembark from the Boeing. Glancing around the cabin, I tried to spot any other passengers who may have boarded this flight to Kolkata to take part in the Rickshaw Run, and a few folks looked likely candidates – young, casually dressed traveller types with an air of excited anticipation about them.

We shuffled towards the door, finally leaving the metal tube in which we'd been cooped up for the past ten hours, and as we did, it hit us: 42°C and almost 100% humidity. We'd just stepped out of the air conditioned plane into a suffocating sauna, and nothing could have prepared us for its impact.

'So, this is India,' said Brummy, as the first bead of sweat began to run down his face.

'Yeah. Nice, isn't it? I thought it would be hotter than this,' I replied in jest.

'I've had nicer,' he replied. 'It's like a flipping oven out here.'

Leaving the airport, the bright sunlight assaulted our eyes after the relative darkness of the terminal, and it wasn't just our eyes which were assaulted – all of our senses found themselves in the firing line. A barrage of noise swept our way from the vehicles and people amassed at the exit; cries of 'taxi, best price' merged with urgent conversations about costs and destinations, all set against a backdrop of the sickly rattle of uncared-for engines. The smells of the tropics reached our nostrils, infused with the odour of diesel exhausts, rich-running engines and cigarette smoke. Having plunged into the pungent mêlée, we soon found ourselves exiting it, crammed into the back of a tired old yellow taxi, our senses being swept along on a kaleidoscopic journey to the hotel. Thousands of lives raced past the grime-smeared windows which separated us from the outside world. People carried their poverty with dignity as they crowded around the shop fronts and apartments which lined the road, the cleanliness of many of their clothes contrasting with the brown monsoon puddles which rippled along our path. The smell of rotting food – or worse – would sweep through the cab, coming into our lives and then leaving in a matter of seconds. And so the city grew all around as the Hindustan Ambassador sped us along for mile after mile, taking us through the curiously-named town of Dum-Dum and on into Kolkata itself, where the damp-streaked buildings reached higher and the city closed in to bustle ever more intensely.

The Hotel Victerrace was everything you'd expect from a budget, two-star place in central Kolkata. The rooms could most positively be described as 'vivid', with a decor that didn't appear to have changed since the '70s, and bathrooms which made the more rustic Mongol Rally side of our personalities feel right at home. But still, at least our room was air conditioned and only cost a tenner a night, so we weren't complaining. Getting to somewhere with air conditioning had been pretty much our only thought since we'd walked out of the plane into the inferno that is early monsoon season in Kolkata.

The skies thundered overnight. Biblical rains drummed on the hard roofs with a jetplane roar through the darkened hours and we emerged into a dripping world of puddles and dampness. We were lucky though. A month before we'd arrived in Kolkata, flooding caused by the arrival of the monsoon had killed hundreds. Most of the victims had been members of the city's 70,000 homeless community; people for whom the Bengal climate provides a continuous battle with heat and disease, and who have come to define life in this most unlucky of cities.

But then, it could be argued that a city built on a low-lying swamp and subjected to one of the most energised climates on earth was never going to have the brightest of futures. However, despite being a byword for urban squalor in recent times, Kolkata hasn't always carried the same reputation. Indeed, a hundred years before our fleeting visit, when named Calcutta, it was the capital of the British Empire in India and was known around the world as the City of Palaces – proof that anywhere can provide an extravagant lifestyle to the luckier stratas of society, provided enough money is flowing through the place. Fortunes were made and lost in the oft-flooded streets of Calcutta as the wealth of the subcontinent flooded through the city's port, en-route back to the Old World.

But the vast majority of Indians saw little of the stupendous wealth which their lands were generating and they continued to live in poverty, at the mercy of the harsh climate, frequent epidemics and the often heavy and uncaring hand of the British Empire. And in more recent times, things have only got worse. First, in the early stages of the Empire's retreat, Britain moved the colonial capital from Calcutta to Delhi, removing much of the city's power and influence. Then, on independence in 1947, the state which Calcutta dominated – Bengal – was split in two, with the eastern half becoming Bangladesh; an event which not only flooded the city with refugees, but also made half the region's agricultural output unavailable to Calcutta, with obvious results. Factor in frequent floods and devastating typhoons, twenty-five years under repressive Marxist local governance and a population explosion, and you can see why the place hasn't had much to shout about in recent times. City of Palaces? City of Jinxes, more like.

Or to put it another way, somewhere perfectly suited to being the starting point of one of our determinedly left-field escapades. The more level-headed tourists might flock to the beaches of Goa or the Taj Mahal, but for us, Kolkata with a crappy rickshaw was just about perfect.

On the morning after we'd arrived in Kolkata, we saw the rickshaw which was to be our steed for the coming 2,000 mile, two week journey for the first time, sat alongside around twenty others which were to form part of the dash across the subcontinent. It was a divisive first encounter. On the one hand, all of the rickshaws were shiny and new, their identical paintwork gleaming in green and yellow and their engines not even run in. Ours was showing an ominous thirteen kilometres on the clock – delivery mileage. But despite their fresh-out-the-factory appearance, other aspects of our new mode of transport were less than confidence inspiring. For a start, the numbers didn't bode well. One cylinder, 150cc, and eight horsepower. Even the Fiat we'd taken to the Arctic had had three times that power, and power would be required,

175

given the Himalayan nature of the challenge that awaited us. And then there were the controls, which were pretty much lifted from a motorbike. We're talking handlebars with a twist-throttle on the right handgrip, and a clutch lever on the left. Rotating the left grip changed gear, while a pedal on the floor masqueraded as the brakes. As someone who'd never ridden a motorbike in their life, it was all rather foreign. Fortunately, Brummy had attended a training day back in the UK in which he'd had the chance to get some time behind the handlebars of one of these, so at least one of us knew what they were doing.

Given that adventures like this thrive on individualism, the fact that all twenty rickshaws were painted identically and were indistinguishable from the millions of other rickshaws on India's terrifying roads was an issue. Customisation was required; a kind of Kolkatan 'Pimp my Rickshaw'. This led to our first afternoon in India being spent roaming a market in search of some paint to give our steed a suitably eye-catching paint job. And naturally, Brummy and I completely disagreed on what colour we should paint it.

'Blue. Dark Blue will suit it brilliantly,' was Brummy's position.

'Dark blue is tedious and will fade into the background,' was my counter. 'Let's go with something ridiculous like orange.'

'I'm not driving across India in a bright orange rickshaw,' said Brummy.

'Well I'm not painting it blue,' I replied. 'Tell you what, how about we have half each? You paint the right hand side whatever dull colour you want, and I'll paint the left side orange?'

'Deal,' said Brummy.

And so it was that we ended up painting our rickshaw's left side orange and its right side blue, finishing off the look by visually tying the two sides together with gaffa tape, to give the visual illusion of it being a cut and shut job. A spot of further pimping involved fitting an extra spotlight on the front, a stereo on the dash and the slogan 'last one dead's a sissy' written in gaffa tape on the rear wing – and so we were ready for the following day's launch. But first, we had to survive that evening's launch party.

It all started gently enough, Kolkata's gritty reality receding into the middle distance as night fell over the open air bar where all the teams congregated for one last beer before hitting the road. However as the event was being sponsored by Cobra Beer, and free drinks were hence very much in evidence, one last beer turned out to be a massive underestimation where almost everyone was concerned – not ideal when you're due to hit the unpredictable roads of India the following day.

It was a fun evening, as everyone there was full of psyche for the adventures ahead, and keen for a laugh. Our fellow Rickshaw Runners formed a young crowd, obviously all adventurous and keen to share stories of past gap year escapades from near and far. But time and time again in conversation, I found there was one thing which seemed to elicit respect from people I spoke to – the Mongol Rally. Or more specifically, the fact I had done it, whereas plenty of the other folk on that year's Rickshaw Run were using their Indian odyssey to test the waters, and prepare them to enter the Mongol Rally at a future date. For the first time in my life, I was being looked up to for the adventures I'd undertaken. Previously, among other pilots or climbers, I'd always been average at best, but here, I was respected. For sure, any of the other teams at the party could have completed the Mongol Rally – it wasn't beyond any of them – but as yet, most of them hadn't. But I had. This feeling of accomplishment stayed with me long after the party; a feeling that even though it was still early days for me, I was on the right track. Automotive adventure was what I wanted from life, and I was finding that I had the right skill set to pursue it.

But first I had to survive my last night in Kolkata, and as we approached midnight, it seemed like doing so would be a formality. Suddenly faced with the enormity of the journey which lay ahead, the more intelligent among us were heading to bed, intent on being on top form for the following day's departure.

Intelligence was never one of my strong points, however.

'Who wants to head to a club in town?' someone said. 'I went there last night, it's not far. We'll get a taxi.'

Brummy's answer was in the negative, while mine was positive, and so along with three other Rickshaw Runners and a local fixer, I climbed aboard a taxi and we headed along Park Street to the venue.

'There's nothing there,' I said, as we got out the taxi in front of a row of dimly lit, boarded up shops.

'Through there,' someone said, pointing to an anonymous passageway heading into the row of buildings.

We walked through the passageway and found ourselves emerging into a brightly lit, yet strangely empty underground car park. It was austere to the extreme – all of the walls were made from unpainted breeze blocks, the roof was a tidy-yet-unembellished array of girders, wires and fluorescent lighting and the floor was bare concrete. We carried on walking, past the empty parking spaces to a corner of the car park, where there was an unmarked metal door. Next to the door, there stood a bouncer in a suit.

So this was the club. Our fixer spoke to the bouncer, and we were in.

I didn't really know what to expect from a nightclub hidden in an underground car park in Kolkata, but even so, this wasn't it. Money had clearly been spent, with the dimly lit venue's glass and pastel décor being similar to what I'd expect from a fancy club back home. And it was packed, with the dance floor being full of Kolkatans forgetting the world outside for the night. Having already spent six hours in the previous bar, we were in the perfect state to join them.

My memories of the rest of the night are somewhat hazy. I remember alternating between dancing, and leaning on the bar chatting to some fellow underdressed rickshaw runners, as the sharply clothed, aspirational young of Kolkata partied around us. I have a vague recollection of several more beers, and a rather more vivid memory of having my glasses – which I'd need to drive the rickshaw – knocked off, and having to crawl around the dancefloor in my half blind state to retrieve them. And I remember that when I finally emerged from the club, the red smudge of the approaching dawn was glowing above the eastern end of Park Street, the clock read five in the morning, and it was time to head back to the hotel.

At seven that morning, the alarm sounded, and my pressure-cooker head struggled with its grating tone. After less than two hours sleep, it was no time to be waking up and my body was confused, lost somewhere between drunk and hung over; passing out and jolting awake.

'What happened to you?' Brummy asked from the other end of the room.

'Nightclub,' I replied. 'I only got in at about five.'

'Idiot.' said Brummy.

He had a point.

We headed down to the school where the rickshaws were waiting, their paint now dry and their crews a mixture of those who were crushingly hung over and dreading all that the day had to offer, and the ones who seemed irritatingly awake and excited for the off. The orange side of our rickshaw was in the former camp, while the dark blue side was in the latter.

We loaded up the machine which was to be the closest thing we'd have to a home over the coming weeks, securely lashing our bags in the back with bungee cords and chatting as we did so.

'So you're driving the first leg then?' Brummy suggested.

'Don't be ridiculous. I've only had two hours sleep and I've never so much as started a rickshaw before.'

'But on the flight over you said you'd take the first leg,' replied Brummy. 'You were most enthusiastic.'

'Things change after eight pints,' I said.

'That's your own stupid fault. If you'd got an early night like me, you'd be all set.'

'That's just utterly unhelpful,' I said.

'Okay, I'll tell you what. We'll toss a coin,' said Brummy.

'Go on then. I call heads.'

And so with a flick of the thumb and a sweep of the palm, the decision was made. Tails. I was driving first.

With this in mind and 40 minutes remaining before we were due to set off across India, I figured that I probably should learn how to drive the rickshaw. Brummy quickly explained the controls to me and I gave it a go, engaging first gear and going forth on a stuttering circle of the parking area, returning to where I'd left from about a minute later, having managed about 50 metres.

'Nicely done. It looks like you're all set to drive across India,' said Brummy in greeting on my return.

'Of course I am,' I replied sarcastically.

And so, after a few speeches from the organisers and the head teacher of the school from which we were launching, twenty tuk-tuks were lined up on the tarmac, revving their asthmatic 150cc engines in anticipation for the off. A wave of the flag, and we were underway.

For the first part of our journey, the Kolkata police were in evidence, temporarily closing off roads and waving our convoy on its way, with a police car driven by the head of police in the lead. This was a definite positive for the event, as given the huge size and chaotic nature of Kolkata's road network, it probably saved several teams from spending the first week of their trip lost amid the urban jungle. However, thanks to the help of the police we raced onto the main road north out of town, our rickshaw jostling for position with those of other teams as if we were in the world's slowest grand prix. But it didn't feel at all slow from behind the handlebars of our blue and orange steed. My first experiences of second, third and forth gear were had only feet from the other entrants and within a few minutes of the off, I nearly crashed into the back of a fellow rickshaw runner when I attempted to stop by pulling the clutch lever, rather than stamping on the brake. But through this baptism of chaos, I quickly emerged as a competent auto-wallah, dicing and jostling with the best of them as we headed north out of town, with Brummy helpfully shouting 'may Ganesh bless you with many sons' at various passers-by as we went.

The lofty apartment blocks gave way to lower slung, mildewed buildings, and soon the famous greens of Bengal began to make an appearance along the roadsides. The rickshaw's odometer flicked past twenty kilometres, and then on to 30. The teams were spread out now, some leaving our route to dash west, picking up the Great Trunk Road across India, while others found their own road north, heading, like us, to Darjeeling. Already I was feeling at home behind the handlebars, as we bounded along at about 30 miles per hour, enjoying our first views of semi-rural India. And then, the whole tuk-tuk began to shudder and squirm, suddenly swerving to the left on its own accord, towards a family who were walking along the side of the road.

I braked and wrestled with the handlebars, dragging our path back towards the centre of the road, avoiding the family and coming to a halt in the process.

'What the hell was that?' asked Brummy from the tuk-tuk's back seat.

'I have no idea,' I replied. 'It just took on a mind of its own.'

'Here's the issue,' said Brummy, pointing down to his right. 'This tyre's gone flat.'

Twenty miles in, and already we'd hit our first problem.

We figured that changing a rear wheel on a brand new tuk-tuk should be a pretty straightforward procedure. We'd just loosen the wheel nuts, retrieve the spare from beneath the driver's seat, tilt over the featherweight machine so the offending wheel is off the ground, swap the wheel over, and then drop it back down again. However, there was one thing we hadn't taken into account – the quality control at the factory which built it.

'Brummy, I can't get the spare out.'

'What do you mean? Just use the key to unlock the seat, and it's in the compartment underneath. How hard can it be?'

'I can't undo the lock. The key goes in, but doesn't turn. I think they've given us the wrong key.'

'What do you mean, they've given us the wrong key? They can't have. It's brand new from the factory. It must be the right key.'

'Trust me, it isn't. Here, you have a try,' I said, handing Brummy the key which he too failed to turn in the lock.

'What a piece of shit,' was Brummy's considered response. 'First the tyre goes down for no reason at all, and then even the sodding key won't work. No wonder they don't sell these things in Europe.'

'I think I have an old chisel in my bag,' I replied. 'I'll see if I can get the spare wheel out with that.

As I began to attempt to prise open the framework which was stopping us getting to the wheel, a couple of other teams spotted us on the side of the road and asked what was up.

'They've given the wrong key to unlock the seat on this piece of shit,' said Brummy.

'No way,' came the reply. 'I bet ours will open it.'

And so I put down the chisel and we tried, and they were right – the lock turned effortlessly and soon the wheel was changed.

Another five miles up the road, we pulled over for petrol, only to find that the fuel filler was in the locked engine compartment, and once again the key was useless. This time there was nobody to help, and so I levered the metal hatch open with a screwdriver so we could fill the tank. 25 miles in, and already the tuk-tuk was vying with the Arctic Fiat for top place in my list of most despised trip cars.

*   *   *

Life on the road in rural Bengal was like nothing we'd experienced before. Our buzzing little locust of a vehicle would bounce its way along at about 30 miles per hour, occupying a space somewhere near the bottom of the highway food chain, above the bicycle, but below the cow. And on these highways, the pecking order was important – if you were smaller, you got out of the way. Buses and trucks seemed to adopt titanic proportions when seen from our vulnerable trike, bearing down on us from every direction, often with their lights flashing and horn blaring, but with no evasive action in evidence. Even without tyres spontaneously blowing out it felt risky, and the number of crashed vehicles and close calls we encountered on those first few days in Bengal drove the point home to us.

But such dangers only really become real when they impede on your life directly, and for us this happened for the first time during our second day on the road. I was resting in the back of the rickshaw while Brummy took his stint behind the handlebars when I was suddenly awoken by a blaring horn as a truck came flying past us in the other direction, so close that it hit our wingmirror, showering me with broken glass and certainly getting my attention. Another foot to the right, and it would have smudged us out completely.

'That was totally his fault. He was on my side of the road, so I had the right of way,' was Brummy's take on the event; a European application of driving etiquette which, we were rapidly learning, was likely to end in tears on these Indian highways.

A few hours later we passed the remains of a truck, lying in a ditch on the side of the road. Its front end was caved in, and a crowd had gathered around the cab. As we passed, we saw the windscreen was missing, and the crowd was lifting the driver's lifeless body out through the gap. But in the background, the verdant greens of Bengal were no less enticing than ever, as the sun sank to be extinguished upon the horizon.

Against this backdrop of danger, poverty and beauty, our lives became suddenly simple. Each night, we'd roll into a town we'd never heard of before and book into a cheap hotel. We lived off dhal and whatever the roadside food stalls had to offer. We got used to a crowd gathering around us every time we stopped, as two Westerners pulling up in a garishly painted tuk-tuk turned out to be a notable event anywhere in India. To produce a map was to risk the crowd rising to a frenzy in their attempts to help; to fire up the engine and leave was sometimes a trigger for begging. But we couldn't escape it. Wherever we stopped, the crowd would gather, intense and drawn tight around us. In towns or villages it was a near instant gathering, but even out in what appeared to be the most remote countryside people would still appear out of the undergrowth to stare or ask questions, and the only place where our personal space remained intact seemed to be aboard a moving rickshaw.

I'm generally quite an introverted person, and so I found this constant mass of humanity wearing. It only took a few days of it before I found myself longing for the wide open spaces of Kazakhstan or Siberia, instead of the intense world of barked questions and close crowds which we entered at every stop. But deep down, I knew I wouldn't have it any other way. Exposure to the sheer weight of humanity which I felt bearing down on me in India was just another way of knocking myself out of my comfort zone and growing as an adventurer, and as a person. The journey was simply another step on the path I'd chosen in life, and besides, it wasn't all hard-edged crowds and near-death experiences. No, behind all that and away from the sometimes-grotty villages, there were moments of beauty like nowhere else, born of a landscape of emerald green, enlivened by the scudding shadows of the monsoon clouds and brought to life by the dust-blurred sunsets of gold.

The monsoon had reached its zenith as we arrived in the state of Sikkim, nestled high against the border with Tibet. The rains strafed us with a hard drama, while the cloud-smothered sky hung low on the landscape. We were denied the famous view of the world's third highest mountain from Darjeeling's tea plantations, as Kanchenjunga's cold white pyramid remained shielded by the weather. Instead, we saw spray being thrown up from the roads to mix with the rain, and people sheltering under shop awnings by the dozen, as the landscape was ensured its verdant greenness for another year.

Time was pressing however, and for us this sodden corner of India was merely a brief overnight stop, as our planned route took a sudden swing to the west, heading into Nepal across the River Mechi, which flows down from Kanchenjunga's glacial meltwater far to the north, forming the border between the two countries as it does so.

As we crossed the border-bridge over the river, things started to get a bit weird. For starters, we gained another 57 years, finding ourselves in the year 2064, such is the standalone nature of the Nepali calendar. We also made a fifteen minute adjustment to our watches, as Nepal's clocks run 5 hours 45 minutes ahead of GMT. No, not five hours, or six. Exactly five and three quarters. And it's not just looking at your watch which will make you think that Nepal is, well, a bit different. Right from the top, its path is entirely its own. In the decade before our visit, the country had seen nine different governments. The standing prime minister had been sacked and replaced in the years 2000, 2001, 2002, 2003, 2004 and 2005, which must be some kind of weird record. But to many, this comedy governance is better than the alternative – rule by the Maoist Rebels who, since 1996, had been fighting to take control of Nepal, and bring an end to the long-running reign of Nepal's royal family.

In typical Nepalese fashion however, the royal family itself seemed to be far more capable of ending its own reign than any rebel group. Six years before we'd puttered across the border in our tuk-tuk, an outrageous spilling of blue blood put to shame anything which Game of Thrones could dream up, by going through three different kings in 48 hours. It all began when Crown Prince Dipendra, the 29 year old heir to the throne was told by his parents – the king and queen – that they weren't a fan of the lady he aspired to marry. His response? To gun them down, in a drunken rage. And not just them. He also murdered his brother and sister, and four other members of the royal family, before turning the gun on himself.

However suicide didn't turn out to be the Crown Prince's forte, and he only succeeded in putting himself in a coma – an interesting twist given that he was the next living person in line to the throne. He therefore became king as he lay in his hospital bed and the last 48 hours of his life passed by, at which point the crown passed on to his younger brother.

Six different prime ministers in five years; three different kings in two days and the small matter of a '70s style Maoist uprising – Nepal promised to be an interesting drive at any time of year, let alone in a tiny tuk-tuk at the height of the monsoon.

But as we passed through the border and hit the road to Kathmandu, it was the calmness which got our attention the most. Whereas the Indian side of the border had been the usual crowd of serious faces invading our personal space, the moment we crossed over into Nepal everyone seemed to take a step back, chill out and smile. The slight tension evaporated, and a feeling of welcome replaced that of intimidation. Even the traffic calmed down slightly, though that's not saying much – an accident still never felt far away.

In some ways however, the relaxed atmosphere of the border town was a lie, for the country which stretched out before us was anything but calm. The Maoist uprising had been going on for the previous eleven years, and so far the struggle had claimed over 14,000 lives. Calm? Not really. We were entering a low-intensity warzone.

Not that it felt like it, as we rolled on into the countryside. All was quiet, and people smiled and waved to us as we passed. But near the towns and villages, the situation was often quite the opposite. The Maoists had called a general strike in an attempt to bring the country to a standstill, and a big part of their strategy focussed on blocking the roads. In our first encounter with such an obstacle, a tree had been felled across the road, making it impassable to cars and trucks. However, the locals were able to nip around it on their mopeds, and we followed, our minds focussed by the sudden escalation in the seriousness of our adventure.

The barriers continued to appear as we rolled deeper into the country. We passed through a barricade of burning tyres, surrounded by a riled up crowd, one of whom made a grab for the handlebars of our rickshaw. At another barricade just up the road, a tree had been felled and a few locals tried to stop our tuk-tuk by jamming bamboo poles under the wheels, but our momentum bounced us over them and carried us on our way. In the next village, a truck was parked across the road, and the only way around it was on a sloping bank which dropped to a river below. The bank was too steep for our rickshaw to negotiate, and so with Brummy at the controls, I jumped out and standing beneath it on the slope, supported it to prevent it from cartwheeling down the bank as Brummy slowly drove around the obstacle. As we rolled onwards, a convoy of United Nations Toyota Land Cruisers sped by, heading the other way.

'You know it's a proper holiday when UN peacekeepers are heading to the place you just left,' shouted Brummy, with a cheeky smile.

And then, just as suddenly as they'd begun, the road blocks stopped, and we dropped into the Koshi Tappu Nature Reserve to spend the night in their tourist-spec huts, some of which were already occupied by other teams of Rickshaw Runners. The police post at the nature reserve's entrance was liberally defended with barbed wire and barriers. A few hours earlier, in the relaxed atmosphere of the border, we would have thought it complete overkill. Now, it made perfect sense.

We opened some Tuborg beers and whiled away the evening discussing how the UN guys would be getting on, as the velvety darkness brought the jungle closer, and fireflies began to dance in the bushes all around.

The next day, we set off in convoy, five teams and ten people hitting the road to Kathmandu. The road blocks may have dried up but the monsoon certainly hadn't, and for most of the day we rolled along beneath swollen clouds, taking the soaking in our stride as the rain swept in through our rickshaw's open sides. Despite the fact we were in one of the most mountainous nations on earth, our progress was surprisingly smooth, as Nepal is very much a nation of two halves, the dizzying heights of the Himalayas which dominate the country's north being balanced by the relatively flat plains which define the southern half. Not that you'd really know it if your only experience of Nepal is a visit during rainy season, as ever since our arrival, the greatest mountain range on earth had remained resolutely hidden behind the clouds. Himalaya? Given the lack of any visible mountains, I might as well have been in Thailand, were it not for the enormous rivers which periodically swept down from the north, carrying the meltwater of the world's highest snowfields to the sea.

However, in spite of the fact that the landscape was strangely ambiguous, signs that we were in Nepal kept on coming. The previous day, these signs had been negative, as we were forced to run the Maoist road blocks, but now, Nepal decided to show us its positive side. Whenever we stopped, rather than crowding into our personal space, the Nepalese smiled and chatted from a normal distance. If it was raining, they were quick to offer shelter; if we'd stopped by a hut with a fridge, they were quick to offer us a cold beer. After India, where at every halt we felt like we were dismounting into an ordeal-by-crowd, surrounded by intense people who often hoped to somehow profit from our appearance, Nepal was a revelation, its people relaxed in their individuality, its welcome seemingly heartfelt. Perhaps that's the difference between a population of 25 million and one of 1.2 billion.

Approaching Kathmandu, we left the main highway to take a more mountainous shortcut to the capital. For the first time in the trip, the road turned to gravel and then began to climb, and we found out just how powerful our little buzz-boxes really were, the short answer being, 'not very.' High revs and low gears were essential to make any form of progress as we gained altitude, and on the switchback roads a race ensued, with passengers in the back of the rickshaws leaning into the corners to help the balance, drivers snatching gears like their lives depended on it and everyone shouting banterful abuse at each other as they tore along through the jungle. Effectively, we'd just invented the world's slowest motorsport, which was just as well when we tore around a corner to find an army checkpoint blocking the way.

The soldier was very much still in his teens, and his combat uniform looked like an ill-fitting hand-me-down from the previous century, though saying that, his machine gun appeared real enough. He seemed rather taken back by the fact that ten Westerners in brightly painted tuk-tuks had just sped around the corner and pulled up at the metal barrier which blocked the roads.

After an awkward silence, he greeted us in the standard manner of people in authority when faced with an unusual vehicle or five: 'documents please.'

Ten Westerners immediately rummaged through their bags and pockets, and then moved towards the soldier, brandishing passports, licenses and sheets of paper covering everything from insurance to yellow fever vaccinations. The soldier's eagerness to check everyone's paperwork evaporated almost instantly, and instead he

189

turned his attention to the hand-written log which occupied pride of place on the checkpoint's only table.

'Enter details here,' he asked.

'Why?'

'Maoists ahead. Very dangerous,' he replied.

We filled in our names and passport numbers, and then the policeman lifted the barrier and our progress continued - for one corner and about 200 metres, whereupon we found our path blocked by another barrier, this one somewhat more ramshackle, and guarded by a Maoist rebel.

His similarity to his army opposite number whom we'd just met was uncanny. Both were short and slightly built, dressed in well-worn fatigues and nervously fingering the automatic weapon which hung from their shoulder like a toy. And just like the soldier, our Maoist acquaintance was somewhat startled by the approaching horde of rickshaw-mounted Europeans.

'You must pay,' he announced. We were cool with that. After all, he had a gun and we didn't.

Each team rustled up 500 rupees, and we handed the money to the young lad, towering over his slight frame as we did so. He took the notes uncertainly, as if he was weary that some trap was being set. But the truth be told, we just wanted to be on our way – the cold beer of Kathmandu was only a few hours' drive away.

'What happens now,' someone from another team asked.

'Well, he's got his money and he seems okay with it. Let's go,' said someone else. And with that, one of the teams lifted the barrier, jumped back into their rickshaw and set off.

No gunfire followed their unauthorised passage; in fact the Maoist didn't seem at all bothered by what had just happened, and so we all carried on, our little convoy of rickshaws winding its way into Maoist territory, and then on to the bright lights of Kathmandu.

The city was a haven of calm as I left the hotel early in the morning. A fume-laden mist hung in the air, enabling the slanting sunlight to tinge the air a golden colour, contrasting with the shadowy half-light that lingered where the sun's rays were yet to penetrate. Those who were already on the streets went about their business silently, almost in deference to the spiritual atmosphere which hung over the city like a veil. I began to walk in the direction of Durbar Square, one of the city's most celebrated sights. As I did so, nobody bothered me. No rickshaw-pullers came along side me with a shout of 'come on, we go now.' No shopkeepers beckoned me into their souvenir stalls, and even the dogs didn't feel the need to bark. I was anonymous, and it felt liberating after the attention of the previous days.

The quiet streets were an uplifting tonic which led me to the square which, for almost a thousand years, has performed a central role in the lives of those living in the Kathmandu valley. Once, the space saw the crowning of kings; today, it is the tourists who give it much of its purpose. I walked among the pagodas, their stacked roofs tiered three or four high against the brightening sky and their intricately calved wooden structures timeless in the evocative atmosphere. Pigeons scattered before me as I walked, and a few locals strolled through casually, beginning their day. And then, as I stood there gazing at a scene whose beauty which spanned the ages, I felt something stir deep inside me. It was a deep, timeless sensation, and as the feeling grew, its intensity built in waves until I could ignore it no longer. As quickly as I could, I made a bee-line back to the hotel room with its toilet, cursing the less than confidence-inspiring roadside curry I'd eaten the previous afternoon, and reaching sanctuary not a moment too soon.

We'd planned on having a rest day in Kathmandu – our only day off the road in the course of our trip across the subcontinent – and fortunately, my stomach righted itself sufficiently quickly that I wasn't forced to spend it in our hotel room's grotty bathroom. After breakfast, Brummy and I headed out into a different city to the one which I'd explored earlier; a city which had come to life with a jarring level of noise and bustle. But we were happy to be there, as on these trips, where you're passing through worlds which are foreign to you for days on end, there's a definite appreciation for those places where life is easy; where the more mainstream tourist trail intersects with yours and familiarity returns. For us, Kathmandu was one of those places, and for the first time in the trip we were able to roam souvenir shops, eat in western-leaning restaurants and take in sights which were sanitised for convenience.

As we sat in a rooftop bar, sipping the first cold beer of the afternoon, those Maoist road blocks seemed a long way away.

But in this instance, the calm was deceptive, and the Maoist's countrywide blockade was reaching the capital in a manner which would still affect us – namely, through a fuel shortage. Kathmandu's petrol stations were running out, and cars were queuing for hours just for a tank of unleaded. We faced the very real risk of being trapped until the situation blew over, which, we were told, often took weeks. Fortunately, we had one thing in our favour when it came to dealing with the situation in a calm and level-headed manner – we'd already had a few beers by the time we'd heard about it. So, with our rest day unthreatened, we filed the fuel shortage under 'tomorrow's problem', and set about enjoying the rest of our time in the city.

Early evening saw us in the Rum Doodle Bar, which takes its name from one of the cult classics of mountaineering literature, and as such was a place I'd long since wanted to visit. Rum Doodle is a focal point which outdoorsy people flock to for a drink, its dimly lit bar serving Everest Beer and its walls covered in graffiti left by passing mountaineers; Edmond Hillary and Reinhold Messner amongst them. Sitting there with a cold drink as I took in my Himalaya-centric surroundings reminded me of who I used to be. I'd long assumed that one day I'd come to Kathmandu, but my assumption was based on my coming as a climber, full of enthusiasm for my first Himalayan expedition. Less than two years had passed since that week when I'd returned home from that washed-out climbing trip to the Alps and heard about the Mongol Rally for the first time, and already my goals had changed beyond recognition. Deep down, I still had some small aspiration to climb in the greater ranges; to summit Annapurna or Ana Dablam, but I now knew that I probably never would. The fire within me which once raged for the big climbs was now barely smouldering, while the flames of automotive adventure were already out of control.

That evening, in another bar, we got chatting to a Dutchman who was in Kathmandu for the weekend.

'I work in Bangladesh,' he told us. 'Legal stuff. But the visa is only for ninety days so I have to do a visa run every now and then. Kathmandu, Bangkok, Singapore. It's nice to have a weekend away every now and then. Bangladesh is a shithole, and you can never trust the people there. They're always trying to rob you.'

Trying to steer the conversation away from our new friend's prejudices, I mentioned that there was a bar in town which I quite fancied finding.

'It's called the Blue Note Bar. Joe Simpson mentions it in a few of his books. Any idea where it is?'

'Nope, but I'm sure we can find it. Let's go,' said the Dutchman, standing up as he downed his beer.

It was dark outside, but there were still plenty of people milling around, and while I was all up for asking directions and walking, our Dutch friend had other ideas.

'Walk? I'm not walking,' he said, flagging down a couple of cycle-rickshaws as he spoke.

'I'll jump in this one, you guys take the one over there,' he announced to us authoritatively, before turning to the rickshaw-wallah and asking, 'Blue Note Bar?'

The thin Nepalese teenager nodded his head sheepishly, looking slightly intimidated.

'He knows where it is, let's go,' announced the Dutchman. We climbed aboard the three wheeled, pedal powered contraptions and our rickshaw-wallahs began pedalling into the night.

I soon understood why our new-found friend was against walking – the route to the bar was uphill. With only one gear, the guys pedalling the cycle-rickshaws had to put all their weight on each pedal just to keep moving forwards. Their effort made me feel sick inside, though fortunately not in the same way as I had that morning, in Durbar Square. No, the conflicting emotions of being propelled up the hill by the physical effort of a stranger over-rode the justification of the small fee the strangers could expect to be paid. It felt wrong, a cruel flashback to the cultural arrogance of colonial times, and I could tell Brummy felt the same way.

Our Dutch acquaintance was clearly less sensitive to such things: 'Can't they go any faster? It's not exactly a big hill, after all. In fact, we should have a race. Come on man, pedal faster.'

Brummy and I were now deeply embarrassed at the situation and I felt so sorry for the guy pedalling us along that I jumped out and jogged slowly along side, as the Dutchman kept agitating for a race, and a bar came into view ahead.

We stopped by its door, and already the Dutchman was shouting.

'This isn't the Blue Note Bar, it's the Blue Moon. I thought you said you knew where the Blue Note was?'

The rickshaw-wallah nodded, his English clearly not equal to an argument.

'You don't, do you? You just said you did. That's it, you're not getting paid for this,' he barked, before storming into the bar in a rage of white privilege.

Brummy and I looked at each other, somewhat in shock.

'I'm so sorry,' we said to our chauffeurs, and paid and tipped them handsomely before heading into the bar ourselves for one last drink, as far from the Dutchman as possible.

*   *   *

We awoke to a city in a state of flux. The Maoist blockades had been very successful in cutting off the road into Nepal from the south and in doing so, prevented any fuel from reaching the capital. The roads were strangely quiet as taxis and private vehicles ground to a halt, and every petrol station had a queue which stretched out of sight. With the tank on our tuk-tuk running low our situation was looking pretty helpless, but we decided to try to get back on the road anyway, sourcing a jerry can and, as nonchalantly as possible, bypassing the queue and walking onto the nearest petrol station forecourt.

Soldiers were out among the pumps, marshalling the queuing vehicles and stopping the pent-up frustrations of the gathering crowd from getting out of hand. These soldiers were somewhat taken aback by a couple of rather cheeky Englishmen wandering up and asking for some unleaded, but like everyone we met in Nepal – including the Maoists – they recognised that tourism is the country's lifeblood, and needed to be supported at all costs. This was just as well for us, as it meant we were quickly on our way with a few gallons of gas, and later that morning, we hit the road towards Pokhara.

No-one seemed to have told the users of Nepal's busiest highway about the fuel shortage, and they drove their vehicles so hard that it seemed their sole goal was to drain their tanks as quickly as possible. Our pace was similar to many of the trucks, and so we tended to cruise along in their company, as the busses and jeeps flung themselves suicidally past in ill-considered overtakes.

Whenever we stopped, the talk was of road closures, with the highway acting as a conduit for rumours to spread across the country. We heard the main borders with India were being closed, and that the blockages were only going to get worse. Bouncing along in our tuk-tuk at about 30 miles per hour, we felt as if we were crawling along as a trap was sprung all around us.

But getting stuck in Nepal for weeks wasn't an option, and we had to do something. That something was taken straight from the Mongol Rally playbook – if in doubt, just keep buggering on. Taking note of the rumours that the main borders with India were already being closed, we decided to aim for a more remote crossing at the far end of the country, which was about 400 miles away. And we wouldn't stop until we got there.

The sun fell to the horizon in front of us as we cruised along with our fuel tank and jerry can brimmed, the monsoon rains leaving us alone for once. At night, driving the rickshaw took on the feeling of a video game, the pale tunnel of light provided by its lights providing only the minimum of clues as to what was ahead. Roadside shacks, signs and shops flickered through our surreal world as we pushed on through the darkness. At midnight, we sped through a cloud of insects, each of them the size of my hand. They peppered me as I sat in the back of the tuk-tuk but I didn't mind at all, as being peppered with large insects while cruising through the Nepalese night just added to the adventure. Sitting there as the night went by and the music of The Cure pulsed through my headphones, I was absolutely content. Just as six months earlier, when I was driving the little Fiat through the Arctic night, everything about the situation felt right. I had found my calling in life, and it was truly blissful.

The sun rose over a sweeping plain of green, the sky clear except to the north, where cauliflower clouds continued to shield the Himalayas from our gaze. We were exhausted, for lazing in the back of a rickshaw as it bounces along isn't exactly conducive to sleep, but the border was now close and daylight lifted our alertness to a level where we were sure we could reach it that morning. We just hoped it would still be open and we could cross it, as we were pretty much out of fuel, and so we risked being stranded there if it was closed.

Luckily for us it was open, and a wave of relief washed over us as our passports were stamped back into India and the tension receded. We'd made it through the Maoist rebels' lockdown, and were nearing the end of the journey.

Once we were back in India, we headed for the Raj-era hill station of Nanital, and on the twisting road which led up to the town, I found myself in a rather exciting race with an old Hindustan Ambassador, belching smoke as it struggled against the gradient, while we wrung every last ounce of power from our steed. This went on for several miles of cut and thrust and ended in a draw, in case you were wondering – probably not something which paints the Ambassador in a particularly good light. At Nanital and in clear need of a good night's sleep, we checked into our fanciest hotel of the trip – The Palace Belvidere – which didn't seem to have changed since the British left, being a rather grand, two story country house which wouldn't have looked out of place on a Dorset estate, even though the tiger skins and taxidermied big-game heads which hung in the hallways may have raised an eyebrow there. The hotel's veranda offered a fine view out over the small lake around which the town of Nanital was clustered, and we sat there admiring the view as the sun passed on the baton to the moon, our cold beers most welcome after the long drive; the outrageously spicy peanuts they were served with, and the huge tarantula which joined us later in the evening, less so.

The landscape gained height as we headed north out of Nanital, the slopes to which the road clung gradually steepening. But the tarmac was good and the weather was fine, meaning the day's drive (or ride, we never did figure out whether you drive or ride a tuk-tuk) went by effortlessly. For much of it, we headed through pine forests and the sense of unspoiled nature and of finally finding ourselves in a place away from the immense mass of humanity which had defined our Indian experience so far, was blissful. Birds and butterflies flitted through the landscape as we drove and the delightful smell of the forest after the overnight rain roused our senses.

There were still people around though, even in this remote corner of India. One afternoon as we puttered through the glorious landscape, we found ourselves sharing the road with dozens of young schoolgirls, walking home from the day's lessons. Where their school was, or where they all lived, we never saw, but there they were, stretching along the road for kilometres in small groups, smiling, laughing and joking as they strolled, their bleach-white uniforms spotless against the unspoilt, natural background.

However, we found that in India you can only go so far before the tough reality of travel in the world's second most populous nation returns, and as we progressed further into the mountains of the Garhwal Himalaya, our journey changed to meet our expectations. The landscape steepened to such a degree that the road clung to it, hundreds of metres above the raging river which marked the bottom of whatever valley we were negotiating. The tarmac became broken and rough, and frequent landslides partially blocked the road or covered it with a layer of mud and rock. Meanwhile, as we rolled along on this thin slither of the horizontal, making plans for how to jump from our flimsy steed if it went over the edge, the buses and trucks just kept on coming, squeezing past each other inches from disaster and setting our nerves on edge. We'd found our stereotypical death road; the sort of highway which generates bus terror plunge stories with such regularity that they cease to become news. Luckily for us however, we made it along the testing road without any time in freefall, and were soon on the road to the city of

Dehra Dun. Or we would have been, if the signage in the towns was up to the job, meaning we often had to stop and ask directions; a task which had variable results.

'Dehra Dun?' I asked one passer-by in a town about ten miles from the city.

The local looked at me blankly, glancing occasionally at the rickshaw.

'Dehra Dun,' I asked again, pointing at the two roads I considered the most likely possibilities. More blank looks and a shrug of the shoulders.

'It's your state capital, dude. How can you not know where your state capital is?' I asked.

The local responded by simply walking off. It felt like a fairly normal occurrence from our attempts to ask for directions thus far.

A few hundred metres on, we pulled over next to about half a dozen guys who were waiting at a bus stop.

'Dehra Dun?'

One guy pointed back the way we'd come, while the other five gestured that we should carry on the way we were going. There was a moment of stillness as the six people continued to point in the two different directions, before the five clocked the one guy whose advice conflicted. Their solution was a few seconds of verbal abuse, before a couple of the guys in the larger group began punching him.

Somewhat mystified, we got the hell out of there, following the advice of the majority and reaching Dehra Dun shortly afterwards, having vowed to be more careful about whom we ask for directions in the future.

We passed through the hippy hangout of Rishikesh and the mountain retreat of Shimla, our final destination drawing closer; India still offering up its usual combination of intensity and absurdity. And no-one could do absurdity better than the authorities, who seemed to be overseeing a quagmire of bureaucracy so deep that no-one really knew how it was supposed to work. We had a brief glimpse into this when we left the state of Uttaranchal, and crossed into Himachal Pradesh.

'They don't have a clue what they're doing,' said Brummy, returning from the offices at the border, while I'd been guarding our bags in the rickshaw. 'I went to one window, and they sent me to another one. There, I got sent back to the first. They just kept doing this, and none of them would help.'

'So what did you do?'

'After a while, I gave up. I just told them both 'I'm bored of you now, goodbye', and left them to it. Let's get out of here. The paperwork can't be that important.'

As we continued our journey north the landscape built up around us, the hillsides rising higher, the wooded slopes giving way to grass and rock. Traffic reduced as we passed into less peopled regions and the number of miles separating us from the finish line at Manali plummeted from triple figures to double, and then on to a situation where only single figures remained. As we approached the finish, I wondered what memories I would take home from India, and found it was the nation's people who'd made the greatest impression on me. The endless mass of people, sometimes overwhelming, often frustrating, always individual. I thought of the sirdars, or holy men, whom we'd passed on the road to Shimla, of the monks who'd watch our progress from the balconies of their monasteries. The crowds of truck drivers who would gather at roadside shacks for lunch, those Kolkata urbanites partying away until dawn in an underground bar and the intense, quizzical villagers who'd surround us every time we stopped. And finally there were those schoolgirls in Uttaranchal, dancing through the pine forest on their way home from lessons, and providing a reason to be positive about the future of this overwhelming country.

Then my daydreams were swept aside by the outskirts of a town, which rose up to meet us as we climbed. We were there. Two kilometres up amid the mountains of the Himalaya in a place called Manali, with another dream journey complete – our third in ten months. And yes, the moment certainly called for a beer.

But a beer didn't quite seem enough when it came to celebrating our achievement, and so we set about one last challenge when we were there – a rickshaw-based ascent of the 4,000 metre high Rothang La, the high pass which marked the road north out of town. With only 150cc and eight horsepower at sea level, the tuk-tuk wasn't exactly the ideal vehicle in which to attempt a spot of high altitude mountaineering, and the power gradually fell away as we climbed. But around us, the landscape made the effort we put into coaxing the tuk-tuk up there worth it. We crawled around the switchbacks of the road which led to the pass, willing our steed onwards in first gear as we passed glaciers which swept down to the road and boulder fields which had been sliced in two by the tarmac. The drops over which the road teetered were sufficiently lethal that quaintly Indian signs were dotted along the route, bearing slogans such as 'License to drive, not to fly', and 'horn is to honk, please do it on my curves'. The altitude strangled our power so much that for the final approach to the high pass, half throttle was required just to make the engine idle and I had to get out and push on the steeper sections. But eventually, we did it. 4,000 metres up, in a rickshaw. From the pass, which was marked by a few bored yaks, the Tibetan plateau stretched away into the distance, the dark shadows of clouds scudding across its surface. And as we gazed upon our first view of the highest plateau on Earth, we found ourselves wondering – where would the next adventure take us?

SEVENTEEN

MONK LIFE

15ᵗʰ May 2013
Qilian Mountains, Gansu Provence, China

The road began to climb, taking us ever higher on slopes which soared from the dusty plains of the Hexi Corridor into the rarefied air of the Tibetan Plateau – the highest plateau on Earth. The tarmac twisted and turned as it sought out the path of least resistance through the barren landscape, and mottled clouds swept in to replace the blue sky which had been a permanent feature of our time in China up until that moment. It came as a relief to finally leave behind the sweltering, scruffy deserts which dominate China's northwest and find ourselves amongst nature once again. The cool air and occasional bursts of rain were greeted with delight, rather than resentment – even if they did make keeping the tail-happy Corvette under control rather more challenging. Despite the welcome return of vegetation, our surroundings retained their bleakness as we climbed, but gained drama with every additional metre of height. Craggy, rough-set mountains rose up to shadow the smooth tarmac, their slopes covered with a dusting of grass which gave way to snow near their summits. Many of the more auspicious points on the road were marked with the tapering silhouette of a Buddhist stupa, and without fail these were covered in a web of tattered prayer flags left by travellers so that the Gods might offer them safe passage, while the prayers themselves were carried to the four corners of the world upon the billowing winds. As the road swerved its way to a highpoint of nearly 4,000 metres above sea level, the thin air imparted a definite lethargy on the cars but predictably, our big V8s had plenty in reserve to cope. With sixteen cylinders and over 500 horsepower between our two vehicles, we'd come a long way since the last time we saw Tibet, pushing that feeble rickshaw up India's Rothang La.

While power wasn't an issue, there was still one aspect of the cars which was less able to cope with the mountains, however – the Corvette's rear tyres. Our excess of exuberant use in the preceding 8,000 miles meant the enormous, 275-section rears were now devoid of tread and while this wasn't much of an issue in the dry, as soon as the tarmac turned wet the big yank's rear grip dropped close to zero. Accelerating away from toll booths or traffic lights with any pace would sometimes find us broadside across the road with the steering on the lockstops to prevent a spin, and twisty mountain roads had to be treated with maximum respect to avoid a rapid, cartwheeling descent as our rear slicks skittered across the tarmac. New tyres had floated up to the top of our shopping list but until we were able to get some, any slippery surface had to be treated with the maximum of care to avoid the back of the car stepping suddenly out of line and spinning us into the scenery. This wasn't a huge problem however, as the Rolls-Royce, with Brummy at the helm, only ever seemed to progress at one speed, which was best described as 'stately'.

Luckily, there are some landscapes on this planet where the scenery is sufficiently arresting that proceeding sedately is the best option, and the edge of the Tibetan Plateau is one of them. The darkening sky, the bare hillsides and the thin, chill air gave the landscape a hostile, Mordor-like feel. It was starkly beautiful, but the overriding sensation of malevolence meant it wasn't somewhere you'd want to be stuck overnight.

The offerings of prayer flags on the stupas which marked the passes seemed a fitting response to this hostile atmosphere. We were passing through a land of the Gods – and not the friendly ones. Against this austere backdrop, I was certainly glad to have graduated from the flimsy Rickshaw to the tough old 'vette.

We traversed several different worlds that day. Firstly there was the natural world, its heavy hills and speeding clouds cranking up the drama. Then there was the human landscape; the towns and villages, some of which were marked by the mosques and minarets of Islam, others by the blandness of modernity. All were dotted with construction sites. Tower blocks and shops were being thrown up to accommodate the influx of newcomers from the east, as a similar pattern to the Uighur areas we'd just driven through was played out. Just as in those areas, minorities lived here, proud people such as the Muslim Hui, and the Tibetan Buddhists. And just like in Xinjiang, these people were now strangers in lands they considered theirs, as the Han Chinese flooded in to dominate the demographics. As if to emphasize this point, that evening we rolled out of the mountains into what was once one of their cities. Xining, where the minorities now made up only a quarter of the two million people who call the place home.

There was little to detain us in what seemed rather a workaday city, and so after a night spent in a hostel on the 14th floor of a tower block, we hit the road early, bound for the Yellow River Gorge, and the town of Xiahe.

We found ourselves driving through a tottering landscape of broken rocks, which somehow still clung to each other to form the sweeping cliffs that towered high above the road. The rain came heavier now, forcing us to drive the 'vette with an abundance of caution as the tarmac swept left and right down valleys which were sometimes so deep and narrow, they brought to mind driving through a tunnel. But the tunnels themselves were something else; China's eagerness to open up the nation's west saw to that. They sliced through hill after hill, speeding our progress and taking us from one landscape to another with such regularity that it brought to mind the trip to the Arctic in the tiny Fiat, six years earlier. At one stage we found ourselves sharing a valley with the mighty Yellow River, a giant torrent of muddy brown water which had already swollen to hundreds of metres across as it swept off the Tibetan Plateau, with another few thousand miles still to flow before it reached the ocean. Then the landscape opened up, the valley was flooded with greenery and the mountainsides turned from jagged rock to a sea of vegetation, interspersed with muddy brown slopes which were sculpted smooth by the abundant rainfall. And finally, the town of Xiahe appeared in the distance.

Occupying a valley three kilometres above sea level, our first impressions of Xiahe were that it seemed to be a rather uninspiring place. In the neighbourhood in which we were staying the buildings looked tired, worn down and stained by the endless battle with the weather. Near our hotel, the stream which passed through town was filthy, choked with litter and foam. Graffiti in both English and Chinese dotted the walls, and muddy water pooled on the pavement at regular intervals.

But nobody comes to Xiahe for the new town. Its appeal is solely focused on its convenience as a stopping-off point for visiting what lies just up the valley.

The Labrang Monastery.

One of the six major centres of Tibetan Buddhism, the monastery's current grandeur is built on a turbulent past, at odds with the peaceful aura which it now exudes. The 1920s saw it providing the backdrop to a series of pitched battles between the Tibetans and Hui Muslims, while in the 1960s it suffered at the hands of Mao's Cultural Revolution, with the persecution of its monks and the destruction of its religious symbolism. As it was beginning to bounce back from all this, the 1980s saw a fire started by an electrical fault which burned down the monastery's largest temple – the hall of philosophy. And then there are the tensions between the Tibetans and the Chinese government which have made life as a Buddhist monk difficult for decades. That the monastery is there at all is a miracle, but it is, and for the two thousand monks who live there, it is home.

While walking the streets of the uninspiring new town, we sometimes caught a glimpse of this sacred place. The gilded, golden roofs of the monastery shimmered against the dull hills which formed their backdrop. Columns of smoke rose up from unseen stupas, suggesting a deeper and more spiritual way of life. And on the streets, amongst the ordinary people, there roamed the monks, whose scarlet robes hinted at the purer world which existed on the other side of town.

We wandered over to take a look.

As you pass from one half of the city into the other, you leave behind the new world and step into the old. The area of the town which contains the monastery is surrounded by a wall, and next to the wall there is a walkway, mostly covered and lined with prayer wheels. Locals and pilgrims alike circle the monastery in a clockwise direction, turning the prayer wheels as they go, sending the messages contained within them to the ends of the Earth. But it is within the prayer wheel-lined walls that you truly find yourself entering another world. From shimmering in the distance, the golden roofs now tower high above you, supported by whitewashed walls and sporting intricate, pagoda-influenced designs, the eves of which are topped with golden dragons and stupa-like towers. Walking past bright, intricately painted doorways, the pulsing hum of the monks' prayers would reach our ears, strangely reassuring and totally in tune with the surroundings. Smoke from burning stupas wafted past our noses, the woody odour mixing with the smell of the yak-butter candles which flickered timelessly to light the interiors of many of the temples.

It is within these temples that the intricacies of the Buddhist faith reach their apex. Brightly coloured images of the Gods adorn every surface, their features representing every state of mind from meditation to aggression. Gold statues of Buddha watch over every space, every one unique and ranging in size from the tiny and easily missed, to colossal, room-filling sculptures which tower over you amid the flickering, candlelit darkness.

Against this restrained and deeply spiritual backdrop, my bright red, shock and awe sports car from Kentucky seemed utterly ridiculous.

The monks loved it, though.

I drove it into the monastery complex a few times, both to take photos and to revel in the unsophisticated ridiculousness of cruising around a Tibetan monastery in a Corvette and every time I did so, the car was mobbed by the monks. They'd gather around it, talking excitedly and firing off questions in Tibetan which we couldn't hope to understand. When they felt no-one was looking, a smartphone would appear from deep beneath their robes to take a selfie with the car, and once the dignified stand-offishness was put to one side, they liked nothing more than to pose for photos in the driver's seat, their red robes matching the interior colour so well that it seemed certain that the car's designers in Bowling Green foresaw this situation arising.

Most excited of all were the youngest monks, who hadn't yet adopted the slightly more aloof demeanour of their older mentors. Overcome with fits of excitement, they would climb into the car and wrap their little fingers around the steering wheel with such looks of happy amazement on their faces, that they made the whole trip feel worthwhile.

But as the youngsters climbed over the car and the adult monks brandished their iPhones and posed for pictures in the driving seat, it did rather call into question the renouncement of earthly possessions which went with their territory – surely that's not the path which the Dalai Lama would want them to follow?

But the Dalai Lama was far away, in Dharamsala, northern India; a place we'd passed in our rickshaw years before. He hadn't been allowed to visit Tibet since he was forced to flee before the Chinese invasion in the 1950s, and the Chinese authorities had waged a sophisticated propaganda campaign against him ever since, describing him as a 'wolf in monk's clothing', and banning anything which furthered his cause – even displaying his image is illegal in China. But he is still revered by the monks here, and his photo sat defiantly proud in one of the temples we entered. In a world where every action taken by the monks is closely watched by the authorities, where informers exist at every level of Buddhism and where even the religion itself has been to some extent commandeered by the Chinese Communist Party as a political tool, the Dalai Lama offers hope, and is admired like nothing else.

When visiting the temple in which his image was rebelliously displayed, I mentioned to one of the monks that I had seen him in Mongolia, years before. The web of emotions which this revelation triggered – respect, jealousy, hope – was so intense, I immediately felt like a fraud; someone unworthy of the experience. After that, I told nobody else. That experience could never mean to me what it would have meant to these people.

*　　*　　*

We drove on through beautiful rolling grasslands which rose to monochrome summits of snow and rock. Whenever we stopped for food or petrol, we were mobbed. Monks would pose for photos with our cars, while local Tibetans peered in to see who was driving these strange cars through their world. The Han Chinese, just as curious but more nervous and standoffish, would watch the spectacle from a safe distance, until the ice was broken by the Corvette's pop-up headlights. In a country which has never before seen such gizmos, nothing causes delight and excitement like pop-up headlights, and out amid the wilds of China's final frontier, they removed barriers, triggered smiles and received a round of applause whenever the switch was turned.

From Xiahe, we headed to Langmusi, where a more modest monastery resided – if Labrang was an epicentre of

Tibetan Buddhism, Langmusi was a more typical outpost. Its buildings were similar in style though, if not in extent. Spreading up a hillside above the town, perfectly tiled golden roofs erupted towards the sky in tiers which shone brightly in the sunlight, while snow-clad peaks provided the perfect backdrop. It was a quiet afternoon and in contrast to this grandeur, the foreground was characterised by solitary monks going about their lives, often wandering past us clutching bags of shopping or laundry. Tapestries depicting religious symbols were draped down the front of the temples and when we entered, we found our eyes adjusting to a kaleidoscope of delicate artwork, with every surface decorated in bright colours. The Gods were apparently everywhere and so we spoke in hushed tones, in deference to the atmosphere.

But Buddhism isn't the only set of beliefs to have swept through these beautiful uplands. Eighty years earlier, Mao Zedong passed through at the head of the Communist Red Army, in a retreat from the Nationalist army of Chiang Kai-Shek. This retreat, known as the Long March, is one of the most celebrated events in recent Chinese history, and laid the foundations for the Chinese Communist Party to eventually win China's long-running civil war and take power, a position it has held ever since. The landscape through which we were driving had born witness to this, one of the most pivotal events in the creation of modern China, but today it is simply an open grassland over 3,000 metres above sea level, fringed by unknown mountains, grazed by cattle and sheep, dotted with traditional yurts and crossed for mile after mile by National Highway 213.

That evening, we rolled out of the endless grasslands and into the ancient walled town of Songpan, where we were immediately mobbed. This wasn't a completely unforeseen occurrence, as parking the Rolls and Corvette anywhere in China without attracting an audience proved almost impossible, but in Songpan, it was something else. Simply opening the boot to retrieve my bag and carry it into the hotel was an event of such magnitude that a crowd of around 30 gathered at a safe distance to watch and take photos. After grabbing a shower I headed to the hotel bar and ordered a drink, and saw that the crowd which had gathered around the cars hadn't dissipated; if anything, it had grown in size.

We weren't the only tourist attraction in Songpan, however. What was once a strategic garrison town guarding the main road from Sichuan to Gansu, now had a theme park air. The over-restored city walls were polished to a smartness they surely never knew in more trying times, while the pedestrian-only main street through the town was sanitised to perfection, with the wooden shop fronts having not a splinter out of place and the window displays being targeted squarely at China's growing middle class. We roamed this sanitised image of China's past as the day turned to night, and the streets were gradually lit by a thousand paper lanterns. Gentle floodlighting brought the town's crenulated walls and their fortress-like gates to a soft yellow life, while the pagodas began to glow against the inky sky and floodlights painted the river which ran through the town centre a ghostly shade of white.

After the moving realism of the Tibetan monasteries, Songpan felt rather contrived; a money making film set for the masses. However, as the deep blue of the sky was washed away by the darkness we had to agree, whoever had made the film set had done a pretty good job of it. It was China's past as its citizens wished to see it – clean, inoffensive and beautiful.

The following day, we drove on through a world of mountain and torrent, and as we did so, we found ourselves flitting between the nations past and near-present on almost an hourly basis.

In a sad contrast, the distant past was represented by further villages and museums which had been over-restored in much the same way as Songpan, while the present was represented by the opposite. Five years before our visit to China, the area we were passing through had been hit by a catastrophic earthquake, which measured 8.0 on the Richter scale. 69,000 were killed; at least a third of the remote region's 15 million people were rendered homeless. Mudslides and collapsed bridges cut off access to those areas which were worst affected and in some of the towns we travelled through, over three quarters of the buildings had been destroyed.

We visited the town of Yingxiu, a place where of 9,000 residents, only 2,300 were lucky enough to survive. The remains of the town's high school had been left in their post-quake condition as a memorial to the hundreds who died there, as well as the thousands more whose lives ended in the other 7,000 school buildings which had collapsed across the region. A chill breeze cut through us as we wandered the site with a local guide, sometimes craning our necks upwards at the tottering four or five story high buildings which had remained standing, but more often gazing out horizontally, at those which had collapsed like so many houses of cards. Vegetation grew up from beneath these silent graves, as a light drizzle fell from a sky of mottled tombstone-grey.

Nearby, a sculpture of a broken clock marked the time when this world was destroyed; 14:28 on the 12th of May, 2008. A half-collapsed building sat directly behind, illustrating the power unleashed at that moment in time.

This fragility of the contemporary world was painted in stark relief when we continued south, leaving disaster tourism behind for a more uplifting take on sightseeing. Because when the largest surviving statue of the pre-modern world is bang on your route, it would be rude not to stop by and take a look.

Carved out of a sheer rock face which overlooks the confluence of the Min and Dadu rivers – which no, we'd never heard of either – the Leshan Buddha gazes out across the world, radiating calm serenity from all of its 71 metre height. We approached the statue through dense, jungle-like undergrowth, for we had finally dropped down from the heights of the Tibetan Plateau into a world of tropical heat. As we approached, passing various other, lesser

Buddhas carved into the rock faces, the smell of burning incense and yak butter candles wafted over from a nearby temple complex, and small birds darted through the trees. Engraved into the floor near one of the temples, there was a legend declaring London to be 7,900 kilometres away, and another which announced that Bangkok was another 1,900 kilometres down the road. We were getting there.

I walked at my own pace, allowing a gap to grow between myself and the rest of the party. Sharing the car with Ian and seemingly always being around the rest of the group, the possibility for solitude was something to be savoured, and as I wandered slowly through the jungle, keeping myself to myself, I thought ahead to South East Asia. To Thailand, Cambodia and Laos. That was, to me, where the holiday would begin. Crossing Central Asia and China, with the schedules, paperwork, bureaucracy and ongoing need to keep the car running was hard work, but in my mind, I'd always viewed South East Asia as being the place where I could take my foot off the gas and relax. Reflect, even, on how this latest trip was changing me, if at all.

As you near the Leshan Buddha, your first glimpse of its enormous, 1,200 year old bulk is surprisingly human. A stylised ear, brought into sharp relief by the slanting sun, appears through the jungle ahead and your mind extrapolates the rest of the head which must surround it. This enables you to pick out the profile outline of a face, and the dimpled sandstone which is dotted with tufts of vegetation, and forms the statues hair.

The Buddha's six-metre tall face gazes out across the confluence of the rivers with a timelessly neutral – if slightly fatigued looking - expression. The eyes have been caught barely open, as if in the transition from alertness to sleep, and the emotions it projects are neither happy nor sad. It is above such human feelings and wears a rather solemn and serious look, as you'd expect, given that it was built to keep vessels safe on the sometimes hazardous waters below.

A series of rickety, pre-health and safety wooden staircases lead down next to the Buddha, enabling you to grasp the dominating scale of the statue. You descend slowly, as inevitably you find yourself held up by a group of Chinese holiday makers, taking on the steep descent with an overabundance of caution and nerves. But this slow descent gives you plenty of time to take in the sculpture. It was carved from the sheer rock face, starting with the head and working down to the feet, and it took 80 years for the figure's full height to be completed. From the walkways around it, the sheer bulk overwhelms. After 40 metres of descent you find you've only reached the Buddha's waist. Its toes alone are two metres in height; each of its hands is larger than a Rolls-Royce. It was something else, but it wasn't the only giant we visited in Sichuan Provence.

The other giants we saw were marginally more dynamic than the 1,200 year old stone Buddha, though not by much. They sat there, slouching back in a reclined position, completely oblivious to us as they kept their movements to a minimum. The only things in which they displayed any kind of interest were the piles of bamboo which they were slowly chewing their way through. Eating is a serious business when you're a giant panda; you do it for fourteen hours a day, which doesn't leave much time for anything else.

The Bifengxia Panda Centre which we were visiting was home to around 80 of the remaining worldwide population of pandas, which stood at around 2,000 at the time of our visit. The centre specialised in the care of young pandas, with an on-site nursery for the priceless young bears. Cute and innocent they may have been, but that didn't stop Brummy levelling at them.

'What a stupid animal,' began one of his rants. 'They have two babies but only let one live and they kill the other. They only live in one type of forest, and only eat one type of food, which happens to be the worst food known to man. They have to eat it continuously whenever they're awake.

Why not just eat something else, which actually contains calories? They're so stupid; it's like they've evolved in such a way that they don't want to survive. Just let them die.'

'They crap 40 times a day, too,' added Ian. 'If that was me, I'd wanna die.'

But the pandas – along with the Chinese state – didn't share the enthusiasm for just letting them die, and from coming close to extinction years ago, they were making a cautious recovery, with rising numbers due to successful captive breeding programmes seemingly guaranteeing their future for some time to come. After earthquake levelled high schools, continuous 1984-style surveillance and the apparent oppression of ethnic minorities, it was nice to spend the afternoon discovering such a heart-warming success story. Even if Brummy thought they should just die.

But as we continued south through China, with our successful crossing of the world's most populous nation beginning to feel assured, it was Brummy's Rolls-Royce which decided to die. We noticed one afternoon that it had begun to mark its territory by leaking fluid whenever it was running, and considering the fact that the Chinese government would probably not take very kindly to the Rolls 'marking its territory for England', we decided to investigate further. And it was just as well we did, as petrol was leaking from the overflow pipe of the carburettor.

With only ten miles to go to the day's hotel we pushed on, leaving a line of fuel all the way. We parked hoping that some Chinese guy wouldn't drop a still-burning cigarette onto the line, even though the CCTV footage of a line of flame snaking through a city for several miles before finally blowing up a 35-year-old Rolls-Royce would surely titillate millions on YouTube. And in the time honoured fashion, instead of trying to fix the problem that evening, we went to the bar and drank a beer because after all, it seemed like the most logical course of action.

The following morning over breakfast I suggested a few solutions to Brummy, but neither the suggestion of ignoring it and accepting it'll cost another few hundred pounds in gas to get to Laos, nor the idea of running a hosepipe back from the carburettor into the fuel filler cap passed the Brummy test for some reason. So, it looked like we were going to have to fix this properly.

Obviously as this was us, stuck in a random part of China with a Rolls, the 'proper' technique relied heavily on the use of a hammer. But as with any situation like this, the skill is in knowing exactly when and where to use the hammer.

So, if you happen to be reading this sat next to a '78 Rolls which is pumping fuel overboard like there's no tomorrow, pay attention. What's probably happened is that the float in the carburettor has stuck in its chamber, causing it to over-fuel. To fix this, first you need to disconnect the fuel pump relay, or remove its fuse. Next, start the engine and let it run until it conks out; something which won't take long. Now, pick up your favourite hammer and liberally clobber the dome-shaped float chamber of whichever carburettor it is that's leaking, to unstuck the float. Finally, reconnect the fuel pump relay, close the bonnet of your wedding-spec Rolls, doff your chauffeur's cap to the bride and groom in the back, say 'sorry ma'am' and carry on driving them to the church.

We didn't have a bride and groom, of course, but we did have somewhere to go that day, and it was even more surreal than spending the morning in rural China, beating an old Rolls-Royce back into life with a hammer.

Dwarf Empire.

Of all the places on the itinerary which I'd presented to the Chinese Government five months previously, this was the one which I thought was most likely to raise an eyebrow. A theme park where around one hundred people suffering from dwarfism live in fibreglass mushrooms and dance for visiting Chinese tourists. Politically correct? Not even remotely. But I'd had a few beers when I put together our route across China, and so a visit seemed like a good idea at the time.

Leaving the Corvette at the hotel, we all piled into the Rolls and drove over to the 'empire', which also housed a butterfly park. The place was deserted, but they were happy enough to take our money and let us in. The butterflies were nowhere to be seen – apparently, it was the wrong time of year for them – and due to falling drizzle and the lack of clouds, all shows involving the park's vertically challenged stars were cancelled. Not for us, the daily dance routines where over 100 residents act out famous operas, miniature tightropes are walked and the empire's king dwarf dons a crown and a golden cape, and rides around the place on a three wheeled motorbike. Given the conflicting emotions the place produced in us, this was in some ways a relief. We wandered the set, its fibreglass caves and houses looking pathetic in the rain; its stage pointless and deserted. A few of the stars of the shows hung around while off-duty, smoking cigarettes and looking considerably more normal than the backdrop against which they worked. What seemed funny after a few beers back in England now felt strangely tragic. Half an hour after arriving, we were gone, back on the road to Laos.

As we carried on south and the climate continued to change to tropical, it was the Corvette's turn to protest. The sudden halving of power and the drone which accompanied it as the engine went into limp mode had become more regular, but the time-honoured approach of 'turning it off and on again' still fixed the problem. We still started the day by slotting a fuse into the holder to fire up the cooling fan before any long drive, but the temperatures were sufficiently high that the Chinese fuses we'd picked up at a petrol station were melting in the heat rather than blowing out, and in slow traffic the temperature gauge still roamed dangerously high in the gauge, calling for ever more frequent cooling stops. And occasionally, after a long drive, the car simply wouldn't restart until it

217

was left to cool down – turning the ignition key brought no response. But despite all these issues, the Corvette still exuded an aura of toughness and dependability. While the electrics were clearly not really up to the challenge, the rest of the car felt as sturdy and dependable as the hammer we'd brought along to fix the Rolls with. It was built in Kentucky after all, and was designed to take the worst abuse the average redneck could dish out as they lived out their Dukes of Hazard fantasies in America's Deep South.

As we drove, the temperature gauge climbing and the electrics failing, I often found myself thinking back to the curvaceous TVR I'd left at home less than two months earlier, and whenever I did I was so glad I'd bought the Corvette. Given their reputation, I felt sure that the TVR wouldn't have been able to cope with such a drive, and it was such a relief that the 'vette was just soldiering on.

Because after all, the jungles of Laos, and indeed the whole of South East Asia, were just over the horizon. And after a surprisingly easy border crossing out of China, we were there, getting stuck into the final leg of the trip.

EIGHTEEN

THE LAST CLIMB

19ᵗʰ July 2007
Plymouth, UK

It's a standard method of passing time for any car enthusiast. You sit down at your computer, click on eBay or the Pistonheads website and see what's for sale. Rapidly, you find yourself descending into a rabbit hole of interesting vehicles of every type, from the weirdness which populates the military vehicle sections of the classifieds to the exotica that's piled high in the Ferrari section, and before long you wish money was no object when selecting a road trip steed. The exercise is most rewarding when carried out on a rainy evening with a whisky to hand and can prove positively dangerous to your finances if you suffer from a concurrent, nagging feeling that your garage is one car short of the optimum number.

The Thursday after we'd said goodbye to the tuk-tuk and flown home from India, the stars had aligned in such a manner that all of the above was true for me, and the combination of a whisky and an urge for another car was a powerful one.

As I flicked through the classifieds, my desire for another city car was still high. The Fiat 126 which we'd taken to the Arctic was gone, but it had left a gap which begged to be filled with another set of wheels, and so I scanned the usual websites to see whether anything would jump out at me. But an old Fiat 500 was too pricy, a Renault 4 wasn't engaging enough and a Citroen 2CV was just too crappy. As I browsed, nothing really jumped out at me, and so as my dram gradually emptied, my wallet seemed safe.

But then I decided a spot of Mongol Rally nostalgia was in order, and there it was.

A 1974 Austin Mini, with a dark brown interior and an exterior which had been painted in such a specific shade of orangey brown, that the nickname of 'Diarrhoea Daisy' was all but guaranteed. It was the standard 998 model, with copious amounts of extra chrome, four extra spotlights lined up in front of its shiny grill, a rather badly made custom dashboard hewn from a sheet of woodstained MDF and the cutest set of little ten-inch Minilite wheels you'd ever seen.

'Six hundred and fifty pounds? Shut up and take my money', was my response. That weekend I headed over to the glamorous suburbs of Camborne, in deepest Cornwall, to collect it.

Sunlight showed new Daisy's paintwork to be more orange than brown, and despite being a little crusty around the edges – as any classic that's endured the Cornish climate for any length of time would be expected to be – it didn't look half bad. Maybe this was down to the excessive amounts of chrome, because let's face it, shiny is good, right? I handed over a wedge of banknotes fresh from the cash point and drove my latest wheels back to Plymouth, with only a bout of mind-focussing misfiring as I passed Liskeard to report.

That evening, after a few hours at the local climbing wall, I went for a beer with some of my outdoorsy friends.

'So that's it?' said Ian. 'You're sacking off climbing to drive to places now?'

'Not exactly,' I replied. 'I'm still going to climb stuff. I'm just doing the driving thing too now.'

'Yeah, yeah. I've heard that one before. I bet by the end of the year you'll be done with it. And fat too, from all that sitting behind the steering wheel.'

'Rubbish,' I replied. 'I still went to Font this year.'

'But you didn't do a Scottish winter trip, did you? And anyway, last year you left Font early to go to that racetrack in Germany. You're losing it already.'

'Fine. Next week, let's climb.'

'Climb what?' said Ian.

At this stage my friend Seb, who'd been quietly listening, chimed in. 'El Naranjo, of course. Still wanna do it?'

'Sure,' I said. 'Let's go.'

El Naranjo de Bulnes, to give it its full name, is a rather vertiginous 2,500 metre high pillar of rock in northern Spain, which is often described as 'the Matterhorn of the Iberian Peninsula'. We discussed our chances of popping over for a quick ascent, but our chances of success seemed slight. Seb only had five days off work, and they didn't line up with the ferry from Plymouth to northern Spain. Flights were a possibility, but I didn't fancy flying on principle – I mean, if you've already driven to Mongolia, why would you fly to Spain? So, I suggested the only option I knew – driving.

'Five days to drive to Dover, get the ferry across the channel, drive to Spain, climb the hardest mountain in the country then get home again?' said Seb. 'I love it, what are we taking?'

'Well, my new Mini, obviously,' I replied.

'Of course we are,' said Ian. 'What a batshit crazy idea. Nothing could possibly go wrong.'

*   *   *

It seemed perfectly fitting that such a daft trip should start from the pub, and so the following Saturday evening we met some friends at Plymouth's Seymour Arms for a send-off. The sun was shining, meaning Daisy looked more orange than diarrhoea as we strapped a bouldering mat to its roof, loaded it up with climbing gear, ropes, tents and other outdoor gear, and hit the road.

Darkness came as we bounced along the M4, getting used to the Mini's cramped interior, in which we'd be spending rather a lot of time over the coming days. Daisy ran well enough though, the simple pushrod engine droning away as we rolled through the night, with 1,200 miles of driving ahead of us to get to the mountain.

The night-time ferry passed without incident and we watched dawn break over northern France, Daisy bumbling along quite happily as we avoided the toll roads because let's face it, there's not much point in forking out for the autoroute when you're not really able to go that much faster than 60 miles per hour anyway. So we bounced along amongst the scenery of rural France, swinging our way around ringroads to avoid the towns and racing down hills before being slowed by the ascents which invariably followed. Every few hundred miles there was a fuel stop and a driver change, and the Mini's brown interior was seemingly always awash with food to snack on, sweets and crisps and biscuits and the rest of the carefree road trip diet I'd become so familiar with.

We rolled into Biarritz as the sun set on our first 24 hours on the road, our grimy and fatigued state matching Daisy's perfectly, and our now raging appetites being calmed by a meal in a Mexican restaurant. And then we pushed on, sweeping over the Pyrenees into Spain with the engine temperature gauge sweeping towards the red as we did so, and eerie mists descending upon our lonely progress through the night, often slowing us to a crawl.

When we finally reached the Picos de Europa in northern Spain, where our mountain was located, the scenery took a turn for the dramatic, the light grey limestone cliffs sweeping upwards in a manner which offered enough climbing to last anyone a lifetime. The road swept up too, and behind the wheel, Seb enjoyed attacking it to the full, Daisy's low ride height and relatively wide wheels making it surprisingly grippy and go-cart like in the bends – not that bends were its problem.

'I think we should pull over,' said Seb. 'It's getting really hot now. Can you smell it?'

'Yeah, I can smell it,' I replied. 'It smells like its barbequing itself.'

We slowed to a halt in a high alpine meadow, the air surprisingly cool thanks to a late morning breeze which brushed its way over the sea of wild grasses in waves.

'I think it's the thermostat,' announced Seb.

'I think you might be right,' I replied. 'There's a village about a mile down the hill. Let's coast down to it to help cool the engine a bit, then change it there.'

'Agreed,' said Seb.

And so, with the engine turned off we coasted down the hill into one of those perfect little stone-built villages which Spain does so well, coming to a stop outside the only bar in the place.

'Beer?' said Ian.

'Hell yes,' both Seb and I answered, and so Ian headed to the bar, returning with three small bottles of San Miguel shortly afterwards.

We didn't have a spare thermostat, and so we decided to simply remove the offending part and see whether it made a difference. Seb got stuck in, unbolting the housing from the end of the cylinder head, while Ian and I chatted about the forthcoming climb.

Though I didn't want to show it, I was nervous, as even though only one year had passed since I'd been rattling across Asia on the Mongol Rally, much had changed in that year. The drive was now my comfort zone, to a degree which climbing had never attained. Seb and Ian had done much more of this kind of traditional climbing than I had recently, and all I really had to carry me up the wall was bravado and a desire not to let the team down.

With the thermostat removed and the cooling system reassembled and watertight, we drove on to the valley in which the mountain was located, parked and set off on the two hour walk-in to the hut at the base of the mountain.

From a distance it stood proud above the sea of lesser mountains from which it rose; a thumb of light grey granite thrusting upwards from the folds of the earth. But distance blunted its sheer scale, and it was only in the latter stages of the walk-in, as we approached its base, that the full impact of El Naranjo de Bulnes made itself felt. From the valley floor it rose 500 metres into the sky above us, its smooth face of vertical limestone a dream for so many climbers. Inspiring and intimidating in equal measure.

But for me, it was already becoming something of the past. As much as I still loved the mountains, it was years since I'd climbed anything like this and my memories of such routes always seemed coated in danger. I thought back to abseiling off the Aiguille de Perseverance above Chamonix in a thunderstorm; to that time we retreated off the Dent de Geant, my climbing partner Lee struck down by the altitude. This was the world I used to inhabit, and had never quite got the measure of. It had always seemed one step ahead of me. The fact I was back in it at the base of this mountain was perhaps down to my stubbornness; that lingering doubt which can make it so difficult to move on from something you know you'll never make work.

Such were the thoughts which swirled around my head as I rested my fatigued head on a pillow in the mountain hut, my alarm set for an early start the following morning.

*   *   *

The mountain's shadow was gradually creeping across the valley as we shouldered our packs and walked towards our chosen route to the summit. Other climbers were waking up, sitting outside the hut or in front of their tents, soaking up the sun's warmth while talking in the hushed, deferent manner which all climbers do when nervously excited about a big day ahead.

The walk in to the start of the climb took several hours, for we were planning an ascent of the mountain's somewhat more welcoming south face which, while not as demanding as the 500 metres of vertical limestone which towered over the hut, still promised hundreds of metres of exposed climbing, as difficult as any route on the high mountains I'd done previously.

At the base of the route we donned our helmets and climbing harnesses, put on the special rock shoes which enabled us to stand on the smallest edges, racked up the climbing gear and tied into the two 60 metre ropes we'd brought for the ascent. And then Seb led off, confidently climbing the first rope length, placing wedges of metal into cracks in the rock face to protect himself against falling, as Ian held the rope below.

The route went vertically upwards for about fifteen metres, before a groove which allowed a rising traverse to be made to the first anchor point. On reaching this seemingly effortlessly, Seb clipped himself into the security of a metal loop attached to the rock, then shouted down 'safe'. It was our turn to climb, first Ian, as Seb belayed on one of the ropes, then myself, protected by the other.

Ian led the next rope length, looking less composed than Seb, but still under control. He always climbed like this, looking like he was going to fall at any moment, but somehow he always scrabbled his way through to the belay. I was happy to let the two of them take it in turns to break the new ground at the sharp end of the rope and simply to follow, carrying the bag which contained our food, drinks, waterproofs, camera and everything else we'd need for the climb.

Once we'd all reached Ian's belay at the top of the second rope length, we were treated to a stunning view out across the mountain landscape of the Picos. It was very much a climber's world, bare rock being the major ingredient, with little vegetation to soften its limestone sweeps. I'd missed this, the remoteness and the sense of being lost in nature. It wasn't the main reason to climb, but it was a happy secondary pleasure to be gained from these trips. I stared out across the abrupt land of sunlight and shadow and as I did so, I spotted a couple of mountain goats grazing far below, my mind lost in the moment.

'You got me?' asked Seb, snapping me back into the present.

'Erm, yeah. On belay,' I replied, threading the rope through the friction device on my harness, so I could check his descent if he fell.

'Good, watch me on this one, it look like a tough pitch.'

And with that, Seb led up the vertical face above us, the water-weathered limestone having formed into vertical runnels which offered little in the way of flat surfaces to use as holds. It was obvious that it was difficult, as Seb's usually flowing technique became jerky, as he thrust and lunged for holds, his forearms getting more and more tired, before he finally breathed out a huge sigh of relief when he reached the next anchor point, high above.

'No way was that VS,' he shouted down to us in climber-speak, as he set up the belay and pulled the rope through, before sending down the order, 'climb when ready.'

I fought my way up the cliff, my rock boots slipping off the smoothly worn limestone and the strength in my arms fading quickly as the heavy rucksack on my back tried to pull me into the void. Upward progress came in short, frantic bursts between small hand and foot holds, and where I should have been using technique to flow up the features in balance, I was instead relying on brute force – a sign that I was out of my depth. And sure enough, when I was still a few metres below Seb, my brute force ran out.

'Take,' I shouted, as my weight slumped onto the rope that was protecting me from above. I was nackered.

'I can't do this pitch, I'm completely pumped. I'm going to jumar the last few metres,' I said, which translated into non-climber speak means I'm going to have to cheat and climb the rope, rather than the rock. And this I did, arriving at the ledge feeling angry with myself that my climbing ability had deteriorated so much that I was failing where my friends succeeded.

'I think I went off-route,' said Seb. 'There's a 7a variation in the guidebook; I'm pretty sure that was it.'

We'd accidently ended up on a harder section of the mountain than we'd planned, but still. I'd failed to climb the pitch in the best style possible. As my road tripping psyche and experience built, so my climbing ability was ebbing away. But now wasn't the time for dwelling on such thoughts, as we still had a mountain to climb. Literally.

The next few rope lengths went in a fairly straightforward manner and soon we were scrambling up the summit slopes of Spain's most coveted mountain on secure holds, with hundreds of metres of exhilarating air beneath our feet. And then the summit was reached and the view swept around us for 360 degrees. To our north, the cloud-dappled Bay of Biscay disappeared over the horizon, while below us, lesser mountains pressed up all around and the rolling countryside of Spain swept south out of sight. Behind us lay 1,200 miles of driving in an old Mini, a long walk-in to the mountain carrying all our heavy gear and hundreds of metres of steep climbing, which we looked back upon with satisfaction. And the summit was only the halfway point, as the old mountaineering adage goes. We still had to make it back. It was shaping up to be quite the adventure.

The south face up which we'd climbed had turned into a sun trap as the day wore on, and we'd become pretty dehydrated by the time we'd reached the summit; a fact which was made worse when we realised that we'd completely forgotten to bring any water. Three apples were all we had for hydration, and so with our mouths parched and dry, we began the long series of abseils down the mountain, the scariest of which was off a single loose peg hammered into a crack in the rock, which moved as we weighted it with our ropes. But we had no other options and so weight it we did, committing our lives to its security in the long dash back to the horizontal world below.

As we descended, the cloud which we'd seen in the Bay of Biscay rolled in around the mountains and El Naranjo became an island above a churning white sea. After completing our abseils, we put away our climbing gear and started the walk out, plunging directly into a swirling white world of mist in which we were lucky to find the hut, where I drank six pints of liquid within an hour, without needing the toilet once.

*   *   *

It was three in the morning. I sat at the wheel of Daisy, guiding us back across France as Seb and Ian slept soundly. The drone of the A-series engine and the wind rustling against the car's rain gutters seemed purpose designed to lull me to sleep, but I knew I wouldn't succumb to the fatigue. We were back in my world now, and I'd been pushing my driving envelope for long enough to know that I could safely make it through the night and get us to Fontainebleau for some bouldering the following morning. The steep walls of El Naranjo now lay behind me, along with my career as an alpine climber. But in front of me, there lay an open road, which led to wherever in the world I wanted to go. I watched it flicker past in the glow of Daisy's headlights, and smiled.

NINETEEN

WELCOME TO THE JUNGLE

25th May 2013
Luang Namtha Provence, Laos

The vegetation looked impenetrable. It crowded around us in a solid, living mass, as dense and unyielding as the bullet-hard ground from which it rose. There was an air of permanence about its endless twisting bulk; the same timelessness which great mountains exude. But mankind's determination to overcome such barriers is strong, and a rough road sliced through it, the jungle bulging powerfully to either side and towering high over our heads to diffuse the watery sky above.

Suddenly jolted from the headlong pursuit of modernity which defined modern China, on entering Laos we plunged into a world which in comparison felt frozen in time, forever destined to reside in the middle of the last century. The broken tarmac and gravel road surface undulated left and right through the unfamiliar greenery, seeking out its own tortuously twisty path through the domed hills and steep-sided valleys which make up the landscape of northern Laos. People were few, and generally stared blankly at our unfamiliar steeds as we roared past their wooden shacks which huddled next to the roads, their backs hard against the dark and omnipresent jungle. A few of the more prestigious folk cruised around the area on mopeds, sometimes with the ultimate status symbol – an AK47 or French-era flintlock rifle – casually draped across the handlebars.

We felt like we'd finally driven off the map into a world beyond ours; a place which existed in another time. A place we didn't understand. After the inflexible itinerary and dull roads of China, it was impossibly exciting, as if by

233

crossing a border we'd been beamed into the first page of a Tintin novel, just as the adventure was getting underway.

It was 60 miles from the border to the first town of any note, and it took us nearly three hours to cover the distance, slowly sinking deeper into the brooding jungle, savouring every moment. Every now and then we'd find ourselves passing through threadbare villages, the huts roofed with leaves, the people sometimes barely dressed. On other occasions, we passed through parts of the jungle which were alive with the sounds of a million insects, buzzing and droning like some giant machine. And it wasn't only insects which lived in the darkened vegetation; somewhere deep in the forest, there roamed Asian elephants, black bears, leopards and tigers. But so dense was the vegetation that we saw little other than the tunnel of ominous green and shadow through which we drove, except on the occasional moments when the road passed a raised point where a view out over the forest canopy was possible, and we'd pull over and stare, delighting in the paths that our lives had taken to lead us there.

We'd just driven a couple of ridiculous V8s to South East Asia. The thought couldn't help but make us smile.

It was dark when we arrived at the town of Muang Xai and the local food market was still open, a few rickety tables bathed in the glow of fluorescent lights, beneath which a tornado of insects danced. But these bugs, whirling around the lamps in confusion, were the lucky ones. On the floodlit tables all manner of well-cooked creatures were spread, from grasshoppers to tarantulas, ants to centipedes. Locals milled among the displays, picking out their evening meals from the forest's natural bounty; we gazed on voyeuristically for a while before unadventurously splashing out on some chicken and a few beers to quench our appetites. And all the while, parked in front of the stalls at which we ate, our cars raised more than a few eyebrows among the locals out shopping for dinner; a pair of lost UFOs from another world, alighting in the timeless past.

But even in the world away from worlds which we'd found ourselves in, there were signs that for the first time since we'd left Europe, the backpacker trail was near.

They came roaring out of the night, three shirtless apparitions on cheap motorbikes, shouting coarsely at each other over the noise of their engines as they parked, their Australian accents unmistakable. Glancing around as they removed their helmets, they first noticed our cars, then us, and then most importantly, they clocked our beers. The die for the evening was cast.

The Australians had bought their bikes in Vietnam – probably while drunk – and had ridden them up to the remote north of the country, before crossing into Laos, leaving a trail of empty beer bottles in their wake. Where were they heading next? They hadn't decided. South probably, or maybe across to Chang Mai in Thailand, but either way, they wanted to end up in Cambodia, and they still had another month to go before they had to fly home. What glorious freedom they were enjoying! After the rigid inflexibility of China, the heady sense of infinite possibilities was delicious; the excited sharing of adventures as we chatted into the beer-fuelled early hours intoxicating. Or maybe that was actually the effect of the beers? Either way, their beers-and-bikes trip around this corner of Asia sounded gloriously fun, an anarchic dash through the jungle on $200 machines.

'We should do something like that,' I said to Brummy.

'Fuck right off,' was the instant reply.

The following morning, the hangover we were all suffering from elicited a similar response from me, and could certainly be described as being as 'character building' as any trip around Asia on an old bike.

*   *   *

Except for the occasional crossing of paths in places like Labrang Monastery and northern Laos, we'd now been travelling in a separate world to the Western backpacker

235

crowd for almost two months, but as we approached Luang Prabang, our two worlds collided. We rolled into a place of freshly washed yoga pants and trekking sandals; mosquito-repellent shirts and Patagonia headwear. T-shirts from far flung places were worn proudly, bestowing prestige on their owners, while every tenth passer-by seemed to be clutching a copy of the relevant Lonely Planet guidebook. After passing through so many different worlds over the past few months and seeing so many unfamiliar faces, we felt like we'd come home. Or at least, we'd arrived at a strange alternative version of home, where the gap year is the norm and a bulging backpack is a statement of intent. Suffice to say, we were somewhat knocked back by the sudden change, as we dragged our filthy cars and dusty selves out of the bulging jungle to the north.

It may have been our fellow Westerners which initially caught our eye, but as the shock faded, we began to notice what had brought them to town. Luang Prabang was a pretty little place, casually stretching along the banks of the mighty Mekong River and striking the perfect balance between the exotic and the homely which appeals travellers the world over. On the main street, restrained colonial style mixed with indigenous flair, and there was everything from pagoda'd temples piercing the sky with their jauntily stacked roofs, to coffee shops and bakeries offering home comforts to the backpacking masses, and naturally charging Western prices for the privilege. Piled-high local shops leaned against smart-casual travellers' hostels, all of which advertised excursions on eye-catching displays out front. Do you want to hire a bike? Or take an elephant trek, visit a local waterfall or find a taxi to the airport? No problem, just pay your money and off you go.

Suddenly, travel was easy. The holiday had finally begun.

But not for all of us; for Ian, it was over. He finished in style though, being chauffeured to the airport in the Rolls-Royce, before flying home to resume his life after a month on the road.

And Luang Prabang not only marked the end of the road for Ian, it was also the final destination of our £4,500 Rolls-Royce. Having covered 12,000 miles since leaving the UK a few months earlier, it was sold to a local hotel for the same amount that Brummy had paid for it in England, and hence proved itself to be a pretty good investment both in terms of money and memories, because let's face it, you can't really put a price on having driven across Asia in a Rolls-Royce. It's the sort of thing which will stay with you forever.

Despite the fact that in the previous few days we'd lost our Chinese guide Shannon, Ian, and the Rolls-Royce, it wasn't all deficit in the V8Nam camp, because while we were in Luang Prabang, we also gained a member – Laura, who flew in the day before Ian left. Laura and I went back a long way and had dated for some time before breaking up the year before V8Nam but despite this, we had remained good friends, and her appetite for adventure meant that the opportunity to nip across South East Asia in a Corvette was not something she was going to miss. Her presence did give us one issue however – three people into a two-seat Corvette doesn't go.

'So, what are you thinking?' I asked Brummy over a beer.

'Simple. I'll just take the bus.'

'All the way to Saigon? Sounds painful,' Laura said.

'Nowhere near as painful as the interior of that Corvette,' Brummy replied.

'So you're really going to go from a Rolls-Royce to a bus?'

'Why not. Or if there aren't any buses, I'll fly.'

'Are you sure you don't want to buy one of these Thai tuk-tuks and convoy the last bit with us?' I asked.

'No chance, not after the last time we did a trip in a tuk-tuk. I'd rather crap in my hands and clap,' Said Brummy, smirking.

'I'd pay to watch that,' said Laura.

'I wouldn't,' I added, before moving the conversation on.

'So I guess the first leg is from here to Vang Vieng, then. That should be pretty easy to find a bus for.'

'I've already spoken to the hostel about it. There's one leaving from out front at nine in the morning.'

'Ideal,' I said. 'Get it booked and I'll race you there.'

*   *   *

It may have taken over 10,000 miles of driving to reach it, but it was the best road of the trip so far. Better than the snow-lined snake of tarmac which had taken Kim and I through the mountains in northern Romania, or the road that flowed up to our overnight stop in Kyrgyzstan's Tian Shan Mountains. Its surface was generally smooth and the landscape through which it swept was endless perfection; a verdant sea of undulating greenery, from which limestone karst towers rose to a mottled grey sky. The road rarely ran straight for long, but neither did it close in on itself with the kind of first-gear corners which could leave the Corvette feeling all at sea. No, it flowed along, its movements dictated by the whims of the landscape, rising and falling, sweeping this way and that, always new, always interesting. The 'vette may have been built to dominate the arrow-straight two-lane black top of America, but it felt equally at home in this jungle on the far side of the world, flowing to the contours of the freshly laid highway.

Yes, we had a lot of fun on the 140 mile drive down to Vang Vieng. So much fun in fact, that we ruptured a tyre.

The first sign that something was wrong came when an unfamiliar vibration began to pulse through the car. On stopping to investigate, we found that one of the rear tyres had worn through all its rubber and the carcass was now split, meaning I guess you could say we'd gotten our moneys-worth out of them. Changing the wheel for one of the two spares I'd brought along was pretty straightforward, but as the spares were barely a third of the

238

width of the original 275-section tyres, we were forced to complete the final few miles to our overnight stop with a fair bit more caution.

We still won the race with Brummy's minibus however, and already had a couple of Beer Laos on the table by the time he walked into the hostel.

Vang Vieng certainly turned out to be an interesting place. If Luang Prabang was where the gap year crowd went to keep up appearances, this was where they came to let their hair down. From our vantage point at the hostel, we watched as a continuous flow of drunken tourists headed to the local river to indulge in what's known as 'tubing', which seemed to involve floating along on a tyre inner tube while others, high on the effects of alcohol – or other substances – made their raucous way around the streets. Back in Luang Prabang, I'd been told that there were 120 different traveller's hostels in the place, which had once been a simple fishing village. Given the state of it, I could quite believe this, and the effect didn't make me in the slightest bit proud to be a Western traveller. I felt like we'd arrived in the dingiest, most embarrassing nightclub in the whole of South East Asia. Though saying that, the views across the river at sunset, when the karst cliffs and watery sky lit up like a painting, were sufficiently stunning to momentarily take your mind off the hedonism that was all around.

The next leg of our Asian odyssey saw us leaving Laos and crossing the Friendship Bridge into Thailand. There, we would head to the house where Laura's dad happened to live, and from him, some exciting news had reached us. The local garage had managed to get hold of a pair of 275/40ZR17 tyres for the Corvette – quite an achievement in pickup-dominated Thailand. But first we had to get there, a task which was slowed somewhat when the Corvette's overheating came to a head in Laos' capital, Vientiane. With the temperature gauge once again pegged to the maximum, we coasted to a halt outside an inviting-looking coffee shop, opened the bonnet and grabbed a drink as we waited for it to cool down. The downside of this enforced stop was that Brummy's bus beat us to Udon Thani, where Laura's dad lived.

'I've no idea what took you, but it looks like one-all in the 'vette versus bus race series,' Brummy said in greeting as we arrived at Laura's dad's house.

'I guess so,' I replied. 'All set for a final showdown on the run to Angkor Wat then.'

* * *

If China was defined by its frenzied pursuit of infrastructure and development, and Laos was characterised by its being stuck in a pre-modern limbo, then Thailand was the happy medium. On every measure it seemed to sit between the two countries. Its roads were far more efficient than those in Laos, without feeling the need to rush headlong into China's level of landscape-scarring development. Its shops were well enough stocked, but lacked the sense of neo-capitalist materialism that's taken hold in China. And its people seemed confident and happy in their own skin, neither as frenzied as those in China's rat-race, nor as laid-back-to-horizontal as those in Laos. Our distinct first impression was of a people who were relaxed in the knowledge that their path seemed to be a good one, blending the best bits of Westernised life with their own traditional rhythms to find a happy middle way.

And they had Corvette tyres too, so they were always bound to find themselves in our good books. We headed to the local version of Kwik Fit to get them swapped onto the Corvette's rims, and soon we had all the rubber we'd need to complete the journey. And while we were in the mood for giving the 'vette some TLC, we saw to a few other jobs – firstly, the repair of one of the cooling fans, which had decided to quit working completely and secondly, an oil change. Having put 12,000 rather hot miles under its belt in the past two months, I figured the long-suffering L98 small block Chevy motor had earned it.

That evening we stayed with Laura's father, who lived in a new house in the city's suburbs. The temperature outside was still well in the thirties as the sun went down, but fortunately for us, a ruthlessly efficient air conditioning system kept the living room temperatures down and we spent a very pleasant evening chatting about our drive from the UK to Thailand, and his life there. The familiar company, the smart and homely surroundings and the cool temperature all made it feel like home, but the moment you stepped outside and the sweat began to bead on your skin, you were reminded that quaint old England was now a very long way away.

Sweating was a definite feature of the next leg of the journey, as our race against Brummy to Angkor Wat got underway. We were at the end of Thailand's dry season and without the moderating effect of the rains, the heat had built to such a level that whatever we did, the Corvette's interior would do its best impression of a sauna. We tried everything, including removing the detachable roof panel to let more air in, but nothing seemed to make things bearable. When we kept the tinted glass roof on, we were rolling along in a 5.7 litre, V8-propelled greenhouse. Remove it and the full, unfiltered heat of the sun would blaze down on us. We even tried to go for a halfway house by gaffa taping a map to the roof to provide shade, but the gaffa tape melted in the heat. And through all this, the hot and clammy leather seats did nothing to aid our plight; whatever we did, there was simply no escaping the temperature. On our first break from the road a few hours out of Udon Thani, Laura looked like she'd been lying in a shallow paddling pool, such was the contrast between her sweat-soaked back, and relatively air-dried front.

'I think I preferred the African Porsche,' was Laura's take on the situation. 'Not only was it quieter and more comfortable, but it didn't feel quite as much like sitting in a fan oven, either.'

But an end to the blazing heat felt near. Clouds were bubbling up thoughtlessly into the stratosphere, their heat-quenching moisture just out of reach. They would release their loads soon enough, bringing life back to the parched plains across which we were driving. But to some of the locals in the villages we passed, 'soon enough' wasn't good enough, and encouragement was needed. But how do you encourage a cloud to unleash its rains? Simple. You fire rockets at it.

On several occasions that day, while gazing out over the unrelenting flatness of the landscape, we'd see a white smoke trail soaring up into the cloudbase - the exhaust from a home-made rocket. We'd had the good fortune to find ourselves travelling through northeast Thailand at the time of year when rocket festivals are held, and tradition dictates that clouds are fired upon to trigger the rainy season. Given that the home-made rockets can be anything up to nine metres long, and are propelled by up to 120 kilograms of gunpowder, the budding Elon Musks who live in the area must really, really want it to rain. Based on their solution to a lack of rain, it wouldn't come as a surprise to hear that they also had a rather short life expectancy, too.

We were just pleased to have made it through the area unscathed, albeit rather sweaty.

After a night in the laid back town of Surin, where the local night market seemed to have an excessive number of inflatable Top Gear Stigs for sale alongside the usual fare, we rejoined the race to Angkor Wat. While we'd been cruising among the rockets on the road south, Brummy had taken a flight from Udon Thani to Bangkok, and then another to Cambodia's capital, Phnom Penh – fortunately without accidently being shot down by a stray cloud-rocket. He was now only half a day's bus ride from our destination whereas we still had a border crossing to get through, and a fair bit of driving to boot. The race was on.

Of course when racing, the last thing you want is a breakdown. The same is true of when you're crossing a border – pushing a broken car past the customs officials isn't exactly the best look when entering a new country. So, when the Corvette decided to pack up at the obscure crossing we were using to enter Cambodia, we weren't best pleased. Especially as it chose to expire in a place where it completely blocked traffic between the two countries.

As I said, not a good look.

Fortunately, it was an electrical issue similar to that which had temporarily halted our progress in southern China, and so we knew exactly what to do – turn it off and on again, by disconnecting the battery then reconnecting it. With cross-border traffic only stopped for ten minutes, we were underway again, the border guards giving us the thumbs up as we roared south towards Seam Reap – a modern city which stands next to what was once the capital of the largest empire South East Asia has ever known. Angkor Wat.

Laura's phone beeped as we got underway.

'Is that Brummy?' I asked.

'It is indeed,' was the reply.

'How's he doing?'

'Apparently the bus is horrific, but he says he's only about an hour away from Seam Reap now.'

'So are we,' I said. 'Time to get a move on.'

The road was open and fast, but the tarmac on which we drove wasn't above suspicion, often being broken and potholed. Despite this, I pushed on as best I could, knocking off the remaining miles to our meeting point as quickly as possible. Laura's phone would often beep with another progress report and we'd try to work out who was in the lead.

'He says he's on the outskirts of town.'

'We're on the outskirts too. Check the buses to see if you can spot him.'

The traffic built and slowed as we got closer to the meeting point, the need to stay alert growing as mopeds and cyclists thrust through the mass. Dust rose from the rainless ground and glowed golden against the cloud dappled sky, as the sun continued to burn us through the Corvette's glass roof.

'He's crossing the river now,' announced Laura. 'He's almost there.'

'So are we,' I replied. 'Look, the bridge is just there.'

'I wonder which route he's taking into the city. He could be on another road.'

'We'll know soon enough,' I said.

Dusty businesses were replaced by housing and hotels as we approached the centre of Siam Reap. Traffic grew ever heavier, and the Corvette's interior ever hotter. And then, as we swung around the last corner and rolled up to the meeting place, there was Brummy, looking smug as he lent forwards and shouted 'losers' through our open window, while gestured the letter 'L' at us.

So that proves it. Those Top Gear races where the car always wins are staged - sometimes, public transport beats even the most over-engined sports car.

TWENTY

THE ITALIAN JOB

26th December 2007
Chepstow, South Wales, UK

It didn't look good. The crack in the driver's footwell of my Mini split the metal for at least fifteen centimetres, maybe more. The metal flexed as I prodded the point of failure with a screwdriver, and through the gap, I could see the driveway below.

How long had it been there? I had no idea. It was the first time I'd ever lifted Daisy's carpets to see what was hiding beneath them. But however the crack had got there, it wasn't an ideal discovery. I was due to head to Turin in the Mini that afternoon.

I attempted to fix the crack with a cheap arc welder, but got nowhere. It had been over half a decade since I'd last welded anything, and the combination of thin, wavy metal and a welder more suited to fixing garden gates than car bodywork meant that all my attempt did was open the crack up further.

There were two hours to go until I had to set off to collect my co-driver and then get stuck into my latest idea for a road trip – an Italian Job-inspired drive to Turin, to celebrate the New Year there.

I tried again with the welder. Each time I raised my cheap welding mask, the world went dark as I slowly inched the welding rod towards the torn metal. Then a flash of blue light would cut through the heavy tinting as the electricity arced to the metal, emitting a fizzing, buzzing noise as tiny sparks bounced around Daisy's interior. The smell of burning paint and underseal wafted powerfully through the air, while dense smoke rose through the crack.

But I couldn't get the crack to close.

One hour to go.

I mulled over the situation in my mind. Thousands of miles around Europe, in a car with a potentially weakened structure? Could we do it safely? I thought back to my days at university studying engineering, and mulled over the maths in my head. My latest adventure hung on barely remembered concepts – second moments of area, monocoque structures, metal fatigue. I ran through the calculations in my mind and came to the conclusion that the split in the footwell was reducing the longitudinal strength of the car by less than five percent, and so I had no doubt that the Mini was safe to drive at that time. How would it be faring a thousand miles down the road? There was only one way to find out.

I gaffa taped over the crack to stop water coming in, replaced the carpets and set off on the first leg of the drive to Turin.

Laura was waiting for me at her mother's house, near Milton Keynes. Pulling into the housing estate, a speed bump made contact with the chunky, centrally mounted exhaust, disconnecting the piping beneath the car from the downpipe. Immediately, Daisy acquired a deep, bass-dominated sound as its exhaust gasses escaped without being dulled by the silencer, and the sound of metal scraping along the ground announced that the piping had slumped down onto the tarmac, somewhere near my feet. I stopped, and using thick gloves, realigned the exhaust and slotted it back together. Normal volume returned and so I pulled up outside the house to collect Laura as if nothing had happened.

'How's the car doing?' Laura's mum asked, as she made me a cup of tea.

'Absolutely fine,' I replied. 'Daisy is a great little car.'

As we left the estate, the speed bump removed the exhaust for a second time and, well practised now, I reassembled it once again and off we headed for Dover.

The various issues had made us rather late for our ferry, and by the time we'd put the M25 behind us and began to race along towards the port, we were having to run at about 70 miles per hour, or to put it another way, about ten miles per hour faster than Daisy's preferred rate of covering ground. With its firm, low suspension, the little car bounced along, sometimes emitting a tinny 'ding' as the exhaust glanced the road. The distance signs to Dover counted down and we were soon sure that we'd make it in time but the engine felt differently, and with twenty miles to go, we lost power and were restricted to about 60 miles per hour for the rest of the trip, as well as being subjected to a rather less appealing engine note. A dodgy valve? A cranky spark plug? We never did figure out the real reason why the engine would sometimes lose power when driven hard for any length of time, but it continued to do this for the entire trip to Turin and back, and could always be fixed by allowing the engine to cool down.

Still pushing hard despite our now limited top speed, we made the ferry with a few minutes to spare and met up with Brummy, who along with some friends, was coming along in his rather more sensible Peugeot 306.

I thought back to the previous New Year's trip in the breadbin Fiat, when we'd lost the yellow Fiat completely and ground to a halt a fair few times before we'd even made it out of the UK. The tradition of early car issues appeared to be continuing with the issues which Daisy had been throwing up, but through my twisted logic, I thrived on the problems. As far as I was concerned, they were what turned the trip into an adventure.

Anyone could get into a well maintained, reliable car – such as Brummy's Peugeot – and drive it to Turin for New Year, but I saw little point in doing so. It would be a fun trip, for sure, but where would the sense of achievement be? It was now eighteen months since I'd taken my first Mini on the Mongol Rally and ever since then, the sense of accomplishment which a journey provided was everything to me. The more problems we faced and the less likely success appeared, the greater that sense of accomplishment would become. That's why an untrustworthy old Mini was the perfect vehicle for me to take on a European road trip – it stripped out the routine assuredness of driving the European highways, and replaced it with an anarchic unpredictability.

In short, it put the adventure back into motoring.

But in many ways, I knew I couldn't cope with too much adventure. When it came to actually fixing cars I was still very inexperienced and deep down, I knew that it was luck as much as judgement which had got me through my previous drives. When I'd set off on the Mongol Rally, I barely owned any tools, and whilst I had an engineering degree which enabled me to understand basic problems in first principles, I was still a very long way from being able to confidently diagnose and fix issues with cars myself. I'd never so much as changed the oil on a car, let alone figured out some complicated breakdown on the Kazakh Steppe, and as I had nowhere to work on cars back home, I hadn't been in much of a position to learn. Behind the bravado and the 'keep buggering on' image which I projected to the outside world, I knew it was only blind luck which was getting me through these trips, and luck can only carry you so far. By definition, sooner or later it runs out.

*   *   *

We rolled off the ferry in convoy, Brummy's sombre, aquamarine blue Peugeot contrasting sharply against Daisy, whose chameleon-like paint had opted for diarrhoea over orange as its colour of choice in the dull winter light. And where did we decide to head, having just rolled onto the continent? Fontainebleau, of course. Or more specifically, to Bar le Bacchaus in Milly la Forêt, where a lock-in with Patrice was all but guaranteed and true to form, Laura and I from team Daisy, and Brummy, Ian, Libby and James from team Peugeot all saw in the early hours there, dancing behind the bar, notching up yet another night in Patrice's. For all our craving for adventure, we really were a rather predictable bunch sometimes.

From Fontainebleau we headed south to Méribel and then took the autoroute over the Alps to Turin. But it had all felt too easy. Brummy's TomTom had navigated us perfectly without any skill being required, Daisy had bounced its way along with only a bare minimum of problems and the presence of Brummy's dependable Peugeot meant we always had a safety net if something did go wrong. I'd wanted to tread the path at the edge of my comfort zone, overcoming problems yet never coming up against something which was beyond my limited mechanical ability. But other than the issues before we'd left, everything had gone swimmingly and it was almost with disappointment that I rolled into Turin and parked Daisy in the famous Plaza Castello which we'd seen in The Italian Job movie, and hence was a must visit for the Mini.

My dissatisfaction with the lack of peril in our trip was probably why I decided to turn up the wick on our continental trip for the return journey to England. Just as in Norway a year before, we had two options – we could either take a nice relaxed drive home, popping into Patrice's en route, or we could strike out east, turning our Italian Job homage into a lap of the Alps.

The choice was only ever going to have one outcome. We opted for the less sensible option, intent on squeezing some more adventure from our holiday by setting off across Italy on New Year's Day, stringing together some compelling destinations with further rolls of the road trip dice.

*　*　*

A chill wind blew through the canals of Venice, keeping the usual hordes of tourists at bay. The Rialto Bridge was almost deserted, the intricate charm of its arches barely softened by passers-by as the low sun cast its shadow far along the canal. The gondolas were mostly at rest, rocking gently as the waves passed them by, while over St Mark's Square, the sky opened up as an angular sheet of cold blue, framed by history. The open space was dotted with well-insulated tourists, huddled together in groups as they braved the low season, while those less inclined to battle the chill sought out the cosy warmth of a café. And all the while, the canals flowed lethargically by, the defining feature of this city without cars, rising from a lagoon half a continent from home.

The nearby Slovenian border presented no obstacle to our progress and we soon found ourselves in Bled, where snow blanketed the silent lands, falling in gentle flurries which swirled on the breeze like dust. The whiteness added a fairytale veneer to the perfect church which rose from the island on the lake, as well as the medieval castle that stood proud upon a rocky bluff high above.

But to me, as pleasant as Venice and Bled were, and as enjoyable as it was to be roaming these highpoints of culture and composition, the experience was leaving me strangely unfulfilled. It was still the journey, rather than the destinations, which I was hungry for. The adventure lay off the beaten track, in the places in between those made famous by guidebooks and documentaries. As much as I enjoyed the effortless appreciation of well-trodden places like Venice and Bled, deep within me I still burned for the unique thrill which only an immersive, edgy adventure could provide.

That's probably why instead of cruising back to the UK from Bled, I suggested we go to Croatia for lunch, and then carry on to Hungary for dinner. It was in no way rational, but I saw it as a way to expand the adventure, to broaden the scope of the achievement while introducing stresses which would guarantee a memorable end to the trip. It's why on the drive back through Austria I suggested we visit the tiny village which went by the rather unfortunate name of 'Fucking', rather than the country's more traditional tourist attractions; in my mind, the preposterous carried more kudos than the sublime. And it's why we ended up running the clock down on our pointless exploration of Central Europe so much that a forced 700 mile dash to catch the ferry was required, battling the elements, reliability and fatigue all the way, a dash we made with only minutes to spare.

The result of all this was that as we looked back upon the trip, it wasn't the dignified splendour of Venice which hung most cherished in our memories, nor the snow-softened beauty of Bled. It wasn't even the New Year's celebrations in Turin; no it was the sheer daftness of the drive home which stayed with us the longest. The silliness of driving to Fucking just because of its name, the weirdness of the service station conversations which happen when wired by coffee at 3am, the unlikeliness of completing the dash across Europe in a faltering Mini in time to catch the boat home.

The destinations were nice enough, but it was the journey, the unlikely vehicle and the seemingly irrational decisions which had elevated the trip to an adventure. They were what made our drive around Europe what we'd been looking for, and they'd brought Laura and I closer together as they did so.

TWENTY ONE

TO SAIGON

04th June 2013
Siam Reap, Cambodia

The alarm pierced the night rudely, jolting me awake. Swinging my arm out urgently, I grabbed my phone and silenced it. The light from the screen illuminated the unfamiliar room with a pale white light and I felt the momentary confusion of someone suddenly jolted from the dream world into the real one.

I glanced at the clock on my phone's screen. It was four in the morning.

Time to get up. Elsewhere in the hostel room, I could hear Brummy and Laura already moving about, beginning to prepare for a day whose dawn was still hours away. Muffled by the night, a gecko's nocturnal cries rose to their usual crescendo, somewhere across the street.

We went to the hostel's kitchen where we each drank a coffee, none of us saying much as sleep continued to sit heavily upon our minds, our thought processes still slowed to a crawl. And then we wandered out of the hostel into the still-warm night where my ever faithful companion, the Corvette, was sat in the street waiting for us.

Laura climbed into the back of the 'vette, lying with her legs stretching forward across the centre console, while Brummy and I occupied the two seats. It took some time for us to all get aboard, but once the doors were shut I fired up the motor, flipped up the headlights and set off across the deserted city of Siam Reap, as the first glow of the coming day crept across the eastern horizon. Three in a 'vette wasn't exactly the most comfortable way to travel, but we weren't going far, and the objective more than justified the hardship.

The sunrise was 40 minutes away, and the incomparable temples of Angkor Wat were just down the road.

Watching the sun rise over the temples of Angkor Wat is a cliché of the travel world. When it comes to predictability, it ranks somewhere up there with taking a camel ride at the Egyptian Pyramids, or being punted through Venice's Grand Canal in a gondola. But things don't become popular without good reason, right? We'd woken early, crammed three in a 'vette and then sneaked it into the temple complex to find out.

The lightening of the eastern sky had built to an electric blue by the time we'd parked among the buses and taxis next to the main causeway to the temple. A crowd was already there, gazing out towards the iconic buildings in a buzz of hushed excitement, cameras held at the ready with both hands. Looking for a quieter area, we wandered away from the car park and found ourselves down by the moat beneath the towering silhouettes of two palm trees, with a clear view of Angkor Wat piercing the sky in the middle distance. And there, we waited.

The watery blue stretched over half the sky now, and above the temples there hung a few portents of the rainy season, their grey bulk outlined gently with violets and pinks. We were close to the equator and so sunrise came rapidly, the hues changing with every passing minute as the sky lightened. The world around us was gradually coloured in by the coming day, and then the sun rose high enough to meet our eyes, glinting from behind the ancient towers and sending shafts of light streaking into the gasping, camera-clicking crowd.

I'll acknowledge that it wasn't a bad way to start the day but was it something which justifies its inclusion on every single list of You Only Live Once, bucket list compilations? I'm not convinced. Just like those posed-on-a-camel photos by the Pyramids, watching sunrise at Angkor Wat struck me as one of those experiences which had been carried beyond its intrinsic value by its own hype.

That's not to say the temples themselves aren't anything to write home about, of course – the complex isn't routinely described as the eighth wonder of the world for nothing, and once the sunrise circus has dissipated around the vast site, it can hold its head high in any company - just don't feel like you have to get up at four in the morning to do it justice.

The Temple of Angkor Wat over which we'd watched the sun rise is certainly a sight to behold. Its name translates as 'Temple City', a most fitting appellation for what is the largest religious building on Earth, occupying a site which covers over 400 acres and is surrounded by a moat 190 metres wide that stretches for over three miles as it makes its lap of the temple's grounds. But this is only a small fraction of what lies scattered amongst the jungles to the north of Siam Reap. For instance, there's the fortified city of Angkor Thom, which was the last capital of the Khmer Empire, and the trippy, enigmatic temple of Bayon, which rises within its walls. Nearby is the 'Tomb Raider Temple' of Ta Prohm, where centuries-old trees still clutch at the ruins, transporting you some of the way back to how they looked before restoration efforts got underway. And scattered around the jungle are many more surreal structures, all ornately detailed with bas-reliefs depicting life eight hundred years ago.

For that was when the Khmer Empire reached its zenith, and its capital was here, in the city of Angkor – a place which could boast a population of a million when London was still a sleepy backwater of 50,000 souls. From here military campaigns were launched, trade pursued vigorously and Gods worshipped on an industrial scale. But of the enormous population whose lives facilitated this, little evidence remains. According to Khmer custom, only the Gods had the right to reside in buildings constructed of stone; mere mortals were permitted only the shelter of wooden dwellings. And so, when the Empire finally succumbed at the end of several long centuries of decline, and the jungle reclaimed the city as the years drifted past, it was only the stone temples which survived to tell the story of this great civilisation. What remains is truly a monument to the Gods, and a fitting one at that.

For several days we rolled around the vast site in the Corvette, marvelling at the sheer level of effort and detail which had been put into even the most seemingly mundane construction. Every man-made surface was covered in sculptures and murals, from the 212 enormous faces which stared out from the Bayon temple, to the smallest pieces of intricate stone carving which jewelled apparently inconsequential walls and walkways.

If the Khmer had put their efforts into conquest instead of stone carving, they surely would have taken over the whole planet with armies to spare. As it is, they still oversaw an empire which stretched from Burma to Vietnam and dominated this corner of the planet for over half a millennium.

When not roaming the jungle-besieged monuments of history, we spent our time in the new city of Siam Reap, where the tourist industry is life. Souvenir shops were scattered liberally along every street; restaurants, bars, hostels and hotels provided the filling between them. And the streets were walked by tourists from the four corners of the Earth, money flowing from their wallets to fuel the growth of the city into a giant of global tourism. They arrived and left in a continuous cycle, circulating through the busy airport and bus station as they ticked off another spot on their South East Asian itineraries, before zooming off to the next destination; Bangkok, Saigon, Singapore, Phuket.

Clearly word of this eighth wonder of the world had got out, and life in this corner of Cambodia would never be the same again.

The tourism-focussed development hit its apogee in the centre of town, where we stumbled upon the rather appealingly named 'Pub Street'. Though this clearly isn't a traditional Cambodian moniker, the locals still seemed pretty proud of it, hanging a large neon sign across the road bearing its name – just in case the multitude of drinking establishments didn't make it clear exactly where in town you were. One evening we took the Corvette down to Pub Street for some photos, and chatted about our plans in a restaurant while we were there.

'So, it was seven years ago that we had the idea for V8Nam while sat in a pub in Plymouth, and now here we are in Pub Street on the other side of the world,' I said.

'Yeah, you couldn't make it up, could you?' said Laura.

'Well you probably could've predicted it,' I replied. 'I am rather partial to drives which end up in the pub, after all.'

'So are you going to take the Corvette to a Vietnamese pub?' asked Brummy.

'I've been thinking about that,' I said. 'Given we're going to buy motorbikes and ride them across Vietnam, it seems kind of pointless taking the Corvette across the border. Especially as there's a good chance it could still be stuck there two weeks later.'

'Wuss,' said Brummy.

'Sensible,' said I.

Where the Corvette was concerned, the Vietnamese border had been a question mark ever since we'd left the UK. Information was sketchy, but as far as we'd been able to gather, it had been closed to foreign cars until just before our trip, and while it may have been theoretically possible to take a foreign-registered vehicle in, we'd been hearing stories of cars getting trapped in No-Man's-Land for weeks by the complex bureaucracy, along with the fact that no-one seemed to know quite whether bringing a car in was genuinely 100% legal yet. Brummy and Laura each had only a limited amount of time left before they had to fly home, and the prospect of spending that time stuck between international borders wasn't an appealing one. So, after much deliberation I decided to leave the Corvette in Cambodia and continue overland to Saigon to complete the land-based journey from England to the South China Sea.

The Corvette's adventure was to continue however, as rather than finishing in Vietnam, I'd decided to extend the trip by a few thousand miles. Singapore was now the final destination. I still had one hurdle to cross in making my plans a reality, however. As we chatted the evening away in the restaurant on Pub Street, the conversation drifted onto the subject, which revolved around two things: Vietnam, and motorbikes.

'Anyway, what makes you think I'm going to ride across Vietnam on a motorbike?' asked Brummy. 'I never agreed to that. In fact, what part of 'sod that' didn't you understand, last time we discussed it?'

'You'll do it,' I replied. 'You've never said no to any of these daft ideas before.'

'But I've never ridden a motorbike in my life,' he said. 'I'll probably die.'

'I've never ridden one either, and neither had Clarkson when Top Gear did it,' I replied. 'It'll be fine.'

'Of course it will, because I'm not doing it.'

'Yes you are. Let's have this conversation later, after a few more beers. Then we can chink on it.' I said.

And predictably, later that evening when the Dutch courage of another few bottles of Chang beer had taken effect, a reluctant Brummy agreed to our own version of the 'Vietnam Special.' But first, we had to get to Vietnam, which was still several hundred miles away.

I spoke to the people who were running the place in which we were staying and they agreed that for the rather agreeable price of about a dollar a day, I could leave the Corvette there for a few weeks while we were in Vietnam, and so we started to look into arranging transport for our final leg to Saigon. Given I'd completed the whole journey from England overland, I refused to fly at this late stage, and so our only real option was an overnight bus. We boarded such a vehicle late one evening, Vietnam bound. Inside the bus, all the seats had been stripped out and in their place a series of what were effectively bunk beds had been fitted. Safe and relaxing it wasn't, but cheap it most certainly was. With a diesel rumble and the whine from the gearbox rising through the floor below, we got underway through the Cambodian night.

It was a disconcerting way to travel. The noise and vibrations from the bus would lull you to sleep, only to be offset by the jolting of potholes, or the sudden deceleration as the bus slowed for some unseen obstacle. We rolled through the Cambodian night neither awake nor asleep, in a bus which echoed to the snores of the old hands of the overnight bus world, and the fidgeting of newcomers like us.

It was two in the morning when we reached Phnom Penh, where we stopped for a while to stretch our legs. We wandered around the darkened bus depot on the edge of town in a fatigued stupor. It brought to mind the surreal caffeine stops that had taken place during the headlong dashes through the night, which had characterised our European road trips years before.

However this time, our fate wasn't in our own hands. The chain-smoking bus driver beckoned us all back onboard, for the drive to the Vietnamese border.

Our first glimpse of Vietnam took place beneath a lightening sky, at a border post which was overcome by the lassitude that infects anyone who is forced to be awake against their will at six in the morning. We drifted across into Vietnam on autopilot, our bags checked by customs, our passports stamped. And then we boarded another bus to the town we'd planned our journey to all those years before, when V8Nam was first dreamed up.

Saigon.

The bus rolled along the last stretch of the road towards the city and I stared through the window, mulling over what the journey meant to me.

Although this was not the end of the journey – I wouldn't reach Singapore for two more months – it was still an end of sorts. The end point of the V8Nam dream which Lee had thought up in the pub all those years before. As these journeys had now been a part of my life for seven years, there was always the danger that the sense of accomplishment would fade with each successful adventure, but that didn't seem to be happening just yet. The pride I'd felt on the completion of the Mongol Rally and the African Porsche Expedition was still there; a pride which was directly proportional to the amount of time and effort which had gone into making the accomplishment happen. But this sense of accomplishment was now part of a cycle, as my life now flowed through a continuous series of trips, more frequent smaller ones interspersed with periodic larger adventures, which grew from small acorns to dominate my life for a period, before being vanquished by success.

The city was all around us now, and the bus moved ponderously along the busy streets as a million little motorbikes darted around it, like shoals of fish around a cargo ship. Buildings grew upwards; the web of cables fanning out from telegraph poles across the road thickened to a tangled web. We were nearly there.

Laura turned to me and asked, 'so, that's Africa in a Porsche and Asia in a Corvette done. What's next? The Pan-American?'

'I'm not thinking that far ahead, I replied. 'Right now, I just fancy a trip to the bar.'

And so that evening, 72 days after leaving the UK, we headed up to the sky bar on the 23rd floor of the Saigon Sheridan Hotel and toasted our achievement with mojitos as the sun set over the city we'd dreamed of travelling to, all those years before.

TWENTY TWO

FIRE AND ICE

03rd October 2008
Plymouth, UK

On the surface of it, the decision to drive my battered old Porsche 944 across Africa owes little to any rational thought process, but in the twisted reality which I'd been inhabiting since completing the Mongol Rally, it was so logical a course of action as to be almost inevitable. I'd completed the Rally and several other smaller adventures, and I was riding a wave as a result. Confident, ambitious and eager to up the ante, I was always looking for a way to take my road tripping up to the next level, which two years after the Mongol Rally meant I wanted to do something which other people didn't, and with a drive across Asia already behind me, there was only one obvious venue – Africa. And as for the car, well I'd already owned the old Porsche for five years, and so it had little chance of escaping some far-flung fate. It made perfect sense for it to be the focus of the adventure.

I was sure the idea was the perfect way to take this newfound hobby of mine to new heights. To cross Africa in a Porsche! The thought was real next level stuff; the sort of adventure people wrote books about. In fact I'd already decided that if the drive was successful, I was going to write a book about it, and on my return from the southern tip of the continent, that's exactly what I sat down to do.

Up until then, I'd never written anything creative in my life, my literary experience being limited to such non-masterpieces as my university dissertation about the design of ships' hulls. But Africa! The things we'd seen, the problems we'd overcome, the way we'd pulled through against the odds; it was a story which had to be put down on paper and so one day, about a month after getting home,

I poured an Ardbeg whisky, opened up Microsoft Word, and began to write.

What followed was every bit as much of a stride out of my comfort zone as the trip itself.

To write a book is to bear your soul; it is to strip away any pretence and say to the world, 'this is who I am, and this is what I do'. And of course in doing so, in putting so much time and effort into something and then putting it out there for the world to see, you risk coming up short if it's not good enough. It's as daunting a challenge as crossing a continent, only the struggle is internal. It takes place in your mind during those long hours sat at a desk, and is fought out on the unforgiving whiteness of the computer screen.

As I got to grips with the challenge, I lived the struggle. I agonised over every comma and spent hours hunting for the perfect adjectives as I strove to find my own style which would carry me through the coming 100,000 words. And as I found my flow, my stuttering progress smoothed out and my confidence increased. On some days everything seemed to align and the writing process would feel blissfully effortless, the sentences appearing on the screen seemingly automatically. But on other days it would be too much. Every word would feel hard won, as if I was dredging up the prose from a dusty and neglected corner of my mind. It was on those days that the writer's life seemed a step beyond me, and the thoughts of futility grew. But I kept telling myself that as long as I kept putting one word after another, I'd get there in the end and sure enough, nine months after I'd sat down to write *Survival of the Quickest*, I had a first draft. That was when the really scary moment had arrived, as I could hide no more. Friends and family were eager to read it, and I couldn't escape the judgement of the world any longer. I had to bare my soul.

Luckily for me, the feedback which I received from that first draft was mostly positive.

It was a huge relief, as while the first draft of *Survival of the Quickest* wasn't remotely perfect – first drafts never are – I hadn't just wasted a large chunk of my life writing something worthy only of the bin. With my psyche restored after its gradual wearing down over the previous nine months, I moved onto the next stage – editing the tome. Once again I agonised over every word, chipping away at the roughness of the text to round off the edges, smooth the flow of the story and make it into something which I hoped strangers would enjoy spending hours of their lives reading. Because let's face it, while it's uplifting to hear that your friends and family enjoyed reading something you'd poured your life into, it's kind of their job to say that, isn't it?

Ultimately, this polishing took longer than the writing, and while the first draft was completed at the end of 2009, it would be several more years and six different drafts before I was confident enough in what I'd written to allow it to face the world. That's not to say I spent all those years after getting back from Africa sat at a desk with only strong coffee and Microsoft Word for company, though. No, adventures were still on the agenda, albeit adventures which were rather different to what had gone before.

While the drive across Africa had taken place during the Great Financial Crisis of 2008, being on the road far from the world's financial centres had meant we were largely insulated from its effects during the trip. However, the expedition book was very much written against the backdrop of its aftermath. At the time, I was a self-employed marine surveyor and work was down, which was a blessing from the book's perspective as it meant I actually had the free time to write and edit it. However the lack of cash didn't exactly lend itself to making any other big future adventures happen. The three months I'd spent in Africa had cost close to £10,000 all in, and it would be a long time until I'd be able to commit to another similarly expensive undertaking, and as a medical student, my co-driver Laura wasn't exactly flush with cash either.

However, that didn't mean we had to reign in our adventurous spirit; rather, we simply had to make the adventures fit our newly shrunken budget. And that's how, eighteen months after getting back from Africa we found ourselves on a budget flight to the land of fire, ice and expensive beer – Iceland. But this time, the adventure wouldn't be taking place behind a steering wheel as in the plane's hold, packed into cardboard boxes, were a couple of mountain bikes which we'd bought a month previously, in a fit of enthusiasm.

Now, I'm no cyclist. I never have been. Generally, I'd rather be driving, of course, but when it comes to exercising in the outdoors, I've always considered Gore-Tex to be way more stylish than Lycra and given the choice, I'd always opted for a climbing helmet over its cycling equivalent. Better a day up in the hills rather than one down on the cycle paths, I used to say authoritatively. Or so it was until Laura and I were discussing what our next adventure should be, and I begrudgingly accepted that if the question is 'four weeks' and 'Iceland', the answer is 'cycle touring'.

This had presented a bit of a problem, as I hadn't ridden a bike in over a decade. I wasn't alone in that though, because Laura had precious little recent experience either. As an additional complication, my hope that we'd opt for an adventure which would give me an excuse to buy another car meant it had taken us so long to finally accept that the answer was 'cycle touring', that we only had three weeks to get everything in place before our departure to Iceland.

Those three weeks became a frenzy of activity. Routes were planned optimistically, without the slightest clue as to what we were letting ourselves in for. Websites giving cycling advice were repeatedly read and taken as gospel. Kit lists were made, and while fortunately much of our existing outdoor kit proved perfectly suited to cycle touring, each of us still had to splash out on a shiny new bike, a couple of panniers, helmet, tools, spares and - most important of all – padded pants. After blowing away the cobwebs with a somewhat wobbly eight mile ride around the New Forest, the bikes were boxed up and we headed off to the airport.

For this first foray into the world of engineless road trips, we planned to follow Iceland's famous Route-1 anti-clockwise around most of the island, before returning through the barren interior, a distance of around 850 miles. It didn't bode well when our plans were put temporarily on hold at mile zero when I somehow managed to get a puncture on Reykjavík's immaculate campground. However, soon the inner tube was changed, twenty kilograms of kit and supplies were strapped to each bike and away we went, wobbling through the city traffic.

And so began my first ever day as a cyclist. It wasn't a gentle introduction, as Route One rushed straight into a range of hills to the east of Reykjavík. On more than one occasion as we slogged uphill, both Laura and I wondered why on earth we'd ever thought we could pedal around Iceland, and it was a pair of very tired and demoralised cyclists who coasted down to the town of Hveragerði that evening.

However over the following days our fitness improved as we gradually adjusted to life in the saddle, away from the comforting shelter of a car. We found that cycle touring in Iceland was a different world to anything either of us had experienced before. A surreal world where it never got dark, the sun merely brushing the horizon for a few hours each night. A primeval world of endless lava flows and bleak oceans of volcanic ash. An angry world of headwinds, cloudbursts and steaming vents. And often, a painful world of tortured legs and sore posteriors.

But above all, as we settled into the routine, it became a world of glorious simplicity, where the sum of our existence each day was to wake up, pack away the tent, and then pedal until we could pedal no more.

During our first few days on the road we made reasonable progress along Iceland's south coast, passing the infamous and unpronounceable Eyjarfjallsjökull volcano – which hid in the clouds, showing no remorse for the chaos it had caused to European air travellers when it had erupted a few months earlier – and crossing endless plains of ash and lava flows.

But in those early days, every mile seemed hard-won. We'd spend whole days pedalling along into a stern headwind, which picked up the volcanic ash and drove it into our faces for hours on end, almost breaking us mentally as we regretted not opting to take a car. On one occasion the wind and ash was joined by a freezing rain squall, and with hypothermia looming we were forced to stop, pitch the tent and warm ourselves up with sleeping bags and cups of tea, before our chill state took us past the point of no return. Every day was a new challenge; every mile felt like an achievement. Every moment in the back of our minds there existed a doubt; *maybe we can't do this*.

In those early days, we'd check our progress on the map in the tent each evening and the enormity of the challenge would hit us, as the slowness of our progress became apparent. At the speed we were going, every day's drive would have taken us less than an hour if we were cocooned comfortably in a car, heater on and music turned up. And given our slow progress, we knew we had no chance of completing the lap of the island, and so we decided to just push on as far as we could. After all, we could always get a bus back to Reykjavik.

Five days on the road saw us reaching Vatnajökull – the largest icecap in Europe. Home of Iceland's highest peak, Vatnajökull is an imposing swathe of whiteness which measures 80 miles across, beneath which several active volcanoes are buried, and from whose glistening dome countless glaciers tumble down to the road. It took three days for us to cycle past the icecap, and so awe-inspiring were the views that I was almost tempted to plan a return with an ice axe and crampons in the future.

Halfway along the icecap, we camped on the shores of the Jökulsárlón Lagoon, in the most stunning location in which I've ever pitched a tent. On the northern edge of the lagoon, a glacier flowed down from the ice cap, spilling into the water and choking the lagoon with a thousand densely packed icebergs. We spent the evening of our arrival drinking tea in silence, listening to chunks of ice falling from the distant glacier as the midnight sun floated just beyond the horizon.

The following day, we completed the 65 miles to the metropolis of Höfn. We'd convinced ourselves it must be a metropolis, as we'd been seeing signs for the place for the previous week. But alas, we still had much to learn about Iceland. With somewhat less than 2,000 residents, Höfn turned out to be a pleasant fishing village, which rather sums up how unpopulated Iceland is – a country the size of England, but with only 300,000 inhabitants. Blissfully empty and quiet. Except for the rather uncouth '80s Camaro which spent the whole evening driving around the town in noisy laps, that is.

Following a rather modest night on the town which left me feeling confused and conflicted – as I'd never in my life felt jealous of anyone driving a Camaro before – we pedalled our way through the Eastfjords, battling a stiff, demoralising headwind for two days running. But still, the scenery made up for it – rugged mountains that would put the Isle of Skye to shame tumbled down to the churning ocean while further inland, the occasional glacier still edged its way into our vision.

The halfway point of our lap of the island was the town of Egilsstaðir, and we reached it with a long day on the saddle – 55 miles into the wind, with a 540 metre high gravel pass thrown in for good measure. Our numbers were improving, and for the first time, we started to contemplate that maybe, just maybe, we could do this after all. Satisfied with how much our fitness had improved in the previous 400 miles of suffering, we threw caution to the wind and celebrated extravagantly that evening, dining out on pizza at the town's petrol station.

From Egilsstaðir, we continued to circumnavigate the island, looping back towards Reykjavík. The Northern Highlands were next and the overcast skies, biting wind and rolling winds initially felt like Dartmoor on a bad day. Fortunately, the biting wind was coming from behind us for once, enabling us to cover 30 miles without pedalling before the road took a turn to the north, resulting in a crosswind which blew us clean off our bikes. Unable to ride, we were forced to walk the bikes for miles until we found a spot sufficiently sheltered for us to pitch the tent.

The active volcano at Krafla was next on our route, offering the chance to explore the still-steaming lava flows and then take a stroll around the Viti Crater, which houses a 220 metre deep pool of the sharpest turquoise. After fifteen days in the saddle, we had our first rest day of the trip at Lake Mývaten - home to more species of duck than you can shake a pair of binoculars at - then another few days pedalling took us to the small settlement of Varmahlíð from where, with five days worth of supplies strapped to our steeds, we got to grips with the most challenging section of our expedition.

Rising 700 metres above the coastal plains, Iceland's barren interior plateau is the very epitome of the remote; a stark landscape of brooding icecaps and geological turmoil into which the modern world has yet to intrude. The harsh sub-Arctic climate has kept the interior uninhabited save for a few hardy sheep, and humanity's only permanent mark on the landscape is provided by a few rough gravel tracks crisscrossing the epic swathe of nothingness. It was along one of these - the Kjölur route - which we aimed to make our crossing.

Finally feeling fit from so long in the saddle, we climbed the 700 metres onto the plateau easily, forsaking the green farmlands of the coast for a barren plain, dotted with lakes. Our first night in the interior was spent camping on a lakeshore, the only people for miles around.

We cycled onwards through a barren wilderness, the track rising and falling with the landscape as the two mighty icecaps on the horizon seemed to slowly drift towards us. There was little conventional beauty in our empty surroundings, no points of interest to draw the eye and provide perspective. But the appeal of the landscape stemmed directly from its emptiness. In the over cluttered, fussy world we live in, there is a magnificent drama to be found in infinite desolation.

The end of our second day in the interior saw us halfway across the wilderness and we pitched our tent next to the hot springs at Hveravellir, between the two icecaps.

The following morning brought – just for a change – a biting wind and heavy rain showers. Our attempt to press on was brought to an end about twenty miles down the rough gravel track, when we became so cold and wet that pitching the tent and drinking tea seemed the only rational option. Fortunately, with supplies running low, our fourth day at the interior's mercy offered some respite, enabling us to reach our first tarmac in 120 miles.

We coasted down to the stunning waterfall at Gullfoss and then on to the geothermal dramas of Geysir – the site after which all geysers are named - all the time feeling a little disorientated by our sudden return to the tourist trail. Our final run into Reykjavík was Iceland's last opportunity to prevent us from completing our mission, and it tried its best, for two days straight blocking our way with mushrooming thunderstorms which unleashed torrents of rain upon us, and pumped lightning bolts into the ground less than half a mile away as we pedalled along nervously, willing our month long ordeal to end.

And then end it did, as we joined the dual carriageway for the final run into Reykjavík and returned to the campsite where it had all began, 23 days before.

Showered and sat in an immaculate bar a day later, we reflected on the trip over a well-earned beer. It had been tough. We'd found there was no such thing as an easy day's cycling in Iceland; the terrain and weather somehow always conspired to find a way of make things difficult. Especially in the beginning when our fitness was lacking, it had often taken all of our willpower and determination to keep pushing on, day after day, against it all.

But from the comfort of the bar, the bad memories were already fading as the warm glow of achievement grew. Iceland hadn't disappointed us. We'd come looking for an adventure, and we had certainly found what we were looking for.

As our drinks emptied and we chatted away, our thoughts were already drifting towards the next adventure.

'So, is this the start of something new for you?' Laura asked. 'Lots more two wheeled adventures to come?'

'No chance,' I replied. 'That was horrible. I'm finished with two wheeled adventures now. Never again.'

TWENTY THREE

THE VIETNAM SPECIAL

13ᵗʰ June 2013
Hanoi, Vietnam

I stood outside the travellers' hostel next to the sorry-looking two wheeled steed, holding it upright with my right hand, unsure of what to do next. I'd just paid $300 for the motorbike in a fit of enthusiasm for a bike trip from Hanoi to Saigon, but as I stood there it dawned on me that actually, I had no idea how to ride the thing.

What was I thinking? I thought to myself, as the sun raged down onto the hot metal handlebars and the baking black vinyl which covered its seat. I remembered the last time I'd done anything on two wheels. It was almost three years ago, amid the cold winds and mesmerising views of Iceland. Clearly, I hadn't learned my lesson.

I looked over the bike's controls, piecing together how it worked. I knew the leaver on the left handlebar was the clutch, and the strange-looking footrest was actually a gear selector. The brake was on the right handlebar, as was the twist throttle. My knowledge of how this contraption worked was coming together, and I began to see how it would be possible to make it move. Except for one thing.

I had no idea how to start the engine.

It clearly wasn't a kick-start, and turning the key did nothing. After being outwitted for several minutes as I failed to figure out the conundrum, I sheepishly wandered over to the hostel and asked if anyone knew anything about bikes.

'Yeah, what's up?' replied a backpacker, in a thick Yorkshire accent.

'I, erm, I don't know how to start it.' I replied.

'Ere, I'll show ya,' came the response.

My newly found – and rather drunk – mentor ran me through the controls before pointing out the starter button on the handlebars.

'Damn, I thought that was the horn,' I pointed out. Which was true, actually. But it didn't convince anyone in earshot of my competence.

'Are you sure you'll be reet riding back t'hotel?' Asked the Yorkshire backpacker, as I climbed onto the bike, donned the far-too-small helmet and prepared to cruise nonchalantly back across town.

'Sure,' I said. 'How hard can it be?'

Thinking back to the rickshaw controls, I turned the throttle to rev the engine, clunked it into first gear with my foot, and let out the clutch. The little 100cc bike responded by leaping forwards much more urgently than I was expecting. Taken by surprise, I jumped off the surging device in an act of pure self preservation, and watched as it fell onto its side and went skittering down the street. As one, the crowd which was gathered in the afternoon sun with their beers erupted in laughter and applause, as I rushed over to right the stricken machine.

I don't think I've ever looked less heroic than I did at that exact moment.

My second attempt to pull away went a little better and I managed to get moving at just over walking pace, with the little bike buzzing away angrily in first gear. It could buzz angrily in first gear all it liked though, there was no way I was going to attempt the change to second. All I wanted was to get the damn thing back to the hotel, park it somewhere out of sight and go for a cold beer, and so I wobbled uncertainly through the churning traffic of Hanoi's old quarter in a terrified panic until I reached the salvation of the hotel.

There, I met up with Brummy, who'd just undergone a somewhat less embarrassing baptism of fire, following the purchase of his 110cc Honda Wave. Both somewhat nervous as to what our immediate futures might hold, we headed straight to the bar.

'How's yours?' I asked him.

'It's a great little thing,' he replied. 'In fact, I'd go so far as to say it's the Rolls-Royce of motorbikes.'

'There's no such thing,' I said. 'I've already decided that all motorbikes are hellish things which want only to kill you.'

'Not a fan of yours then?'

'Nope. In fact I've already named it The Little Bastard,' I replied. 'Why oh why didn't I bring the Corvette across the border, instead of buying that two wheeled piece of crap?'

'I told you buying bikes was a terrible idea,' replied Brummy. 'But did you listen?'

Of course I hadn't, and suffice to say at the start line of our planned 1,200 mile journey across Vietnam, things weren't going well. In fact, I would even have considered the decision to fly up to Hanoi and buy bikes to ride back to Saigon to have been a mistake, were it not for the evidence all around us.

In Vietnam, the motorcycle is king. The country is home to over twenty million of them, and they meet almost all the transportation needs of the nation's 87 million people. This means that if you're not on a bike, you're going nowhere fast. They flow down every street in shoals, moving together around obstacles or less agile vehicles such as buses and cars. They're pressed into service as delivery vehicles, transporting everything from construction materials to livestock. They function as family transport, and seeing four or five people on a single bike is a pretty common sight. They're status symbols, ambulances, heirlooms and anything else you can think of, and they provide the pulse to which the Vietnamese nation lives.

Our bike trip may have got off to a laughably bad start, but it was the right decision. If you *really* want to see Vietnam, two wheels are the only way to go.

Worryingly, the trip didn't get any more auspicious the next day, when we set off on the long journey south. Rush hour was in full swing as we joined the thousands of other bikes on the main road out of town. My clutch control was still jerky at best, and wasn't helped by the fact the clutch itself had begun to slip, but I found that once I was part of the traffic stream, with all the other bikes flowing along with me, it wasn't too difficult to make progress – just focus on not hitting any of the other bikes and all is good.

Unless you break down, of course.

I'd managed to cover a grand total of three miles before the first breakdown occurred, the bike losing power before the engine cut out. I slowed to a halt in the middle of the road, the twelve-wide flow of other bikes parting around me before reforming their tight formation further on. I tried to restart the engine, but it wouldn't fire, and so I had no choice but to set about the biggest challenge of the V8Nam Expedition so far – getting the bike to the side of the road. As I pushed it along, drifting to the right towards the safety of the kerb, half of Hanoi continued to come rushing past me on their fully functional bikes, beeping or shouting at me rather than slowing down. A few of them almost clipped me as they left their avoidance to the last minute, and it took several minutes of stop-start pushing to get the bike to the kerb.

Whereupon it fired up immediately, at the first push of the starter.

Brummy had already disappeared off up the road and so I set off in pursuit, breaking down a second time, and then a third time, before catching him.

'What took you?' he asked, waiting for me by the side of the road, just out of the city.

'The Little Bastard is living up to its name,' I said.

'You should have got a Honda Wave,' he replied. 'The Rolls-Royce of bikes. Now come on, let's get moving. It's still a long way to that Ninh Binh place.'

With The Little Bastard finally behaving itself, I began to settle into life in the saddle. Progress was certainly far easier than it had been during the pedal-powered Iceland ordeal, but that's not to say it was even remotely comfortable. After a few hours, the seat became rock hard and the helmet which came with the bike was far too small for me, meaning it dug into my forehead, leaving a bruise. However, the worst pain of that first day was reserved for the back of my hands. In the frantic efforts to get ready for the trip, I'd neglected to apply any sun cream to them, and the sun beat down relentlessly onto them all day. By the time I reached the evening's hotel, two layers of skin were done for, with a deep burning pain serving as a reminder not to make the same mistake again.

Suffice to say, I wasn't particularly enjoying my initiation into the world of motorcycling.

However, things improved as I got used to the bike, and my prospects of surviving the planned 1,200 mile ride from Hanoi to Saigon increased dramatically. For several days we swept down Highway One towards the bullet-scarred city of Hue, dodging buses and trucks as we joined the flow of local bikes and got used to our slow life on the open road, swerving around the pushbikes and donkey-carts, but being treated with a relative distain by everything else. However, despite our better progress, life with the bikes hadn't suddenly become smooth and routine. My starting issues continued, with The Little Bastard often dying for no apparent reason and remaining inert for five or ten minutes before it could be coaxed back into life, though this issue paled in comparison to just how painful it is sitting on a tiny bike for hours on end, as our purchases weren't exactly designed with long range touring in mind. We quickly learned that covering any more than 100 miles in a day turned the ride into an exercise in pain management, an aspect made worse by just how slowly the hours ticked past.

For the previous 12,000 miles and three months, I'd been covering the miles quickly, effortlessly and painlessly in the Corvette, but suddenly I'd found myself in a situation where progressing a mere 30 miles meant an hour's painful ride, cooking under the sun. However there were a few benefits to being on a bike. Fuel costs ran to about £3 a day, while 500 miles down the road in Hue when a trip to a garage was called for, a new clutch, a full service and some other fettling came in at the equivalent of £11 – a definite improvement on the Corvette's appetite for burning through money.

South of Hue, on the way to Da Nang, the road changed. Mountains forced the previously straight Highway One closer and closer to the coast, until it was pushed up and over the undulations, clinging to the precipitous hillside as it rose high above the azure sea. The twists and hairpins piled up on top of one another as we climbed through the mountains and for the first time in my life, I was flying along a fantastic driving road on two wheels. While my tiny 100cc Honda was a far cry from being the bike of choice for such a road, it was still great fun to ride as hard as I dared along the fantastic strip of tarmac. From never having ridden a motorbike five days previously, I was finally beginning to find some confidence, leaning into corners and banging up and down the gears at each hairpin in an urgent manner which still somehow approached smoothness. On that twenty mile tangle of tarmac perfection, I experienced first-hand why, to some people, two wheels are the only way to enjoy the roads.

Following a rest day in the preserved old town of Hoi An we headed inland, joining the Ho Chi Minh Trail which snakes south through the Vietnamese Highlands towards Saigon. These lightly trafficked mountain roads offered a further opportunity to get the hammer down and we continued to enjoy hustling our tiny steeds through the twists and over the hills, and also through the odd tropical downpour, which would always put a halt to the fun – although even in the worst weather, the sight of Brummy in his $1 poncho could still raise a laugh. We spent almost a week crossing the highlands, passing dusty villages, flooded rice paddies and bulging hills while spending the nights staying in remote towns, far from the tourist trail. We'd cross high bridges and gaze down upon floating villages far below, and drone through dense jungle as the sun sank to our right, and the sky turned golden.

Our ride across the highlands wasn't totally idyllic however, as pretty much every day saw one of our bikes breaking down and predictably, it was usually mine which 'failed to proceed'. On one occasion, I was riding along when the sump plug decided to fall out of the motor, depositing all the oil onto a stretch of mottled tarmac in the middle of nowhere. On another occasion, my handlebars came loose, leaving me without much in the way of steering, but the winning issue was probably the time The Little Bastard's chain came off the sprockets and jammed against the frame, locking up the rear wheel. I was doing 40 mph at the time, and so I was rather lucky that I didn't come off the bike and end up a rather reddened mess. In total the bikes suffered twelve breakdowns during their journey across Vietnam, though usually they cost no more than a pound or two to put right at the many small roadside garages spread throughout the country, and as I result I guess they rather added to the adventure. Because after all, riding the length of Vietnam isn't supposed to be easy, right?

Two weeks and 1,200 miles after leaving Hanoi, we crossed our fingers that the breakdowns were over as we dropped out of the cool mountains and re-entered the world of tropical heat on the final run-in to Saigon. As the city traffic thickened around us we bustled our way through the melee with a confidence that I couldn't have imagined a few weeks previously, when I took my first faltering steps into the world of motorcycling. Soon, we were back in the bar on the 23rd floor of the Sheraton Hotel, toasting our second road trip to finish in Saigon in three weeks, as the city's two million motorbikes swarmed through the dusty streets far below. And as Brummy and I chinked our beers together with satisfaction, I only had two words to say on the subject of two wheeled adventuring: 'Never again.'

TWENTY FOUR

HUNTER'S MOON

10ᵗʰ April 2011
Shaugh Prior, Dartmoor, UK

The lean years which followed the African Porsche Expedition drifted to memory, as the world's financial engines began to get back into gear following the 2008 Great Financial Crisis. The cargo ships began to arrive in the ports of South West England with increasing frequency and with them, my survey work picked up, meaning I could once again afford vehicles with more than two wheels, and so thoughts could return to those dreams which had been lingering untouched for the previous years. Dreams of cars and travel.

While I was certainly in no position to rush into making the omnipresent idea of the V8Nam drive happen, I was still able to indulge in my passion for cars. And it needed indulging. Daisy the Mini had been taken off the road in dire need of a restoration (on its return from Europe, its MOT failure sheet had run to two pages), and to save money, for the previous eighteen months I'd been running a '90s Toyota Avensis, which was painted in a depressing shade of silvery grey and answered to the name of 'Britney'. Now, as anyone who has spent eighteen months driving an Avensis knows, such an experience is like a prison sentence to anyone with petrol in their veins. Even its reason d'être – its bulletproof reliability – was somewhat dull, and it was almost a relief when it showed its human side by eating its own gearbox as it approached 180,000 miles.

But as 2011 went on and the work began to build once again, there was no need to continue to exist in the petrolhead desert I'd been inhabiting. It was time to buy another sports car.

285

Naturally, given my past history with old Porsches, an aircooled 911 was the first thing I considered. Iconic and practical, such a car seemed to tick every box, but I was worried that in rushing back to the Porsche brand, I would be missing out on the disparate interests offered by other marques. I considered a Lotus Esprit, but decided it would be too impractical because after all, if you can't take your sports car camping in Fontainebleau for a week, what's the point in even owning it? Then I considered a TVR Chimaera, but I was put off by the stories of unreliability, and the kit car image.

However, as there was one for sale at a garage a few miles from where I lived, I decided to go and check it out anyway. At least that way, I would know whether the boot was big enough for my climbing gear.

I didn't plan on buying it. In the photos on eBay, it was a dull shade of green which seemed to do the curvaceous shape no favours. But my curiosity led me there and I found that in the sunlight, the pearlescent paint shone like glitter and the magnolia leather interior was far more appealing than I'd ever considered possible. And then, with a turn of the key the big V8 fired up and the garage's forecourt filled with the intoxicating sound of drums and thunder.

Resistance was futile. I was buying that TVR.

I collected the car one sunny Wednesday and a few days later it was loaded up with camping and climbing gear, ready for the yearly pilgrimage to Fontainebleau. I'd been delayed by work for a few days and my friends were already there, and so I drove through the night to the campsite, pulling up just as people were getting ready to head out for a day of climbing.

'So you brought one then?' said Brummy in greetings. 'Looks good, how many times did it break down getting here?'

'None actually,' I said. 'But the temperature gauge packed up near Paris, and I think it's only running on about five cylinders.'

'What did you expect? It is a TVR, after all,' said Brummy.

'Oh wow,' Said Laura in greeting. 'It looks amazing, so much better than in the pictures. Sorry to hear it's playing up already though.'

'Don't worry,' I said. 'It's nothing serious, touch wood. Being a TVR, if it makes it home without blowing up, I'll consider it a win.'

'So, what are you going to call it?' she asked.

'I was thinking about that on the way over and so far, I've came up with two options. Greenpeace, because it's green and has a V8, or Kermit, because it's green and looks like a frog.'

'You're so unimaginative,' said Brummy.

'It has to be Kermit,' Laura added. 'It really does look like a happy frog.'

'Yeah, that's definitely the better name,' I said. 'Kermit it is.'

And so I found myself the proud owner of a TVR Chimaera named Kermit.

The purchase of a TVR wasn't the only big change to come about that year. Shortly after Kermit had made it back from France with only a tyre blowout on the motorway 80 miles from home to further dampen its record, Laura and I started to look into renting a small place out in the Devon countryside. Internet searches brought up all manner of barn conversions and cottages, but one place stood out above all the rest – a 6-bedroom house in a Dartmoor village, which came complete with a swimming pool, sauna, two bars and plenty of parking. It was way too big and also way over budget, of course, but it got us thinking.

What if other folk could be convinced to move in with us and spread the cost?

As it happened, it wasn't a hard sell and soon we had enough people onboard to make a communal rent happen. Everyone who joined us there brought their own unique brand of adventurous spirit to the house – there were people who were into travel, climbers, runners, kayakers and hikers, all bubbling with a contagious enthusiasm. A small climbing wall and gym was built in what was originally the dining room, the bar was well stocked with whisky and ale before being turned into a planning room packed with books and maps, and the garage was stacked with tools. The name of the house was Hunter's Moon and it had a huge effect on all who lived there, not least in its role as a breeding ground for all manner of daft ideas, with barely a week going by without some harebrained occurrence taking place.

There was the time Tom – who'd joined us on the AfricanPorsche Expedition – wrote off his Vauxhall Astra by hitting a cow one night, then replaced it with an old Porsche 911 which he proceeded to bounce off various bits of Dartmoor scenery with aplomb, much to our amusement. Then there was the New Year's party which saw 30 people packed into the swimming pool at the stroke of midnight, and barely less in the hot tub which it was adjacent to. There was the time a storm took down a tree in the garden, destroying the house's heating oil tank, and the time we all clubbed together to buy a house Range Rover, complete with an ex-TVR pre-serp V8 and sports exhaust. And what about the night when Kim attempted to drive home from a party only to kill her MINI by driving headlong into a flooded road one stormy night, only for Laura to almost do the same with her Alfa Romeo Spider the following morning?

Hunter's Moon became a place where anything could happen, where no idea was too daft and where living a life less ordinary was to be encouraged. The impulsive nature of life there can be summed up by one week in November, a few months after we'd moved in.

'I can't find flights anywhere for under £900 return,' I said to Brummy.

'Neither can I,' he replied. 'I'm not paying 900 quid just to go to The States.'

'Agreed,' I said.

We both had a week off, and I'd decided that the best way to spend it was to head to Texas and find an old Ford Mustang to buy and ship home. Unfortunately, our dates coincided with Thanksgiving, which is one of the busiest times of the year on the other side of the pond, and so the flights had all been booked up for months in advance. It was Thursday evening, and our week off work started in twenty hours.

'What shall we do then,' I asked.

'Let's go to the pub, have a beer, and come up with a plan,' Brummy said.

An hour later, we were sat in The White Thorn with beers on the table, and ideas in our head.

'What have you came up with then,' I asked Brummy, who'd been looking for cheap flights on his tablet.

'Brazil. Rio de Janeiro, in fact. £500 return, flying out on Saturday morning. What about you?'

'Pretty similar,' I replied. 'Fancy a trip to Venezuela? We could hire a car and then head out to see Angel Falls. Flights are the same price as you've found for Brazil.'

We discussed the options and found that really, there was nothing between them. But it was already ten at night and the bar would be closing soon, and so a decision was needed.

'Let's toss a coin,' I suggested.

'Good plan,' Brummy replied. 'Heads, Brazil. Tails, Venezuela.'

The coin landed heads side up. We were going to Rio de Janeiro.

Forty hours later, we were in a traveller's hostel with a fine view over the city. Climbing movies were showing on a big screen in the bar, and a party was in full swing as one of the staff members celebrated their 21st birthday.

I brought us a couple of beers and we chinked them together, sitting at a table as Brazil's hip young folk danced all around us.

'Cheers,' I said, grinning.

'Cheers indeed,' Brummy replied.

'I can't believe that 40 hours ago we were sat in The White Thorn not sure what to do with the week and now here we are, gatecrashing a birthday party in Brazil.'

'I know, crazy isn't it?' Brummy replied, as he gazed out over the city.

Just occasionally, life is awesome. That was one of those moments.

I may not have got to buy my '60s Mustang, but that week in Brazil was a fine consolation prize. After a few days of taking in the sights of Rio, we hired an old Fiat Uno and set off out of town to explore Rio State, having abandoned our original plan of driving to Iguaçu Falls when we noticed just how big Brazil actually is. So instead, we went to the old colonial town of Paratay, where cannons sit idly on the quayside, facing out across the azure blue of the sea, with the town's brightly painted houses behind them. We headed up into the hills to visit Peropolis, where Brummy managed to crash the Fiat into a Volkswagen Golf, but such occurrences were by this stage fairly routine on our trips, and no lasting damage was done. And we returned to the UK a week later, our minds filled to bursting with the joy de vivre which seemed to burn brighter in Brazil than anywhere else we'd been.

After that week, whenever I glanced at the map on the wall of Hunter's Moon's bar, South America would now stare back. I'd had but the briefest taste of the continent, but I knew that one day I would be back to do it justice. First though, I had to turn that idea which had spent the past five years on the backburner into a reality – it was time to make V8Nam happen.

TWENTY FIVE

GOING SOLO

28ᵗʰ June 2013
Saigon, Vietnam

I was alone in Saigon. All around me the city of nine million people bustled, but I knew not one of them. For the first time since leaving the UK three months earlier, I had no travelling companions, no friends in the next room. Laura had flown home from Hanoi and Brummy had sold his bike the previous day, before heading back to his job in the UK. Of everyone who had latched onto the V8Nam dream, I was the only one left, sat in a traveller's hostel in the backpacker part of town. All that energy and vigour which had swept us across Asia over the past three months seemed to have disappeared; fading like the light at the end of the day.

I sat on the fifteen-dollar-a-night hostel bed feeling strangely melancholy, my energy reserves suddenly drained and my spirits plunged into the doldrums. I knew I had to be proactive, to keep pushing on with the trip, but at that moment I couldn't. I had to ride out the low tide, knowing my positivity would flood back soon. When it did, I would sell the crappy bike which was sat in front of the hostel to some unsuspecting backpacker and board the night bus back to Cambodia, where the Corvette was hopefully still in one piece, awaiting my return.

Hours passed and as the afternoon wandered into the evening, hunger began to build, first balancing against my inertia and then overcoming it, driving me outside to find something to eat.

Sat at a busy street-food stall, I fell into conversation with some other travellers. They were a worldly bunch, having paused their lives in Holland, France and Argentina to cut loose in Asia for a few months, and the talk flowed along at a breakneck speed, propelled by their passion for the sights they'd seen and the experiences they'd had. This reconnection with the world put the wind back in my sails and as the evening progressed, carrying on with the trip and ultimately getting the Corvette to Singapore alone didn't seem like such an insurmountable challenge.

Unfortunately, none of them wanted to buy a motorbike, though – not that this was surprising, given the abuse I'd given it when I told them the story of my trip down from Hanoi. However the following day I did find a buyer – an Australian backpacker who was planning to ride it back up that well worn groove to Hanoi. And I got my money back, pocketing $300 before boarding a night-bus back to Cambodia.

*　　*　　*

Tired and dazed after an almost sleepless night on the bus, I wandered through the streets back to the hotel in Siam Reap where we'd been staying three weeks previously. The sun was just rising above the fatigued buildings, flooding the city with a golden light which always made me feel as if I was trespassing upon the past.

I rounded the corner and walked towards the hotel, spotting the Corvette still parked where I'd left it, albeit now covered in a layer of dust which burnt gold in the sunlight. In a chair next to the car, there sat a middle aged guy in well-worn clothes, dozing with a shotgun resting horizontally across his lap.

In the hotel, I asked the receptionist how long he'd been there.

'Since you left,' he said. 'He's been taking turns to guard it with his brother. They each do twelve hours a day and were expecting you to be back a week ago.'

'Wow, I didn't expect that. Sorry I'm so late, how much money are they expecting?'

'Whatever you want to give them,' came the reply. 'A dollar a day should cover it though, so about twenty dollars.'

'Twenty dollars isn't much for sitting next to a Corvette with a shotgun for three weeks,' I said.

'Just give them whatever you think it's worth,' I was told once again.

I went back outside, and woke up the guy with the gun – very gently, as people with loaded shotguns aren't the sort of folk you want to startle. He didn't speak English, but I managed to thank him through a series of clumsy gestures, before handing him $50. His eyes lit up as he was released from his twelve on, twelve off routine by a payment of double what he was expecting, and he strolled off merrily down the street, chattering happily to himself as the city came to life.

Though the temples of Angkor are by far the most famous sight in Cambodia, this beguiling little country has far more to offer besides them. On leaving Siam Reap that morning, I continued my tour by hitting the road down to Phnom Penh.

The change in the weather began gently, a few droplets of rain thudding into the Corvette's steeply raked windscreen, but the looming blackness in the sky ahead told the full story. The rain got heavier and heavier, and even the wipers' fastest setting couldn't maintain a clear view ahead. Water rushed into the Corvette's cabin through the perished door seals and the glass began to mist up relentlessly, as the white heat of lightning strobed through the blackened dome above.

Traffic slowed to a crawl, and barely able to see and not wishing to cause an accident, I pulled over. Motorcycle taxis splashed on past me amid the puddles, while buses and trucks stormed through the maelstrom casting great sheets of spray into the scenery. And through it all, people on scooters and bicycles wobbled along, sweating beneath cheap, brightly coloured plastic ponchos as they carried on regardless, grinning at the absurdity of it all. And then the horizon brightened and rainbows arced delicately across the sky, the road surface reappeared from beneath the muddy torrent which had swept across it, and it was time to carry on into the town, for somewhere in Phnom Penh, there was a beer with my name on it.

I found it in an Irish bar named 'Rory's Pub' which, with total logic, was run by an American who definitely wasn't called Rory. However, he and his ex-pat clientele did their best to maintain a drunken Irish vibe, seemingly congregating at the bar early in the afternoon and staying until the night was old and walking had become a challenge. From what I gathered, most of the customers worked in the offshore industry, and it seemed that hitting the bar was their answer to the question of what to do with the month off between trips to the rigs. Conversations seemed to drift around a few predictable subjects – the apparently unjustified spending habits of their local wives being one, and the inferiority of life back home in the West being another. However, they expelled their arguments with such venom that it seemed they were trying to justify their decision to move to Cambodia to themselves, and the understanding echo chamber of Rory's Bar was the place to do this.

After a few evenings there, I didn't go back, preferring to spend the evenings sat at the tables in front of the hostel; an environment which somehow felt more representative of the city. And not just when rats would run across our feet before disappearing back into the drains, or boisterous groups paraded down the street, blowing trumpets and flying political flags with a raw, almost religious fervour you never see back home.

Phnom Penh struck me as a strange place, inherently unbalanced in much the same way as I'd found Rio de Janiero to be when I'd visited a few years earlier. It was a place of very visible wealth, which shone starkly amid a sea of poverty. Rolls-Royces sat apart in garages, their windscreens bearing enormous price tags, while beggars sat hopeless in the dust down the street. It was that kind of place. Decadence amid the decay.

While I was in Phnom Penh, I didn't undertake the usual tourist excursions. I didn't visit the Royal Palace, the National Museum or the famous Killing Fields of the Khmer Rouge. I think this was because after three months on the road, I needed some downtime; a break from continuously rushing across the map, going to new places or seeing new things. I made the hostel on Street 278 my $10 a night home, and let my mind and body catch up with the frenzy of travelling which the previous three months had been. And once the recovery was complete, I did what everyone does when they visit South East Asia.

I went to the beach.

*   *   *

It was the South East Asia they want you to see; the version of the landscape which bursts forth from a thousand tourist brochures and adverts. Soft golden sands occupied by the merest sprinkling of people, and lapped by the gentle caress of the waves. Palm and tamarisk trees provided shade from the heat of the sun, while down at the bamboo café which sat alone on the sand, smoke from the barbeque drifted across the scene, as the freshly caught fish were prepared for the evening's dinner.

And the best bit? It was happy hour, which meant you could get two beers for a dollar. Yes, Otres Beach was a pretty good find.

But a few miles up the coast, there was a more typical beach experience. In the town of Sihanoukville the waterfront was crowded with restaurants and bars, all of which were very protective of 'their' patch of sand. Holidaymakers crowded in regardless, crammed ten-deep between the unattractive town behind them, and the waters which in this situation, had seemed to lose their romance.

But as a decent sized town, Sihanoukville was easy to get to from elsewhere in South East Asia, and made the traveller's life easy with its hotels, shops, restaurants and bars – especially the bars; the large population of Russians living there saw to that. But it was more of a crowd than I was looking for. It didn't live up to that tranquil image of South East Asia which I'd been fed for years before the trip, and so I'd taken advantage of having my own wheels in-country and headed down to Otres, where I could spend a few days living in a beach hut like in the brochures, next to a beach which didn't so much as garner a mention in my guide book. And then, with my stress levels reduced to zero, it was time to fire up the Corvette and head to Bangkok.

Rolling into the city at the end of a long day on the road, my fatigued mind perceived a malevolence in Bangkok which it didn't possess. Tired, I allowed my imagination to continue its strange fantasy and as it did so, the great city felt positively dystopian. The hulking, anonymous buildings rose tight to the road, lit inconsistently against the night. Traffic raced around aggressively in a frenzy my mind perceived as panic, while dust and rain fought a half-hearted battle in the stifled air around me. The low overcast sky glowed a sulphurous orange and seemed to take on a liquid form, an inverted ocean bubbling overhead, illuminated by a million bulbs in the streets below. The flashing lights of airliners swept down from within this poisonous-looking ocean to the airport, or rose up to be enveloped by it. It was a city from a future gone bad. It was Gotham, or the backdrop to Tron, or Judge Dredd.

The Corvette's big V8 roared with a Mad Max urgency as I plunged into this uninhabitable metropolis of danger and deceit, as car alarms wailed all around. Fighting the fatigue to stay awake, I was the hero in my own delirious fantasy, purposefully strapped into the high-tech cockpit of my hero car. And the heroism came from the fact I was going into lands unknown; enemy territory. These racing concrete overpasses, this bleak urban jungle, the poker-faced tuk tuk drivers; it was no place for tourists.

But then the roads widened into boulevards and people appeared on the sidewalks, smiling, laughing and joking as they strolled carefree through the night. And I swung around a few more corners and found myself floodlit and centre stage amid another extreme.

Koh San Road.

And there, the fantasy ended. Bangkok is no place for Tourists? Definitely not true; this street was pretty much built from the ground up with them in mind. In fact, it was so tourist-focussed that it had been declared pedestrian-only, and the police politely told me to turn the Corvette around and come back on foot.

Koh San Road is the Vegas of Thai travel. A brash, tasteless celebration of the culture from which it rose, it takes delight in its wafer-thin dignity, and wears it with pride. Its nods to a deeper culture are unashamedly only skin deep, its motivations are solely financial and its methods of achieving said monetary goals are sufficient to raise even a Thai's eyebrows. But its transparency is so complete that it is hard to hold this uber-tourism focus against it. Koh San Road is how it is, and it works for both those who frequent it and those who own its businesses. It may cross the line into vulgarity on occasion, but you can't really complain when it does. Not for you? No problem, there are plenty of other places to go in Asia.

From my perspective, one of these places was rather close by; a must-visit location whose significance ran so deep for my family that there was no way I was going to pass it by.

After a few days of sleeping late and eating well in the area around Koh San Road, I solemnly climbed into the Corvette and set off out of the city to visit it.

*   *   *

The rain came down in a continuous deluge. It didn't sheet down as it often had done during my time in Asia, varying its intensity in a way which suggests a break will come

299

soon enough. No, it fell like a never-ending shower of soft molten metal. It fell as if it had always rained in this place, and always would. It quickly soaked my trousers and seeped in through my Gore-Tex jacket as I walked. But I barely noticed. I was hemmed in by a narrow cutting which stretched for hundreds of metres through the jungle, the sides of which rose seven metres above my head. I stopped walking and rested my hand against one of the cutting's wet rock walls. It had a rough texture and for decades vegetation had slowly been taking it back, but the coarsely gouged limestone had been unmistakably shaped by man. The smooth anonymity of machine work was lacking; here, every inch of the surface bore the mark of a person. Every inch told a unique, personal story. I stood there, my fingers moulding into the rock's rough grooves, their history being recreated within my mind.

I was standing in Hellfire Pass, and for six-week period in 1943, it had been the worst place on Earth.

The story of Hellfire Pass is in many ways a microcosm of the story of the suffering which took place during the construction of the Burma Railway, as it was pushed through the jungle by the Japanese forces at breakneck speed, to resupply their forces in Burma during the Second World War. During the six weeks in which Hellfire Pass was cut, thousands of Allied prisoners of war and local labourers slaved away with their bare hands and rudimentary tools to create the cutting, driven on by the brutality of their Japanese and Korean guards. They were forced to toil around the clock for weeks on end, as the work and the tropical climate preyed on their malnourished bodies. Malaria, cholera and dysentery were rife, but such ailments weren't allowed to slow the work. Anything other than 100% effort was met with a beating, or worse.

It was a brutal story which played out throughout the 258-mile length of the Burma Railway; a story which many didn't live to tell. The disease, malnourishment and starvation combined with the indifference and brutality of the guards to take a huge toll on the forced labour. Twenty percent of the 60,000 prisoners of war forced to work on the railway never lived to see its completion; the 80% who survived did so having endured a living hell.

One of those survivors was my grandfather.

A member of the Royal Medical Corps, he was posted to Singapore in 1941, shortly before the Japanese captured the city. He then endured three years as a prisoner of war, most of which were spent working alongside captured Australians on the Burma Railway. When he was finally released from captivity, he weighed about forty kilos.

He was six feet four inches tall.

I lingered in the railway cutting as the rain fell, my fingers flowing across the hand-cut rock as I slowly drifted along, lost in my thoughts. Was he here? What did he go through? What would he have seen? I'll never know. He'd passed away five years earlier when I was in Africa, having never talked to me about those years he'd spent in hell.

Some wounds are best left unopened.

The eternal rain kept falling and the warmth began to drain from my body. Involuntary shivers pulsed through me as my soaking clothes clung to my skin, and I felt a sudden urge to leave this place. I shuffled hurriedly back out of the past, leaving the dark pages of history to return to my lucky life of sports cars and traveller's hostels, as the rain mixed with the tears in my eyes.

TWENTY SIX

A BARGE ON THE BALTIC

10ᵗʰ February 2012
Shaugh Prior, Dartmoor, UK

Hunter's Moon quickly became the perfect breeding ground for outlandish ideas. The combination of a well stocked bar or two, a library of maps and guidebooks, plenty of parking spaces and half a dozen like-minded people was an irresistible one, and many evenings were spent dreaming up outrageous adventures. It provided the atmosphere in which V8Nam was finally turned from a dream into a reality, allowing us to hit the road in the spring of 2013. But the intoxicating effect of life there also resulted in some smaller outings which took place in the year before the V8s roared, generally sized to fit into a fortnight away from work and providing an excuse to buy a vehicle which would have otherwise gone un-owned. The first of these trips took place early in 2012, and came about purely from an observation I'd made in passing while browsing the internet one evening.

In Estonia, they drive on the sea.

More specifically, every winter, as temperatures plummet to 30 below zero, large swathes of the Baltic relinquish their liquid state and freeze, forming vast ice sheets off the coasts of Estonia, Russia, Finland and Sweden. Where the ice freezes thick and hard enough, it is able to support the weight of a car, and industrious locals build ice roads across the sea to islands offshore.

A chance to drive across the frozen Baltic Sea? It was such a simple yet compelling idea. And what's more, it provided the perfect basis for a two-week road trip, and so a vague plan was drawn up, a charming old Jaguar XJ6 3.2 purchased for £900 and for a few weeks before our departure, quizzically perusing Baltic Sea ice charts became part of the daily routine.

To give us the best chance of finding open ice roads, we planned to leave in early February, but due to an unseasonably warm winter, with one week to go none of the ice was thick enough to support the weight of HMS Jag. However, a couple of days before the car's departure for the Baltic, a late freeze sent things into overdrive, and our dream of driving on a frozen sea on a 22 centimetre-thick layer of ice became viable. Work commitments meant I wasn't able to travel with the Jag on the first leg of the trip from England to Estonia and so instead I made plans to fly to Tallinn and join Laura and Tom on the trip, five days after they'd left the UK and just in time for the first planned ice road.

*　　*　　*

For once, I'd bagged a window seat, and as the Boeing dipped its wing to turn onto finals to land, it revealed a frozen ocean, dotted with islands and glistening in the sunlight. As the plane touched down, the soon-to-be-launched HMS Jag was still 200 miles further south, purring its way through the snow from Riga. Once I'd effortlessly cleared customs at Tallinn's airport, I got the bus to the old town and slotted into the tourist rhythm, passing time until the car arrived.

And arrive it did, at six o'clock that evening, covered in 2,000 miles of grit and grime and looking rather sorry for itself in the half light, with its trademark chrome grille swathed in gaffa tape against the cold. Tom and Laura jumped out surprisingly full of energy after their six day marathon and promptly dragged me back into the pub I'd just vacated for a cheap pint or two.

And so the following day we nursed our hangovers 50 miles east from Tallinn towards the coast, where the town of Haapsalu marked the beginning of our ice road adventure. At the time of our arrival in Estonia, two ice roads had been opened – a six mile route across the sea ice to the island of Vormsi, and a shorter one from Haapsalu to the Noarootsi peninsula - a far cry from the previous year, when all six of the possible ice roads were in condition, stretching up to fifteen miles across the Baltic. We headed for the longest of the open ice roads first, attached a Union Jack to the back of the HMS Jag, and were soon driving along a track of compacted snow as the shoreline passed unseen beneath us.

Estonia's Ice roads have a rather esoteric highway code – no seatbelts, no vehicles over 2.5 tonnes, no stopping and no cruising at speeds between 30 and 45 kilometres per hour. After firing up a stirring rendition of 'Rule Britannia' on the stereo, we accelerated up to a comfortable 45 miles per hour cruise and wafted across the ocean, a ferry slowly plying its channel in the ice a few hundred metres to our left.

There was no unusual sensation which accompanied driving on the frozen sea ice, nothing to differentiate the experience from driving on a wintery back road other than the constant niggling thought that there was less than 30 centimetres of ice keeping two tonnes of car and the Baltic Sea a safe distance apart. But in my mind, that realisation was sufficient to justify the adventure. It was another way of using a car to create the memories which counted for so much in my life; a new and different experience which justified the effort we'd put into making it happen.

We soon wafted up onto the shores of the island of Vormsi, having put a six mile sea crossing behind us. However, it quickly occurred to us that out of season, there's not a huge amount to do on said snow-smothered island, and so we promptly spun the Jag around and headed back across the frozen sea, beating the ferry back to the mainland by a couple of minutes.

After a spot of pizza, we drove over to the second ice road. Shorter but more twisty, it offered a similar experience but with the bonus that the corners provided the opportunity to have some fun with the rear wheel drive

Jag, drifting it like a rally car on the frictionless surface. This quickly lead us to the conclusion that lairy oversteer on the Baltic Sea is, quite frankly, a box which every car enthusiast should tick at least once in their life.

Satisfied with our first taste of driving on a frozen sea, we headed back to Tallinn feeling fulfilled, and spent the evening sightseeing in the old town, before boarding a ferry to Finland the following morning.

The pack ice fractured easily as the ferry bulldozed its way into the Port of Helsinki. Still in the European Union, entering Finland was a formality and we were soon heading north across an endless landscape of rolling forests and lakes with just over 400 miles to go to the day's goal of Oulu, a port and university town near the northern end of the Bay of Bothnia, and home to one of Finland's more famous ice roads.

The first 200 miles of the drive were fairly uneventful, despite the roads being an unconvincing mixture of grit, tarmac and ice, banked by snowdrifts and covered in veils of blown spindrift. HMS Jag wafted on through the unfamiliar surroundings with a businesslike nonchalance, while we relaxed in the warm, leather-bound comfort of its cabin. However after dark, things changed. The spindrift worsened, becoming so blindingly illuminated by oncoming headlights that it was impossible to see the road for worryingly long periods of time. For four hours we pushed on through the grit and ice patches in various degrees of blindness until we reached our evening's destination, full of relief. Once again, the Jaguar had never missed a beat, purring through the day's drive without so much of a hiccup.

Feeling refreshed by a full night's sleep, the sun shone brightly through the cold air as we approached our next ice road the following morning. We stopped at the point where the road set out across the sea to take some pictures, and as we did so a local car returned from an attempt at the road, stopped, wound down their window and advised us not to attempt to drive the five mile route.

But attempt it we did.

Everything went smoothly until we were a few miles from shore, when some patches of waterlogged ice appeared in the smooth surface of the road, suggesting that it had thinned to such a degree that it would be unable to support the weight of a car. As stopping and turning around wasn't an option, I was forced to swerve around the rotten ice, forcefully ramming the poor executive saloon through snowdrifts at the side of the road when there wasn't room for us to drive round the bad ice cleanly. Plumes of white powder were sent high into the air, and at times I found that I was driving blind, as waves of thick snow covered the windscreen. But the track was narrow, and I had no choice but to push on regardless, with Tom visibly panicked in the passenger seat, and Laura pensive and silent in the back.

After about 500 metres of this the conditions worsened yet further, and our luck ran out. A narrowing path between the snowbanks forced us onto one of the rotten sections of ice, which promptly gave way beneath the wheels on the right hand side of our hefty steed. Fortunately, I had been driving rather quickly since the dangers began and 40 miles per hour was just sufficient to skim the Jag's driver's side wheels over the disintegrating ice, aquaplaining on the surface of the sea, before reaching more solid ground. Speed was now our only safety, and I kept my foot hard down, swerving around further patches of thin ice and Baltic potholes, until we reached an area of bad ice which spanned the entire ice road. Fortunately, this obstacle was preceded by an area of ice which was both sufficiently large and solid to turn around on. There was only one thing for it. Mustering Monty Python's rallying call of 'run away', we spun the car around and headed back to shore, ramming into the snowdrifts at the side of the track to avoid the worst looking ice – including the bit we'd broken through, two sea-filled tire tracks now marking the point where HMS Jag had almost sunk.

And even through this, the raffish Jag never missed a beat. There can be few more satisfying ways to spend £900 than on than a two decade old XJ6.

Following our close encounter with a non-frozen part of the Baltic, we decided that heading inland to terra firma was the order of the day. And when in Finland, inland destinations don't come much more appealing than Arctic Lapland – hence a 60 mile detour from the Baltic coastline to Rovaniemi, Arctic Finland's most hyped tourist destination. After a day spent taking the Jag across the Arctic Circle, wafting past Santa's official residence, failing to spot the northern lights and hooning around on snowmobiles, we spun our gripless, wafty steed around and began the long drive home.

Entering Sweden, the first sight which greeted us was, fittingly, an Ikea – so meatballs all round were the order of the day, before we carried on south through a worsening blizzard, which for about 100 miles made both visibility and grip distant memories. Given the poor ice forecast, the relatively high temperatures and our recent near-sinking, we decided to give our planned attempt on the ice road near Lulea a miss, and so drove on to the university town of Umea, halfway down Sweden's coast and on first impressions, home to a population which was almost entirely drunk.

We then continued to Stockholm where we spent a pleasant day wandering around Sweden's beautiful capital city, its canals choked with dense pack-ice which glistened in the sun. The next day Copenhagen beckoned, followed by a final stop in Amsterdam. The Jag took these long days on the road completely in its stride, wafting along in perfect comfort and winning us all over to the inherent rightness of Jaguar's approach to things.

And so, fourteen days and 4,950 miles after it left the UK, the unflappable, wonderful Jag returned home to Hunter's Moon. Predictably, the car remained completely unflustered and reliable to the last, and hence the trip around the Baltic became the first adventurous road trip

I've ever completed without actually breaking down, even if nearly sinking in the Baltic Sea probably counted against a clean sheet. The lack of any breakdowns made any comparison with my previous trip to the Scandinavian winter, five years earlier in the little Fiat, most profound – I'd come a long way since we'd nearly flown backwards into that fjord.

But, while our lap of the Baltic represented the beginning of the Hunter's Moon road tripping tradition which would ultimately see us setting course for across Asia in our V8s, it also marked the end for Laura and I. A relationship which had begun amid the baking sands of Africa ended three years later amid Estonia's icy winter, with us never again having quite equalled the intense highs which had brought us together.

TWENTY SEVEN

TO BURMA

17ᵗʰ July 2013
Kanchanaburi, Thailand

Hellfire Pass wasn't the only remnant of the Burma Railway to be found among the jungles to the west of Bangkok. From the hostel in which I was staying, walking a few miles up the river brought you to the most famous relic of all – Bridge 277, better known as The Bridge on the River Kwai. While the Burma Railway required a total of around 600 bridges to be built, this is the one which looms largest in people's minds, and it has become a symbol of the suffering which took place during the railway's construction.

But as you approach it, it doesn't shout of suffering in the same way that Hellfire Pass does. In appearance, it is simply a bridge spanning a river; eleven steel spans resting on concrete pillars which rise from the waters between the two banks, which are about 100 metres apart. It's no ordinary bridge though; it is a monument to the pain of those who were forced to build it and as such, you approach it respectfully, accompanied by a strange feeling that the past is watching you, even judging you. Deferentially, you throw your mind back to the past sacrifices, and find yourself attempting to recreate history in your mind's eye.

But it is impossible to immerse yourself in the past fully. Brightly coloured stalls stand in the shadow of the bridge, selling souvenirs and tours. Crowds mill around the riverbank, cameras raised and poses perfected.

Today, the past is just that; a faded memory in sepia and black.

I walked across the bridge, continuing down the tracks past a few closed up tea-stalls which marked the edge of town. Dappled sunlight lay upon the sleepers and tracks, and grasses were pushing up through the gravel of the rail bed. Ahead, the remains of the Burma Railway drifted around a corner, and out of sight.

258 miles.

100,000 lives.

It all seemed like the ultimate nothing.

But I wanted to understand, if only for my grandfather. Standing there on the railway sleepers as butterflies flitted through the shadows around me, I wanted to know more. Just as I have a constant craving to see what lies around the next corner of a road, so the Burma Railway, curving out of sight into the jungle, drew me to look closer.

Two days later in Bangkok Airport, I boarded a plane to its terminus – Yangon, the Capital of Myanmar, as Burma is now known.

*   *   *

While the past was one of the main factors which made me feel the need to go to Myanmar, there were other, more recent reasons. The month I visited marked the 25th anniversary of some of the most significant events in the history of modern Burma. In early August 1988, mass demonstrations for democracy had been violently suppressed, and thousands of people had lost their lives. A few weeks later Aung San Suu Kyi stepped into the limelight by enthralling half a million people with her rallying speech calling for democracy, before going on to lead her party – the National League for Democracy (NLD) – to a resounding election victory, winning 80% of the available seats in the 1990 election. Unfortunately, the military government's response to this humiliation was to declare the election void, make the NLD illegal, and place Aung San Suu Kyi under house arrest for much of the following twenty years.

For most of those years, she had campaigned against tourists visiting Myanmar, as their presence both lined the pockets of the military junta which was ruthlessly holding onto power, and also appeared to legitimise the regime. However, in 2010, Suu Kyi and the NLD had changed their stance, suggesting that independent travellers should come and see the country for themselves, and tell the world what they saw.

Taking a week out from the road and leaving the Corvette parked in a Bangkok monastery, I answered the call and did just that.

So what did I see? I saw a thousand smiling faces belonging to the most friendly, unprepossessing group of people you're ever likely to meet. I saw a proud traditional culture where men still wear sarongs and women take pride in applying shimmering yellow thanaka paste to their faces. I saw golden pagodas soaring skyward, exotic monkey-thronged temples clinging precariously to mountainsides and endless wildernesses untouched by man's destructive tendencies. And I learned just how unlikely the smiles and beauty are, for I also saw police heavy-handedness, political injustice and people struggling to eke out an existence in a nation left impoverished by 60 years of military rule.

Like many tourists who visit Myanmar, my first port of call was the Shwedagon Pagoda in northern Yangon. A stirring sight, this spectacular tower of gold sweeps skyward from its broad base to a needle-like summit 99 metres above the ground, upon which sits a crown made from thousands of diamonds and rubies. Monks and ordinary Burmese folk circulated around the sacred behemoth, lighting incense and prostrating themselves, for this pagoda is most sacred Buddhist site in all of Myanmar and in many ways, can be considered to be the symbol of the nation. Because of its importance, the Shwedagon Pagoda has often been the centre of both religious and political struggle, and it was here that 25 years before my visit, Aung San Suu Kyi had given her famous pro-democracy speech which inspired half a million Burmese people who were desperate for change.

After visiting the pagoda, while wandering aimlessly around the scruffy-yet-charming city centre I found myself in the middle of a confrontation between locals and the police, who were aggressively loading up trucks with the confiscated belongings of every street trader around me. As I walked away from the confrontation, for hundreds of metres word was spreading, and traders who'd not yet been targeted were frantically packing up their stalls and moving them out of reach of the heavy-handed police.

To escape the kerfuffle, I turned up a side street, and a few minutes later I was passing more police trucks, each one with about 60 regular looking guys shoehorned inhumanely in a cage covering the load area. Not wanting to linger and ask potentially awkward questions, I once again walked on, but despite not knowing the full facts of what I'd seen, my scepticism regarding the government continued to grow.

My second day in Yangon coincided with a public holiday worryingly named 'Martyrs' Day'. As I walked near the Shwedagon Pagoda, large crowds were arriving, both on foot and crammed into buses, all waving the flag of the National League for Democracy party. Predictably, the area had been sealed off by a large number of well-armed, strutting policemen, and reinforcements in riot vans shadowed the gathering. Not one to linger around heavily policed political gatherings – especially ones held on 'Martyrs' Day' – I kept my distance, as in recent memory such gatherings had been suppressed violently, for instance during the 2007 Saffron Revolution, when the protests of 15,000 monks and their supporters were broken up with tear gas, beatings and deaths.

That evening, I hit the road to Mandalay. No longer the romantic pilgrimage of the famous Kipling poem, my journey consisted of about nine hours on an overnight bus, the windscreen of which bore the slogan 'Thy kingdom come, thy will be done in earth, as it is in heaven.' As we pulled onto the road to Mandalay, I wondered just how far 'in earth' the slogan was referring to, and hoped it didn't mean six feet under it, as the journey took us along a road which the UK Foreign Office had recommended not to travel by night.

Other than the bus's headlights, the darkness was complete. Unforgivably, in 2013, three-quarters of Burma's population still didn't even have electricity, meaning the countryside was utterly black at night. With nothing to look at other than the rain flickering past the headlights, my tired mind pondered the nation I was travelling across, and tried to make sense of its current situation.

When Burma gained independence from the UK in 1948, it was the second wealthiest nation in South East Asia. Unfortunately, the subsequent 65 years of independence have not been kind, due mainly to its governance by a military junta which took power through a coup in 1962. Military rule meant things went downhill fast, and Burma is now not only one of the poorest nations in SE Asia, but was also recently found to be the second most corrupt nation on earth, with only Somalia scoring worse. At the time of my visit, the nation's GDP per capita was a shocking $450 per person, and the regime is accused of indulging in many of the human race's less noble traits, including ethnic cleansing of minority tribes, use of child soldiers, slavery, holding political prisoners and the oppression of freedom of speech. However despite the government's general incompetence in improving the lot of its citizens, it had managed to line its own nest rather well, both through sales of raw materials and the fact that virtually every decent-sized business in the country is forced to divert a fair amount of money to the regime.

As the bus rolled along, I mentally added up how much of the money I would be spending would be diverted to the regime. According to my guidebook, of the $350 my visit was costing, around $80 would end up in the governments back pocket. Thinking back to the way aid agencies often advertise for donations using statements such as 'your $80 can provide food and shelter to a family for 2 months…', I wondered how such an advert would read if penned by the recent military junta. Possibilities included your $80 paying for one child soldier, complete with their transport to one of the many areas of civil war between the regime and minority groups. But child soldiers are cheap, and your $80 won't even come close to paying for a mobile phone SIM card (shortly before the time of my visit, the average cost of a SIM card was $1,000, and hence mobile phones – the ultimate tool for organising popular protest – were still solely the preserve of the rich). It would also be barely be a drop in the ocean when it comes to the 1.2 billion dollar cost of Naypyidaw – the new capital city which the regime had indulgently decided to build on a greenfield site in 2005, despite the fact that Yangon had been a perfectly serviceable capital for the previous 130 years or so, and a third of the nation was living below the poverty line and hence could probably use the cash.

At three in the morning, our bus pulled into a service area halfway along the road from Yangon to Mandalay, not far from the expensive new capital city. To the right of our bus, a 24 hour cafe was doing reasonable trade from the passing night-buses, but the story to our left couldn't have been more different. A row of ramshackle roadside stalls stretched through the night, each consisting of a table about a metre square, on which lay a few items of fruit bathed in the sombre light of a battery-powered bulb. There were around ten of them, and hunched over on a stool behind each stall was an old lady, hoping their night spent in a grotty bus stop in the middle of nowhere wouldn't be in vain. But it was three in the morning and nobody was buying, and they all had a look of resigned failure on their weathered faces. As our bus pulled away I felt more moved by the situation of these ladies than by anything else I'd seen during my previous four months of travel.

Mandalay turned out not to be the exotic city which persists in the imagination of the West, but rather a dusty ex-capital which seemed to do everything required of a nation's second largest city, but little else. After a few days there, I decided that I needed the spectacular back in my life, and so I hit the road to Bagan.

Between the 8th and 12th centuries, an unprecedented frenzy of construction took place on this flat plain on the banks of the Irrawaddy, with temples and pagodas ranging from the size of a shed to 40 metres high being built wherever there was space. It is estimated that at the height of construction there were around 4,000 temples shoehorned into this area of a few dozen square miles, and 2,500 remain standing today. In isolation, each of the temples would constitute a fine diversion, but it's the sheer number of them stretching into the distance which makes Bagan such a remarkable sight, especially at sunset when the glowing horizon is serrated by hundreds of their delicate spires.

Once I'd taken in the sights of Bagan, my whistle-stop tour drew to a close and I headed back to Yangon feeling sadly pessimistic about the future, despite recent changes in the way the country is governed. It's true that the military had opened up somewhat and handed over some power to a civilian government. It's also true that elections had been called for 2015, but it still wasn't clear how transparent these elections would be, especially as back in 2010 the NLD – the main opposition party – wasn't even allowed to contest the election. It's true that many political prisoners had finally been released, but this was counterbalanced by the fact that the government continued to wage wars against minority peoples; wars which, every year, were turning tens of thousands more people into refugees. And it's also true that at the time of my visit, Aung San Suu Kyi was at that time more free than she has been at any stage since 1989, but as a perennial thorn in the side of the regime, she wasn't exactly going unwatched, and had seen more than her share of false dawns over the preceding two-and-a-half decades.

So the big question was, would her – and her supporters – bravery and determination pay off? On the surface things were changing. The Burmese government was being feted by foreign leaders for its recent conciliatory attitude, the political arena was more open than it has been for a very long time and a trickle of inward investment had begun. However the nation had seen false starts before and at the time of my visit people remained sceptical. As the Yangon taxi driver who took me to the airport to catch my flight back to Bangkok said to me, 'Change? There is never change. Too many very rich people have too much to lose. Maybe things will get better in 20 years, but not before.' The fact that simply uttering this sentence to a foreigner risked a lengthy jail sentence is an interesting reflection on just how much change was still needed.

So ended my time in Burma – a wonderful nation whose people both desired and deserved the opportunity to finally control their own destiny. With the support of the rest of the world, there was a chance that the elections which were due in 2015 could prove the Yangon taxi driver wrong and yield the right to self-determination which the Burmese so sorely deserve. However there was also a possibility that the elections could turn out to be just another false dawn in this nation's sad recent history.

As I boarded my flight back to Bangkok, where the Corvette sat waiting for the final run down to Singapore, I had my fingers crossed for this long suffering nation of wonderful people, for whom false dawns had sadly become a way of life.

TWENTY EIGHT

MOROCCO V8

15ᵗʰ April 2012
Shaugh Prior, Dartmoor, UK

On our return from the Baltic, thoughts started to turn towards making V8Nam – which for years had existed only as a dream and an occasional pub conversation – happen, and a major consideration was what season to make the journey in. Winter in Central Asia looked brutal, with the Kazakh Steppe dropping to minus 40°C in January, while crossing Europe, the Ukraine, Russia and China at a similar time of year looked almost as challenging, thanks to the combination of icy roads, short days and tough camping conditions. Taking all this into account, as well as our Mongol Rally experience, we decided to make the trip as early in the following year as possible by hitting the road in spring, with a spring in our step. This timing had other benefits too – we'd be able to drop into our traditional Easter gathering in Fontainebleau Forest en-route and all going well, we would catch the spring wildflowers on the Kazakh Steppe.

With the Baltic Jaguar having been sold on eBay for more than we'd paid for it, we had a year in which to prepare ourselves for the coming trip across Asia.

'Well I guess that gives us time for another road trip this year then,' said Brummy one evening, while sat in the trip-planning room at Hunter's Moon. 'Any ideas?'

'Of course,' I replied, standing up and walking over to the map on the wall. 'Look how close Morocco is. We're practically there already.'

'Africa?' he replied. 'You want to go back to Africa? Don't you remember how horrible it was last time round?'

'It'll be fine,' I said. 'A two week run down to the Sahara and back. What could possibly go wrong with that?'

'That's what worries me,' he replied.

Given all the logic and consideration we'd applied to the climatic implications of our V8Nam departure date, it's ironic that we chose to make our trip to the Sahara Desert at the worst possible time of year - the high summer.

Our choice of vehicle could be considered ironic, too. A gloriously brown 1976 Rover P6 V8.

As was now traditional, I'd bought the Rover in the pub one Saturday evening, via eBay, for the paltry sum of £800. It was only the following day that I realised I'd just bought the worst car in the country – literally. The year before my new purchase had rolled off the intermittently striking production line at Longbridge, the AA had awarded it the title of 'the worst new car in England'. And they had good reason to. The brand-new P6 they'd bought the year before had gone through three engines, two gearboxes and two clutch housings in only 6,000 miles.

The perfect vehicle for a 2,800 mile trip to Africa and back, then.

One April morning, I took the train to London to collect this quality automobile which I'd still never so much set eyes on, handed the previous owner a wedge of £20 notes, and set off to drive it the 240 miles back to Devon.

First impressions were that it wasn't actually that bad a purchase. The interior was in pretty good condition and the shelf-like dashboard which stretched across the car pleased me with its functional style. Up front, the old V8 may have been sluggish in the extreme but it at least got the car moving okay, though on the motorway I found that full throttle was needed just to cruise at 70 miles per hour. This wasn't too much of a problem though, as cruising at 60 seemed to suit the old thing. My opinion of my new purchase was further improved when I had a rummage in the glovebox and found some old 8-track cassettes which, amazingly, actually worked in the car's player. So, with

Elvis's greatest hits on the 8-track, I cruised slowly along the motorway, bound for Devon.

On reaching the West Country, the landscape began to undulate and the Rover started to have real trouble dragging itself up the hills. Despite the 3.5 litre V8 up front, it could barely climb the gentle motorway slopes on which it found itself. I was forced to use momentum to make progress, getting up as much speed as possible on the downhills, so as to be able to make it up the next incline. But as I approached Exeter, with 40 miles to go, the engine lost power completely. I managed to restart it as I coasted, but a few miles later, it was gone for good.

I had a look around the car and was at a loss as to what was wrong. It seemed to be turning over okay and would sometimes try to start, but couldn't quite manage it.

But then I took a closer look at the carburettors, and found they didn't have any fuel in them. A faulty fuel pump maybe, or a blocked fuel filter? No, like an idiot, I'd run out of fuel.

I did the maths. I'd put £60 of unleaded in the tank leaving London, and had covered about 180 miles since then. The fuel should have got me home, but given the running issues, it was totally possible that the car had chewed through it all already, even though the fuel gauge was still showing a quarter full.

I called the AA, a gallon was added to the tank and the Rover fired up straight away, before getting me the rest of the way home. What an idiot.

With the car home, we had a couple of months to get it ready for its trip to Morocco. To begin with, I looked into the running issues and found the cause of them pretty quickly, thanks to the simplicity of the old V8. The first problem was that the motor's two carburettors are supposed to be linked by a metal bar, which allows the accelerator pedal to open both of their throttles simultaneously. This bar was missing, meaning that for the whole drive back from London, only one half of the motor was responding to my right foot as I begged it for power. Additionally, on the side of the engine which was working, two of the high tension electrical leads had gone bad. So, out of the engine's eight cylinders, only two were supplying any significant power. No wonder it ran out of fuel; I was just amazed that it made it all the way back to Devon like that.

With the engine once again running on all eight cylinders, the only additional jobs which needed to be tackled before we hit the road were to stop the radiator leaking and to make the exhaust louder. The radiator I tackled using steel epoxy glue, while the central exhaust silencer was cut out by a friend of mine named Ross as unlike me, he could actually weld reasonably well. So, with the car pretty much running as it was supposed to and sounding like a proper V8 for the first time, we began the long drive to Africa. The initial ten mile journey to the ferry port went by without a hitch, which was a good sign as the previous time I'd tried to drive the Rover that far, the cracked radiator had resulted in the temperature gauge getting dangerously close to the red. Fortunately, this time my last minute repair was holding.

The 27 hour ferry journey across the Bay of Biscay to Santander was characterized by the predictably passable entertainment and more memorably, the several hundred members of the various Harley Davidson clubs who were also on board – and who entertained us with two-wheeled banter and free top-ups of whiskey into the early hours.

We rolled off the ferry at lunchtime on Monday, straight into an epic storm. Lightning and rain surrounded the car as we climbed onto Spain's Central Plateau, before easing as we got closer to our day's destination of Salamanca, 225 miles down the road. Five hours after leaving Santander, we arrived and spent a relaxing afternoon exploring the ancient university town, before staying the night in a hostel with amazing views over the floodlit central plaza. The big Rover had completed its first real run since it had came back from London without a hitch, using only a little water and no oil, and behaving impeccably throughout – a feat it repeated the following day, when it covered another 250 miles to the town of Evora, in Portugal, and then on to the ferryport of Algiceras, where we boarded the ferry to Morocco, with the adventure all set to begin in earnest.

The Rock of Gibraltar shimmered to our left as we floated gently across the gateway to the Mediterranean, rolling onto the African continent in the Spanish enclave of Ceuta. After leaving the ferry, we drove the two kilometres across town to the border, where the usual collection of hustlers and chancers surrounded us as we pulled up, eyeing us opportunistically and hoping to profit from our presence in some manner. Avoiding them, we got our passports stamped and then imported the car – a process which fortunately didn't require the 'Carnet du Passage' documents which had cost us so much on our previous visit to Africa with the Porsche, four years earlier. Instead, a simple form, completed in triplicate and stamped into officialdom, brought the car across the border – one of the simplest we'd encountered on the continent. Twenty-five minutes after our arrival at the border crossing, we were dodging cyclists, donkeys, pedestrians and Mercedes grand taxis as we headed south.

As no insurance was available at the border, we pulled into the first town we arrived at to purchase some. This attempt proved unsuccessful, but a second try in the next town, ten miles down the road, got the job done and for the cost of 700 dirhams, or £50, we were on our way, driving legally in Morocco for the first time.

Several hours of boiling, signless towns and twisting mountain roads then took us to Chefchouen, where we explored the steep, bustling streets before heading to the campsite for our first night in Africa. That evening, the Rover elected to play up for the first time on the trip, by refusing to start. The engine was getting fuel and a spark, but it wouldn't run. We guessed the problem was fuel vaporisation caused by the build up of heat in the engine bay, and after leaving it to cool down for a few hours, it coughed into life, much to our relief.

The following day was spent cruising slowly south to Fez, one of the old imperial capitals. The drive took us through spectacular gorges before crossing rolling, empty arable land for hours until it brought us to our destination. The drive's only real car-related interest was provided by the exhaust mounting bolts gradually working loose, a simple fix with a couple of half-inch spanners being called for before we spent the evening exploring the labyrinthine alleys of Fez, a maze of cobbled streets where 150,000 people live within the old city walls, crowded together beneath the burning sun.

The following morning saw the traffic in Fez's new quarter bustling roughly around us as we headed south out of the city, but it wasn't so dense that it slowed our departure by much. Soon, the last cluttered remnants of Fez shrank in our rear view mirrors as we took the two-lane tarmac south towards the Atlas Mountains. A few other road users raced along with us, Mercedes grand taxis, tinny Peugeots and hustling minivans all joining in the aggressive overtaking manoeuvres which marked each encounter with a slow moving lorry, tractor or bus.

The rolling arable land allowed good visibility and we made fine progress for the first hour or so until, enjoying the meandering road, I flew around a corner at a rate of knots, the wallowing Rover attempting to touch the ground with its wing mirror, while pitching comically on the bumpy tarmac. The big V8 roared as I powered out of the corner, but soon quietened down when I spotted the Policeman, with his radar.

Flagged down, I pulled over and attempted to talk my way out of the predicament; however it's pretty hard to argue with a photo showing you doing 81 kilometres per hour in a 60 zone, and so I had little option but to accept my guilt and pay the 500 dirham fine. Following this intermission in our rapid progress, we hit the road again in a somewhat more sedate manner, reeling in the High Atlas Mountains which formed the horizon ahead of us.

The High Atlas is rather aptly named, given that it is the highest mountain range in North Africa. It also marked how much my life had changed in the previous years, as I'd visited the range once before, on a climbing trip which saw me making a winter ascent of the highest mountain in the range – Jebel Toubkal, which soars to 4,167 metres above sea level. But on this visit, those mountaineering memories may as well have belonged to someone else, as such adventures were no longer my calling. No, on this occasion there would be no ice axes and crampons, only bad roads and a tatty old Rover. We planned to complete a 140 mile north-south crossing of the range, starting at the delightfully named 'El Kebab' before rising to an overnight stop at Imchil, then dropping down to the Todra Gorge the following morning. Even before we reached the start of our planned route at El Kebab, the road soared enthusiastically upwards and the tarmac lost its smoothness to become potholed and crumbling. Within five miles of the start of our crossing, the coolant temperature rose towards the red before the engine started to splutter, losing power. We coaxed the Rover to a spot of shade beneath a tree and began to investigate. The air temperature was well above 30°C and the heat in the engine bay was something else. Clearly, the car's cooling system wasn't up to the job in a situation so far removed from what it was designed for, and so we decided to give it all the help we could. Off came the grille, numberplate, bonnet insulation and sealing strips to increase the airflow. We worked out that the breakdown was caused by the carburettors overheating and vaporising the fuel before it reached the engine. Using the heat shield from my camping stove, we tried to insulate the fuel lines as best we could and also re-sealed the crack in the radiator, which had re-opened in the heat. After half an hour, we were ready for Rover vs Atlas, take two.

The road climbed higher and higher, and soon we were rolling across sweeping plains almost two kilometres above sea level. The surface beneath our wheels remained tarmac, but unhelpfully it also remained potholed and broken. And then the gently rising plains carried us into the mountains, the smooth giving way to the jagged as conglomerate peaks soared all around us.

With the mountains came more steep ascents, along with areas of rough gravel where the road had been swept away by flash floods. The exhaust broke once again as we climbed, the silencer rattling uselessly beneath the back of the car. When evening fell, we were over 2,000 metres up, crossing our fingers that the car would survive and get us to Imchil before nightfall. It nearly managed it but the last, steep ascent before the high plateau on which we planned to spend the night was just too much for the long suffering Rover, and we overheated to a standstill for a second time.

Half an hour later we chugged onwards and upwards in the rapidly-cooling air, on a road which clung to the side of a mountain, over a mile-deep chasm which drew our attention as the sun began to set behind us. Dusk was all around as we pulled into Imchil and found a room for the night, whiling away the time discussing Islamic marriages and mule prices with the locals in broken French, before sleep took priority.

The following morning dawned bright and clear as we climbed aboard our steed – which we now knew had cost the same as a decent mule is worth – and carried on south. A livestock market had taken place in the village that morning and we shared the mountain tracks with a variety of vans, all with a bemused selection of goats or sheep balanced in cages on their roofs. The road climbed up to 2,700 metres above sea level before the mountains gave up trying to stop the Rover, allowing it to coast down through its precipitous northern reaches into the other-worldly Todra Gorge, a snaking alley of soaring rock which terminates at a selection of cafes, nestling beneath beautiful sweeping walls of granite; one of Africa's greatest rock climbing destinations, but alas, no longer for me.

The Rover had survived the High Atlas – and one of Africa's highest roads – but it now faced a new challenge as it dropped down into the Sahara. The outside temperature hit 40°C as we cruised through the desert, sweating away within the cramped cabin. With temperatures rumoured to be hitting 50°C further south we decided to abandon our original plan of heading to Western Sahara, instead choosing to explore some of the oasis towns which mark the periphery of the world's greatest desert. We spent our first night south of the Atlas at Skoura, which once hosted epic camel trains as they emerged from the Sahara. During our visit, the place was deserted, and the Mosque's call to prayer rang out into a twilight which seemed to be hosting only four friends and their Rover, exploring ruined Kasbahs amid the sea of palm trees.

The following morning brought cloud, which instead of heralding lower temperatures merely provided us with an increase in humidity. We drove on to Ouarzazate where we toured the Atlas Film Studios, taking in sets from films as diverse as Gladiator, Lawrence of Arabia, Black Hawk Down and Seven Years in Tibet. A quick tip to a security guard enabled the car to gain access to the film sets, its backdrop phasing from Egypt to Tibet to Jerusalem in about twenty minutes.

We then continued to Ait-Ben Haddou, a hillside of ruined kazbahs and palm trees which has also proved to be a valuable resource for the Moroccan film industry. Exploring the twisting alleys and mud-coated buildings was a trip back in time, but the heat was unrelenting, striking down one member of our group with heat exhaustion. Because of that, we stayed put for the rest of the day, before heading north over the Atlas to Marrakesh the following day.

Given the problems we'd had with overheating on mountainsides, that afternoon we rigged up the screen wash system to jet its water onto the carburettors, hoping the evaporation would keep them cool enough to allow the Rover to make its return crossing of the Atlas Mountains without a hitch, before retiring to bed, wondering what the following day would bring.

Thirty-one degrees and rising rapidly was our answer, at nine in the morning.

It was definitely time to head north, back across the High Atlas Mountains to cooler climes. We loaded up the Rover, checked out of the Auberge and set off along the main road linking Ouazazante with Marrakesh, about 130 miles away. The driving conditions were considerably better than we had encountered on our two day southward crossing a few days previously, but the tarmac still climbed to 2,100 metres above sea level as it baked beneath the omnipresent sun.

As we climbed, dicing with grand taxis, tour buses and crawling lorries, the engine temperature rose as usual, but the modification we'd made the previous evening – directing the screenwash system onto the carburettors to cool them – meant that thanks to a squirt every kilometre or so, we didn't have any of the fuel vaporisation issues which had plagued our previous attempts to drive slowly up hills. The brakes weren't so fortunate however, and shortly after crossing the high pass the pedal went straight to the floor, necessitating a cafe stop to allow them to cool down, before coasting the vertical two kilometres down the northern reaches of the High Atlas, almost back to sea level. Ahead lay Marrakesh, and by mid-afternoon we had located the town's old medina, avoided the hustling chancers who stalk tourists incessantly in Morocco, found a Riad in which to stay the night, and headed out to take in the sights.

Marrakesh's old town is like no other in Morroco; it is a living pantomime which gives your senses no respite. By day, you take centre stage as you explore the twisting souqs, eyed opportunistically by every stallholder and hustler as you studiously feign disinterest, for interest is something which will be expertly latched onto as a means to coax open your wallet. The cries ring out around you: 'bonjour', 'come look at my shop', 'good price for you'. All around, locals fly through the twisting alleys on scooters, donkeys wander through the melee and life goes on with a frantic intensity.

But at night, the tempo increases. Dejemaa el Fna Square in the centre of the medina becomes a caricature of the great city's past. Snake charmers, performing monkeys, musicians and storytellers jostle for the crowds, and a swathe of food stalls compete for business – 'come, my kebabs are the best in town', 'you're from England? Here, my food is bloody marvellous'. Aromas drift through the balmy air; mint tea, spices, tagines, drains. The whole square animates with a vibrant rhythm, a liveliness which assaults your senses and brings you to life.

But there are nodes of stillness within the extroversion. Here, an old lady is kneeling to beg for change, her look of hopelessness refined to perfection. There, a weary man roams the crowds, trying to sell an old belt for a few dirhams. And just out of the square, staring into the middle distance, someone holds four packs of tissues in his hand as the crowds rush by, a white stick leaning unseen against their leg.

Every extreme of life competes for your attention as you wander the Medina, demanding your attention every step of the way. A million stories of tragedy and triumph.

We took the two-lane motorway north out of Marrakesh, heading for Casablanca and dodging stray dogs and bored mules all the way. The Rover seemed happy to be heading north, growling along the smooth tarmac without a complaint. Inside the car, the cooler air – a mere 34°C – was most welcome, but open windows and plenty of stops for cold water were still essential to preserve sanity.

Casablanca turned out to be just as we'd imagined; a dull commercial centre which four million people call home, and which has little to recommend it other than the Hassan II mosque, the largest in the country, built by its modest namesake as a 60th birthday present to himself. Despite its audacious numbers – its minaret reaches 210 metres skyward and is topped by a gold ball 12 metres in diameter, while 105,000 people can worship there simultaneously – I found it strangely underwhelming.

Even considering its bold outline, obsessive detailing and grandiose size, the fact that it was only completed twenty years before our visit acts to reduce its impressiveness. In a world where skyscrapers are completed somewhere on the planet every day of the week, the impact of a self-congratulatory 210 metre tall minaret is negated somewhat.

We left dull-but-businesslike Casablanca for Rabat, where we wandered the evening away taking in the 'real' Morocco. Tourists were nonexistent and instead of souvenirs, the souqs sold the essentials for everyday life. Clothes, food, music and household goods. No-one hassled us; we were blissfully invisible in comparison to our experiences in the tourist towns. All around us, Moroccans went about their everyday lives rather than competing for our attention through displays of drama or helplessness.

The road north from Rabat to the ferry port took us past a few pleasant ex-fishing villages, which had become beach venues for Morocco's middle class, as well as plenty of fellow Europeans. We stopped for coffee at a couple of these relaxed places, enjoying the cool sea air, clean streets and old forts around which they were invariably centred. And then we hit the road again and reached the border with the Spanish enclave of Ceuta, where our 1,100 mile lap of Morocco ended as we boarded the ferry back to Europe. And so the Rover returned to its home continent, having completed the border crossing without any major issues other than its ability to attract a thorough going-over by customs – and their sniffer dogs – every time it crossed a border. There must just be something about four young people in a grubby 37 year old Rover with 'The Marrakesh Express' written down the sides which, in the mind of the average customs officer, screams 'boot full of hash'.

On our journey north, we stopped off at Gibraltar for a taste of home; a place which felt like a caricature of England with a sea of Union Jacks and bunting flying proudly in the Mediterranean breeze. Here, we enjoyed the view from the top of 'The Rock' and donned head torches to explore some of the abandoned tunnels which perforated it, hewn for defensive reasons during various conflicts over the past 300 years. We then stopped off at the Alhambra, a fourteenth century Islamic palace whose relatively plain exterior belies the exquisiteness of the spaces within: walls covered with intricate arabesques which rise to ceilings of delicate Muqarnas and courtyards where ornamental ponds are framed by fine marble arches and their slim supporting columns. And further north we wandered the Guggenheim museum in Bilbao, trying to make sense of the contemporary art housed within the stunning building.

And finally, two weeks after we'd left England, we boarded the ferry back to the UK and began to reflect on the journey. Despite its general lack of preparation the Rover had done amazingly well, only breaking down when forced to crawl slowly up mountainsides in temperatures approaching 40°C. It had proved comfortable and dependable – if not economical – and had lent our journey a unique character which no other mode of travel could have come close to providing. And most importantly, it had filled our minds with unique memories. But these memories were already moving aside, making space for dreams of the next adventure.

A few days later, back home with the 2,800 mile, two week odyssey complete, it struck me that it's amazing just how quickly such a vivid experience can revert to being a dream. Driving the Rover from the ferry port back to Dartmoor, I had tried to mentally recall its time in Morocco only to find that the memories of a week before had already acquired a hint of unreality. The edgy bustle of the souqs, the glaring heat of the desert, the calls to prayer echoing through the sultry night; all these memories, so vivid at the time, had softened into experiences which might just as easily have happened to someone else. After months of planning and two weeks on the road, already the trip had receded into the past, leaving a space in my mind to be filled with new dreams. Future dreams. Bigger dreams.

It was time to make V8Nam into a reality.

TWENTY NINE

THE ROAD TO SINGAPORE

30th July 2013
Bangkok, Thailand

There was only one road left to drive. It ran due south for 1,200 miles down the Malay Peninsula, from Bangkok to Singapore. There, only a dozen miles from the Equator, the end of the road was waiting, literally. I could drive no further on the Asian continent. The thought was an exciting one. Soon I would have driven my old Corvette clean across Asia – what a great thing to have done! It felt like the logical progression from my trip across Africa in the Porsche almost five years before, and already I was allowing my mind to wander forwards; to start to wonder about what the next adventure would be.

But while the thought of finishing the trip was an exciting one, it was inevitably marked with a slight sadness and uncertainty. Once I'd completed the final 1,200 mile run down to Singapore, I'd have nothing to do but to head home. But what was home? For four months now, my home had been this car, the open road and whatever cheap room I'd found in which to spend the night. Hunter's Moon had slid into the past. It was now a memory of a previous life to which a return felt as unlikely as, well, as crossing Asia in a Corvette.

Early one morning, when it was still dark and the rush hour hadn't yet got into its stride, I fired up the Corvette and took the road south out of Bangkok, heading towards the time and the place where my life would, once again, change.

It was no exaggeration to say there was only one road south. In places, Thailand thinned to a strip of land as little as five miles wide, pressed between the border with Myanmar and the sea. Even further south in Malaysia, the

1,200 mile long peninsula reached a maximum width of only 150 miles, with few roads to speak of. I literally couldn't miss Singapore, all I had to do was keep on heading along the peninsula and I'd hit it.

That morning as I drove through the thin mists of the Thai dawn, I began to visualise the journey having an end for the first time. I'd found a drive from England to Singapore to be too large to consider as a single entity, and so in my mind, I'd broken it up into a series of smaller, less intimidating prospects. Across Europe, through Central Asia and then China, then the journey from Laos to Vietnam. Now, I was on the last leg. After the next waypoint, there was nothing else; just a plane ticket home, and a return to what passed as the real world.

However, there were still enough diversions to keep the real world at bay for another few weeks, at least. Three hundred miles into the final drive, I parked the Corvette at Chumphon and took a boat to the island of Ko Tao for a few days of relaxation on a Thai island.

But would I really find it relaxing? Early on in the trip, Kim had told me that I'd hate the Thai beach tourism machine, with its huge numbers of budget flight holidaymakers, all intent on having a good time. Ko Tao was my first taste of this aspect of Thailand and as an island I'd hoped it would provide me with a gentle introduction and sure enough, what I found wasn't nearly as irritating as I had primed myself for. Sure, there were plenty of other tourists, but the numbers weren't overwhelming, the boisterousness wasn't crushing. I found the island to be a nice place in which to pass a few days by getting up late – for the fatigue of being on the road for four months was starting to make itself known – and spending the afternoon sat in a beachfront bar, either reading a book, chatting with like-minded folk or doing some writing. The place didn't feel like it was being smothered under the sheer weight of visitors and despite having spent most of the previous four months well off the tourist trail, I decided that Thailand's industrial-scale tourism wasn't actually that bad. I could handle it. With that in mind, on returning to the mainland, I drove the 'vette to Krabi.

I'd only been out of the car for ten minutes, but I was already overwhelmed. Everywhere I looked there was a backpacker's hostel, travel agency, bar or restaurant and wandering between them were crowds which defined the gap year stereotype. Sometimes drunken, often loud, always impossible to ignore, they'd flocked to Krabi for the essential travel ticks it served as a jumping off spot for – scuba diving in the bay, climbing lessons on Railay, social media-worthy snaps of longtail boats floating on the blue, mojitos on the beach and various illegal substances in the darker corners of the bars across town. Arriving alone, I was the odd one out and I felt like a rabbit caught in the headlights as I wandered through town, like I'd just walked out of the desert into Vegas. I wasn't prepared for the shock. I tried to escape it by taking a boat across to Railay, but just found more of the same. Maybe I'd been on the road too long, or maybe I was jaded, but in Krabi and the surrounding area I'd found my own personal hell in what was, for others, paradise. Two days were enough to leave me craving silence and space and luckily, I had a car at my disposal. I fired up the 'vette and headed down the coast, looking for somewhere which would redeem Thailand's beach scene in my eyes.

I found it in a place called Hat Yao. A little fishing village nestled down south by the Malaysian border, Hat Yao is home to about 200 friendly Muslim souls, and is the perfect antidote to the experience machine further north. Life is simple there. Early in the morning, small boats leave the village for the daily fishing trip, bringing their catch in around lunchtime. For the rest of the day, the villagers busy themselves with fixing the nets, boatbuilding and enjoying a gloriously slow-paced life.

I spent three days in Hat Yao, and they numbered among my favourite of the entire trip. In the mornings I would walk the town's deserted, four mile long golden beach, feeling lucky to have it all to myself after the free-for-all further north. I'd collect shells as I walked, or stop to do some climbing on the boulders which sat above the tide line. My time in southern Thailand coincided with Ramadan, and so no restaurants were open during the day. When the sun went down, I'd wander over to the village's only shop and feast on crisps, chocolate bars and whatever else they had in that day, as the moon rose over the Andaman Sea, its reflection shimmering upon the water like a sprinkling of broken glass.

My guidebook dismissed Hat Yao as a 'scruffy little village', while raving about the overcrowded beach spots to the north. I decided that on this one occasion, my guidebook had rather missed the whole point of travel.

Pulling myself away, I carried on south, crossing into Malaysia at a grubby border crossing before continuing to the island of Penang, my desire to reach Singapore growing with every mile. When journey's end had felt incomprehensibly far away it hadn't impeded upon my thoughts but now, with the end being so close – in the next country, in fact – I had a compulsion to reach it and finish what I'd started all those years before. I began to think about what life would be like once I was back in the UK and as I did so, I was struck with an urge to get stuck in, hit fast forward and find out. But first I had to finish the trip.

Arriving in Penang, I found another place where the weight of tourism blunted my enthusiasm – however good the food was. I was jaded by the endlessly boisterous backpacking masses, and by the routine of moving from place to place in the Corvette, alone on the road with my thoughts, which were now almost exclusively of the future. Feeling struck by one of the lows which all solo travellers far from home periodically have to ride out, I went out that evening, found a bar and bought a beer, hoping to wash away my moroseness. Sat alone, my ears drifted to attention as a familiar song sounded out across the bar. The lyrics jumped out at me from a previous trip.

'I don't know why she's leaving or where she's gonna go. I guess she's got her reasons but I just don't wanna know, cos' for 24 years I've been living next door to Alice... Alice... who the f... is Alice?!'

Immediately, a smile began to creep across my face.

I'd last heard the song blasting out across a bar in Slovenia, when we'd taken my Mini on that New Year's lap of Europe. I started to grin uncontrollably as the memories from that night in what we called 'Bar 2000' cut through my low mood; the endless Laško beers, the time late in the evening when the bar staff had gone outside for a smoke and locked us alone in the bar – the ultimate lock-in. It was a road trip high which swept back to the forefront of my mind, switching out my low mood like a switch and illustrating to me just how far I'd come as a traveller in the five years since that night out in Bled.

It might be tough in places, but this life I was leading wasn't bad overall. I had certainly made sacrifices to live life as I was, but you can't put a price on having a store of positive memories to dip into as the years go by. The following morning I resumed my journey with a newfound enthusiasm, and was rewarded by one of the high moments of the trip, which provided another entry in that memory bank of positivity.

It started innocuously enough. Darkness had fallen as I was rolling through the dense jungle of the Cameron Highlands and Kuala Lumpur, my objective for the day, was still some way off. Now usually, I do everything I can to finish the day's drive before nightfall, and so by rights, the situation should have grated with me a little. However in this instance, the wave of energy which had been triggered by wondering who the f... Alice was while in Penang kept me positive and anyway, the dusk light was far better appreciated in the countryside than the brightly-lit city. As the darkness became complete, I found myself dropping out of the highlands with the lights of Kuala Lumpur spread out below as far as the eye could see. And rising from the centre of this welcoming swathe of civilisation, two bright columns of light thrust up into the air.

The Petronas Towers.

They took me almost by surprise. In my urge to get to Singapore I'd pretty much forgotten that they existed, but all of a sudden, there they were. Two of the tallest structures in the world, piercing the sky above the city. The shock of seeing them rose to a euphoric joy as I chewed over the situation in my mind.

I'd just driven a Corvette to the Petronas Towers! Somehow, the sudden realisation gave the thought a greater impact than the other milestones on the trip. Even the memory of reaching Saigon paled in comparison.

The towers were about ten miles away when I'd first caught a glimpse of them, but they flickered in and out of my vision as I drove towards them, sometimes being hidden by cuttings or hills, on other occasions growing steadily in the windscreen through which for the past four months, the journey of my life had been framed.

And then I was in the city, and buildings rose all around me as I drove on, but the towers continued to dominate, growing bigger and bigger until they loomed over the Corvette, and I had to crane my neck to appreciate them, looking up at them through the car's transparent roof panel.

It was one of the most memorable arrivals I'd ever experienced, and it was all the better for being so unexpected. Kuala Lumpur had snuck up on me and charmed me before I'd even known what was happening – my memory filed it alongside reaching Ulan Bataar and Cape Town as a moment to treasure, even if the question of who the f... Alice was, still went unanswered.

With the benefit of a night's sleep and a day's rest, the Petronas Towers possessed even greater gravitas. They rose from the manicured ground in two columns of light, tapering to a pair of points 450 metres above my head. Their presence was that of a couple of Saturn V rockets, swiped from the pages of a science fiction magazine, given an oriental makeover and rendered real against the tropical sky. The only thing missing from the space-launch illusion was a countdown to lift-off, clouds of vapour venting to atmosphere and the frantic anticipation of the press jostling for vantage points a dozen miles away.

On my travels, I've found that it's rare to encounter a modern structure which generates as much of an impact as the historic sites you visit. Morocco's Hassan II mosque was proof of that, its minaret seeming somewhat hollow due to the assumed ease which modern technology had lent its construction. But the Petronas Towers, both through sheer scale – for nothing succeeds like excess – and by adopting a style and design all of their own, sidestep this disappointment. They aren't trying to be something they're not. They merely represent the high point which Malaysian architectural design, inspired by Islamic cues, had reached thirty years previously. Even if their architect, César Pelli, was from Argentina.

The towers set the tone for the time you spend in Kuala Lumpur. They soar over the park where locals and tourists alike wander at sunset and appear in your vision half-unexpectedly as you walk the streets. It's a nice city, a most liveable city and what it lacks in the big, hashtag-worthy hitters of history, it more than makes up for by simply being an effortless place in which to spend a few days. The food is varied, good and readily available, the transport system works and the streets are clean. It's comfortable and safe. But it's also only half a day's drive from Singapore, and when that's your ultimate destination and your desire to return home is building, it becomes a fact which always plays on your mind.

However, one does not simply drive into Singapore. To bring a foreign car onto the city-state's road network requires a customs document; a rather expensive one known as a Carnet du Passage. We'd needed one for the African Porsche trip, but as none of the countries on the V8Nam route thus far had required a carnet, I'd saved myself several thousand pounds by giving said document a miss. However, this meant I wouldn't be able to drive the

Corvette triumphantly into Singapore; instead, I'd have to have it met at the border by a car transporter, onto which it would be loaded and taken to the port, where it would be locked into a container, ready to be shipped home.

Of course, all this needed to be arranged. Shipping companies and agents needed to be engaged, a car transporter had to be booked and customs officers needed to be informed. This all took time and initially I worked on it during my afternoons in Kuala Lumpur but, after a few days, I decided to find somewhere cheaper in which to await the final permission to take the car into Singapore.

That place was Malacca, and one Thursday afternoon in August, I drove down there in the 'vette, roof off and loving the freedom of driving around South East Asia in my own sports car to the last.

I ended up staying there for a week, waiting for the cogs of shipping and bureaucracy to turn sufficiently for me to be granted permission to take the Corvette into Singapore. It was a pleasant enough place, clean and tidy in a colonial-town-made-good-for-tourism kind of way, and there was a great Bengali restaurant just down the road from the hostel which made a fine tandoori chicken, meaning the evenings could certainly have been worse. But I was impatient. After almost five months on the road, looking after the Corvette, willing it to keep on going for day after day, I was on the brink of being freed from the continuous cycle. With 14,000 miles already driven, there were only 150 left to go. Like a marathon runner on the final straight, I had that urge to just keep going, to get across the finish line, and this meant my time in Malacca, though pleasant, was also tinged with frustration.

I'd reached the point where I'd travelled enough. I just wanted to go home.

But for a week, while the paperwork was all being arranged, I waited in limbo, wandering the town and the shops by day, chomping my way through tandoori and beer by night. Time seemed to slow further with each new dawn as my groundhog day continued until one afternoon, when I received an email from the shipping company in Singapore telling me everything was now in place. I could head to V8Nam's final country the following day.

*   *   *

I rose before dawn, and the chill night air felt luxurious as I silently carried my bag down from the shared room in the traveller's hostel, placing it in the Corvette's surprisingly large boot for the final time. The cycle of my life, which I'd been following for almost five months, was about to be broken. I fired up the V8 and rolled onto the road out of town, feeling not only like I was leaving Malacca, but also like I was leaving the life I'd been living for the previous months.

But did I feel any different to when I'd started the trip? I was too close to the coal face to know at that stage, as the road to Singapore was not somewhere which was sufficiently distant from the experience to allow hindsight. I was a confusion of emotions, sad to be leaving this adventure yet also happy to be heading home; to be getting back to the life I'd put on hold and kick-starting it back into motion. But a proper understanding of how the trip had affected me would have to wait, because as dawn broke upon the Corvette's last day on the road, the trip was still underway. Anything could still happen.

The mists seemed to vent from the palm trees which lined the road. Coloured gold by the low sun, they drifted and eddied and swirled around the Corvette as it made its way across southern Malaysia, and I felt as if I was driving in a dream. With so few cars around, the cruise control on and Muse playing on the stereo, I rolled on as if in a trance. If there was one thing which could be taken from my relaxed mental state, it was that I probably should have had more coffee that morning.

There were less than a hundred miles to go now, and one border crossing. I set about enjoying the final hours on the road, in the company of the Corvette which had done so well to get me so far. It may not have had the cheeky character of Daisy the Mini, or the connection which five years as a daily driver had given me with the African Porsche, but it had still been a great ally during my trip across the globe. If it wasn't for the V8Nam idea, I would never have owned a Corvette C4. It simply wasn't a car which most Englishmen would consider buying. But I was glad I had; glad that I'd experienced this particular outpost of motoring – the straight-line brashness of the American muscle car. From the tuk-tuk in India to the Fiat in the Arctic, adventure road tripping was drawing me into areas of car culture I simply never would have otherwise encountered, and I was thankful of that. And already, as I droned along towards the border crossing at Johor Bahru, I was looking forward to what was next. I was unsure exactly what was to come, but every hostel I'd stayed in over the previous five months seemed to have a map of the world on the wall, and every time I looked at the map I would see the world in two halves – the half which I'd already driven, and that which was still to be experienced. In this respect, my eye was always drawn to the long roads of the Americas, and this had become something I could certainly see in my future. But first, I had to finish this road trip.

It was mid-morning when I met the low-loader in No-Man's-Land at the Singapore border. We got the Corvette loaded and strapped down, and then proceeded to customs.

Now, in every other country in South East Asia, the customs checks had been cursory at best. A quick glance at the bags in the boot sufficed, and I could quite easily have carted a rucksack full of drugs and half a dead goat down from Laos without anyone being any the wiser. However in Singapore, they took this stuff rather more seriously. The car transporter was backed up to one of the platforms which are generally used to allow access to lorry cargoes, and three customs officers descended upon it. My bags were taken to a table, emptied and their contents inspected. The bonnet and boot were opened and given a thorough going over, with no interest being shown in the car or its journey. The customs officers had a job to be done and unlike their counterparts in the rest of South East Asia, smiling or conversation wasn't part of the job description.

They set about the interior, looking behind the seats and in the footwells, and rummaging through the glove box. While doing so, one of the customs officers found the copy of Chairman Mao's 'Little Red Book' which I'd brought months earlier in China, as a souvenir.

'You cannot bring this into Singapore,' the customs inspector announced triumphantly, holding it high in the air as he smiled for the first time. 'It is communist propaganda.'

'It's just a souvenir,' I said. 'I bought it in China. I can't even read it. It's just a joke really.'

'It's communist propaganda,' he replied. 'It can't come into Singapore.'

'Do I look communist?' I replied. 'I'm from a capitalist country, and I've just driven here in the most capitalist car in the world. Do you think a communist would drive across the world in a sodding Corvette?'

The ridiculousness of the situation certainly wasn't lost on me. You can't get a much bigger symbol of capitalism than that symbol of America – the 'vette; especially one which is on a jolly across the globe. I looked about as communist as a Texan oil baron. Fortunately, one of the other officers agreed.

'I don't think he's coming into Singapore to promote communism,' he said to his more hot-headed colleague. 'Leave it be.'

I said thank you, and tried not to laugh at the surreal situation, as they continued their checks of the car.

'What are these?' The first officer barked as he looked in the storage compartment built into the central console.

'Cigarettes,' I replied.

'You can't bring these into Singapore.' he said.

'No worries, just bin them then.'

'You don't understand. You can't take these into the country. They have to be destroyed,' he said.

'Fine, destroy them then,' I replied. I don't even smoke, anyway.'

He looked at me quizzically for a moment, before asking, 'why do you have 200 cigarettes if you don't even smoke?'

I was starting to get bored of this.

'Well, you know,' I replied. 'Bribing police officers, border guards, that kind of thing.'

He didn't get the joke, instead staring at me harshly, uncomprehendingly.

'You must destroy these cigarettes.'

Under the watchful eye of the customs officer, I carried the cigarettes into their office, where I was handed a pair of scissors and a bin.

'They must all be cut in half,' I was told.

And so, for about five minutes, I sat there with the scissors, cutting every one of the 200 cigarettes in half and throwing them into the bin.

Welcome to Singapore, I thought, as I did so.

Eventually, with the cigarettes all sliced in two and the customs officers unable to find any further communist propaganda in my capitalist Corvette, I was free to go. I climbed into the cab of the car transporter with the driver and we rolled out of the customs depot.

And so, 14,000 miles and five months after leaving the UK, the Corvette finally, triumphantly reached the end of the road - strapped to the back of a lorry, being taken directly to the port to be shipped home. It wasn't quite the glorious high on which some of my other road trips had ended, but hey, it was still quite an achievement, and a definite moment to remember.

348

THIRTY

MOMENTUM

01ˢᵗ August 2012
Shaugh Prior, Dartmoor, UK

With our jaunt to Morocco complete, thoughts naturally turned to the next adventure, and this time there were to be no more fillers – it was time to make the big one happen. V8Nam. I got stuck into working towards making my dream of driving a V8 to the far side of Asia into reality, pouring over guidebooks and maps, digesting travel advice and piecing together in my mind the possible routes from Dartmoor to South East Asia.

Two routes were obvious contenders, but neither was perfect. The first possibility swept across Europe and Central Asia to China, and then crossed this huge nation to the border with Laos, before winding its way down through South East Asia. The second option reached the same point, but would see us driving across Europe to Turkey, then passing through Iran, Pakistan and India, before taking a boat to Malaysia via the Andaman Islands, the overland route to South East Asia via Burma being impassable at the time. While some people had merged the two routes in the past by driving to the subcontinent before taking the Friendship Highway through Tibet and heading on to the border with Laos, we didn't really consider this to be an option as it combined the worst of both worlds financially, with both the expense of entering China and the cost of a Carnet du Passage for Iran coming together to make it a rather pricy option.

So, the choice was between an expensive, bureaucratic crossing of China, and an expensive, slightly edgy crossing of Iran, followed by a sea voyage which felt a little like cheating. But how were we to decide which option to go for?

Simple. Brummy and I went to the planning room, grabbed some beers, talked it through, and the decision was made. China interested us more than Iran, and so China it was, even though our desire to give a significant sum of money to the Chinese Communist Party for the privilege of negotiating their lands was negligible at best.

So, we had our line on the map. Now, it was time to turn it into a trip. Countries needed to be researched, places of interest found and our route adjusted to take them in. I spent hours in the planning room at Hunter's Moon, dredging every resource for possible places to visit, the weirder the better. I found a Cold War missile silo in the Ukraine and a mountain retreat in Kyrgyzstan; an unspoilt beach in Cambodia and a theme park populated only by dwarfs in China. And with every new attraction, the line on the map was drawn tauter, running between cities, points of interest and border crossings with a decisiveness which we couldn't wait to act on.

With the line on the map marking a route, a timescale needed to be overlaid. As had become traditional with these trips, to some degree this was dictated by the amount of time Brummy could pull together in paid and unpaid leave, and on this occasion, it totalled about three months. So, that was the goal. To reach Vietnam in twelve weeks, with the additional constraint that we wished to cross China as quickly as possible, to keep costs down, as it was looking like it would be costing us somewhere north of £100 a day to have each car in the country.

So, with our start date lined up to coincide with our Easter climbing trip to Fontainebleau, and a goal of reaching Vietnam twelve weeks later, we pieced together the rest of the plan. Driving from the UK to Ukraine at a sensible pace would take around two weeks. Kiev to the Chinese border could comfortably be done in three weeks. Crossing China would require four weeks, and the remaining time was to be spent heading across South East Asia to Vietnam. However, this wasn't the end of the trip I wanted to undertake. Once Brummy had flown home, I planned to spend a further two to three months in South East Asia, slowly making my way to Singapore; effectively tacking a backpacking holiday onto the end of the trans-Asian drive.

The decision to break the trip up into these bite-size chunks made it accessible to other people to join for shorter periods, and so the group grew. A Scotsman called Grant moved into Hunter's Moon and was quickly talked into coming along on the Central Asian leg of the trip and Ian, who I'd already completed several European adventures with, committed to co-driving the Corvette on the Chinese leg. The more accessible European leg got the greatest interest, however. Takers included a friend named Fred, who ironically took the opportunity to head to his climate conference in Vienna by road and a girl named Kim, whom I'd only just met through the Hunter's Moon social scene and begun spending time with at the climbing wall and pub, was fairly easy to talk into co-driving with me as far as Kiev. And so, the pattern for the trip was set. By the autumn of 2012, we had a route plan, timings, team members and costings in place.

'I guess we probably should get some cars brought then,' I said to Brummy one evening in the local pub.

'Well I already know what I'm taking,' said Brummy.

'Ah yes, the legendarily unimaginative Rolls-Royce. Found one yet?'

'There are two that look good on eBay at the moment, both under five grand.'

'Well get one bought then.'

'I will,' he replied. 'Have you figured out what you're taking yet?'

'Not exactly,' I replied.

This was true. I'd put a lot of thought into car choice for the trip, but as yet I hadn't found anything which fitted the bill. My first choice was to get another, tattier V8-powered TVR, as I wasn't willing to risk trashing my pride-and-joy Kermit on the adventure. However with a maximum budget of £5,000, none of the Chimaeras on sale seemed quite trustworthy enough and I dismissed the wedge-shaped '80s TVRs due to the perceived tiny boot and the vulnerability of their convertible roof.

I considered plenty of other options. A Porsche 928 would have been perfect, but I'd already done a trip in a Porsche, and so I felt my choice of car for V8Nam should be more imaginative. I went to look at a Mercedes SL, but walked away because it was simply too dull; I looked into the possibility of a hard top Triumph TR7 V8, but such a machine is a rare beast, and none were available. A Jaguar XK8? Too modern and sensible. A Triumph Stag? Too fragile and overheaty. A BMW 840? Too terrifyingly complicated. Gradually, the need to have a car became more and more pressing and I remained at a loss. And then late one evening, I was browsing eBay and I saw it. Details were scarce, but the gist of the advert was inescapable. A bright red, utterly tasteless 1990 Corvette, for £4,000.

The following morning, I contacted the seller and headed up to mid Devon to take a look.

I first saw it sat in the corner of a rural industrial estate, the bright red paint and confident sweeps of bodywork looking somewhat incongruous against the surroundings. It was huge and brash; my TVR seemed like a retiring little pedal car in comparison. It's interior, with its Cessna-like smell, was possibly the least classy thing I'd ever seen, with fake-looking red leather being combined with red carpets to create something which I imagine looks like the insides of a Texan. But the one thing which struck me above everything else was that as far as the trip was concerned, it looked *right*. Given that whatever car I brought was going to provide the backdrop to my life for almost half a year, this was important. It had to look right; it had to give V8Nam a vibe which worked for me.

I had to fight to suppress a grin as I walked up to it on that autumn day. This was the car I was looking for.

Karl – the guy selling it – wanted to buy a boat, but his wife had put her foot down by enforcing a one in, one out policy when it came to big boy's toys. For Karl to buy his boat, the Corvette had to go. And he knew just what was going to sell it. The engine.

He fired it up, and the loud, offbeat pulsing growl of a V8 with a 288° cam, performance ironheads and uprated manifolds and exhaust filled the air. It was a definite 'shut up and take my money' moment. We then went out for a drive and the second gear performance just added to the effect. As the rev counter swept past 7,000 and the air filled with Kentucky thunder, I knew I'd found my car.

'£3,800, and I'll pick it up tomorrow?' I said once we'd parked.

'Deal,' was Karl's reply.

V8Nam had its first car.

The following day, Tom gave me a lift up to mid Devon in his aircooled Porsche 911 to collect the 'vette, and we had a great drive home, both enjoying our wildly different steeds, Tom working the flat-six hard while I gradually learned what life behind the wheel of a Corvette was all about. I quickly came to realise that what I'd bought wasn't really a sports car in the traditional sense. It didn't flow up the road like the TVR, or my old Porsche 944; instead, it thundered along the straights on a wall of torque, before the numb steering and stiff suspension sapped your confidence in the corners. It was a muscle car, a one trick pony. But I didn't care. It was different and cool in its own strange way, and that's all that mattered.

That evening, the Corvette was sat on the drive of Hunter's Moon as the other residents came home from work. Just as with the TVR a few year's previously, I'd brought it under a cloak of secrecy, and the responses to its sudden appearance varied greatly, from a 'no way, that's amazing' from my friend Ross, to a 'what the hell did you buy that piece of American crap for,' from Brummy.

A few weeks later V8Nam's second car arrived, as the Rolls-Royce thundered up the drive amid that stormy Halloween night, and we had our convoy. A Rolls-Royce and a Corvette. Chalk and cheese.

And the chalk and cheese continued as we prepared the cars for the trip. I say prepared; the Corvette required virtually no work, proving reliable straight out of the box and promising to be a dependable companion on the roads of Asia. The Rolls, however, wasn't quite so promising. It was a few weeks after purchasing it that Brummy had taken it to an independent specialist and told them: 'It only needs to do 12,000 miles. I don't care after that; just make it do 12,000 miles as cheaply as possible.' Following the cut-price work on the brakes and carburettor, it was as ready as it was ever going to be - meanwhile, in the few months before our departure the Corvette had notched up 3,000 miles without fault, and so was also good to go.

In the weeks before any big trip, there are always lots of last minute tasks to get done. The time prior to our departure to Fontainebleau on the first leg of V8Nam was no different, and daily tasks amounted to a full time job for me, as I put my marine surveying business on hold and got stuck into making sure everything was in place. Daily, I exchanged emails with the Chinese regarding our transit of the country which was still two months away, kept up to date with the security and red tape situation in the countries we'd be travelling through and refined the itinerary as I learned more about the road conditions and places en route. And eventually, it was almost time to go. On the morning of our departure, I fired up the TVR for my last drive of it in months, heading to the supermarket to get some supplies for the early stages of the trip, along with a big pile of Euros and some gaffa tape. On the drive back to Hunter's Moon, as I swept through the still-wintery scenery I thought about what the future would hold. I dwelled on who I would be once the trip was over; how it would change me and what I would become in the course of the next five months and 14,000 miles. And as I flicked the TVR along those Dartmoor lanes, revelling in the engine noise echoing off the drystone walls and delighting in the tight manual gearchanges, I felt a sense of loss at leaving this life behind, but it was tempered against anticipation for the adventure which would be starting in a few hours, when I'd fire up the Corvette, head into town to collect Kim, and begin the journey.

THIRTY ONE

HOME

24ᵗʰ August 2013
Singapore

The journey was over. I'd watched the Corvette being loaded into a container at the Port of Singapore and I wouldn't see it again until it arrived back in the UK. That moment was still seven weeks away and for me, home was still half a world away.

I wandered Singapore's baking streets for a few days, feeling like a ghost, lost without the constant of the Corvette in my life. I gazed over Marina Bay at sunset and visited the food halls to hunker down over a curry and a Tiger Beer each evening, but I felt empty. A combination of fatigue and my sudden loss of purpose dragged at me like an anchor. The limbo I entered when I waved goodbye to the Corvette had turned to an anticlimax. Ultimately, I needed to go home; to put some distance between myself and the adventure and so allow myself to process it, learn from it and reconnect with who I was, away from the Corvette's plastic cabin.

After three days of what felt like a transient nothingness, I took a taxi to the airport. Singapore Changi Airport. The name rang a bell; it was where my grandfather had been based when he was captured by the Japanese, 61 years earlier. I boarded the plane and began the long journey home.

Because direct flights were rather costly, I'd came up with a cheaper, more roundabout route for my journey back to the UK. The first leg saw me fly to Taipei, the capital of Taiwan, where I spent a few days as a tourist. I toured Taipei 101, the building which had finally taken the 'tallest building in the world' crown from the Petronas Towers nine years earlier, wandered the national museum and spent

357

the evenings sat out on plastic patio furniture, bathed in fluorescent light as I fuelled myself with noodles and beer. But just as in Singapore, my existence felt strange. I wanted to be the epitome of the traveller, dashing this way and that, delighting in new places and new experiences, but my heart was no longer in it. My desire to experience Taipei butted up against a wall of homesickness which made my brief stay there feel strangely pointless.

When the time came to continue my journey home, I almost didn't make it out of Taiwan. A tropical cyclone rolled out of the Pacific and as the city battened down against it, my plane climbed out on the buffeting winds, a stormy wall of black cloud rising powerfully to its starboard side. It was one of the last planes to leave Taiwan for a couple of days, and I was most relieved I was on it, homeward bound.

We landed at Shanghai where I changed flights, and then flew on to Hamburg. From there, I boarded an early morning flight to London City Airport. All around me, unsmiling businessmen in their grey suits prepared for a day of meetings, intent on doing deals in the capital. After the technicolour east, it all seemed so bland, so drab. My life had followed a very different tangent to those around me and my spirits rose through the fatigue of travel, pleased beyond measure that I'd refused to follow the crowd, and instead pursued my very own life less ordinary. And as I walked out of the airport into a beautiful English summer's morning, I smiled as I recognised that my V8Nam adventure wasn't yet over. Home was still 240 miles away, so there remained one last opportunity to create some memories before drawing a curtain over the five-month odyssey. So, I did what any right-minded car enthusiast would do in the circumstances.

I bought a Porsche.

Not a shiny new one, but the cheapest one in the country – a rather tatty white Porsche 944 which I'd found for sale in a north London garage while passing time online in Taiwan. It was identical to the one I'd previously driven to

South Africa and straight away, the memories came flooding back, from the slightly rubbery, though still satisfying gearchange, to the way the steering would lighten strangely as you approached full lock.

With a deal done and £1,800 handed over in exchange for my new daily driver, I wished for reliability and set off on the last 240 miles of my journey. Destination, home. Or more specifically, my homecoming BBQ at Hunter's Moon.

The drive went without incident and as I pulled up outside the house, friends were gathered on the decking, smiling and laughing. The reappearance of a white Porsche in my world immediately raised eyebrows, and I enjoyed living up to my random approach to life. Sausages and burgers were then cooked, beers opened, and the evening whiled away with talk of adventures near and far, and of the five months of everyone's lives which had passed since I'd last been there. But I was exhausted. The three flights from Taiwan followed by the drive had run me down to nothing, and I was first to bed that night, as thoughts about what the past five months meant to me churned around my blunted mind.

The following day, I took my beloved TVR to the supermarket. It felt so different to the angry Corvette, so much deeper in terms of character and refinement, yet still just as capable of unleashing hell when the mood took you. As I drove along that Dartmoor B-road, where the tarmac swings left and right between the drystone walls, the gearchanges slot home tight and fast and the exhaust noise echoes of the scenery like thunder, I thought back to the person who had come this way in the TVR almost half a year earlier. He seemed so remote, his future so different, but yet so familiar. Had the trip changed him? Was I a different person to that guy who had set out for the far side of the world with Kim in the passenger seat, five months earlier? I didn't feel any different. I'd slotted back into life at Hunter's Moon effortlessly, and had quickly started to feel as if I'd never left. But surely I must have changed in some way? After all, every previous big adventure had seen me come back a slightly different person.

I mulled over the question as I drove, and it dawned on me that all the big changes in who I was had actually happened during the years which preceded V8Nam. It was that feeling of success which came from completing challenges such as the Mongol Rally and the AfricanPorsche Expedition, along with the many other road trips on two, three and four wheels, which had gradually made planning and undertaking such adventures feel routine to me. But to pinpoint when the changes which had set me on the path towards a life of adventure had begun, I had to think back even further – all the way back to that fateful day of my first solo flight, when I found that the skies weren't my calling. That was the day on which the story began, and it was all the changes which had occurred to me during my long journey from that first solo flight, via countless mountain summits, motoring miles and roadside repairs, which had brought me to the start line of V8Nam. From epiphanies beneath the northern lights to summiting snowpeaks at sunrise, from roaring through Siberian wilderness to wild camping beneath African stars; these were the experiences which had truly moved me. In doing so, they'd made this life of wheels and wonder so compelling that I had committed everything to normalising it. I was seduced by adventure, and for over a decade I had pursued it as my calling. And in doing so, this life of adventure and my everyday world had become as one.

The V8Nam Expedition hadn't needed to change me. There was nothing to change, as this life of adventures was already who I was. The big trips were routine now. I had come of age as an adventurer, and so they were now simply what I did. That's not to disparage them, merely to say that they had become a constant in my life; a life of spanners and maps and the dusty haze of unknown tracks and distant horizons, built upon the changes I'd faced and the sacrifices I'd made in pursuit of my dreams.

But that's not to say that nothing had changed. In some ways I was returning to a very different life to the one I'd left, as my life had always been an existence defined by the next ambition. And just as completing the Mongol Rally had led to follow-on dreams such as African Porsche, and just as success there ultimately set the scene to make V8Nam a reality, so the pattern would repeat itself.

There would be another adventure. At that stage it was a blank canvas as I didn't yet know what form it would take, or even what car I would be driving, but I knew it would happen. Beer would be drunk and ideas would be had, and the clock would once again begin to count down to the next big drive.

I dropped a cog and fired Kermit's big V8 towards the redline, riding the wave of torque as the instant acceleration pressed me back into the seat. I smiled to myself as I revelled in the TVR's noise, looking forwards to the next big, as yet uncharted drive.

I'd only been home for a day, but already I couldn't wait.

Printed in Great Britain
by Amazon